NEW ILLUSTRATED

Bible

FOR CHILDREN

Written by

E.B.R. Hirsh

Advisory Board

Rabbi David Goldstein
Father James O'Hara
Reverend Kingsley Smith

Popular Press Limited • London

Contents

Hebrew Scriptures

The Book of Genesis

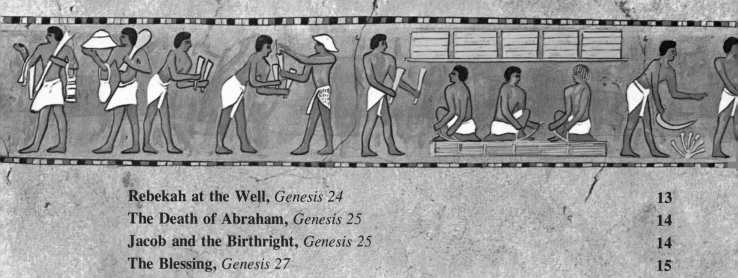

The Book of Exodus

The Book of Leviticus

The Book of Numbers

The Book of Ruth

The Books of Samuel

The Book of Daniel

The Book of Esther

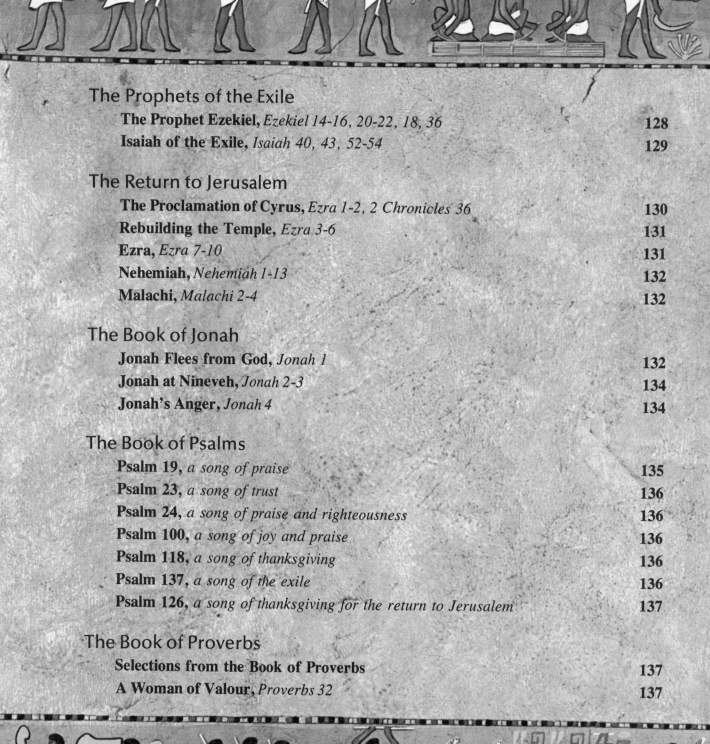

The Acts of The Apostles

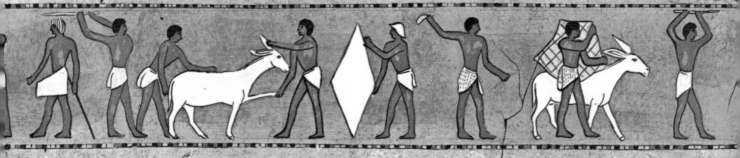

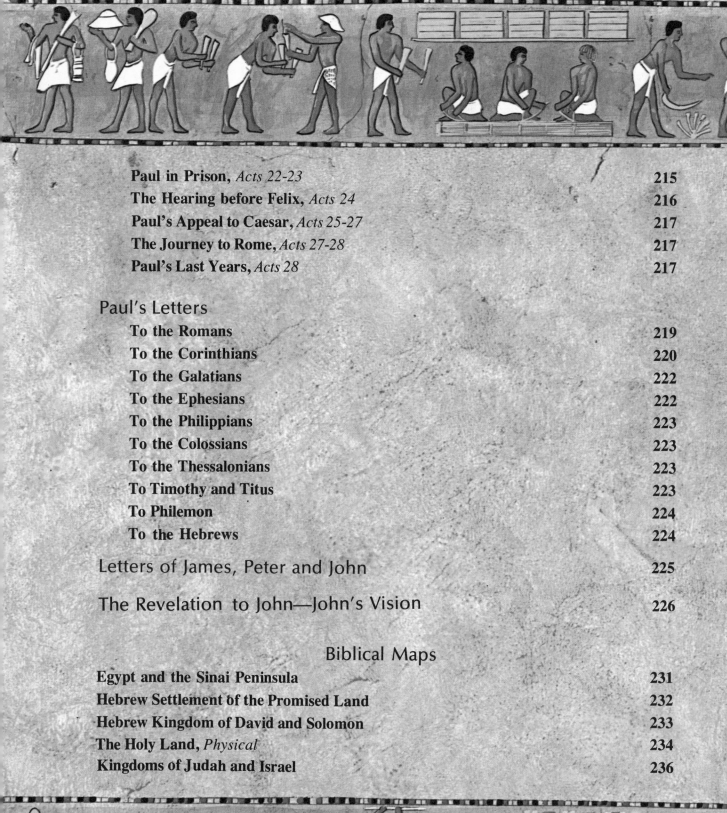

Introduction

The *Bible for Children* helps youngsters discover exciting people, places and ideas from the world of the Bible. It is a special edition of the Bible *for* children, rather than a collection of Biblical stories.

Reading the *Bible for Children* enables children to develop a knowledge of history, literature and human nature. It helps both Christians and Jews understand the bases of each other's beliefs.

What Is the Bible?

The Bible is the sacred book of Christians and Jews that tells of God's relationship with men. The word "Bible" comes from the Greek word "biblios," which means "book."

The Bible is a collection of many books, such as the Book of Exodus and the Book of Ruth. The books of the Bible were written over a period of hundreds of years by different authors in different places, all inspired by God.

Each of the books of Hebrew Scriptures, called "Old Testament" by Christians, was written for a different reason. Some are historical and tell the story of the children of Israel, of kings and of battles. Others tell of love, adventure, heroism, sacrifice and faith. The books of the prophets teach wisdom and the meaning of life. There is poetry in the Bible, and the Book of Psalms is a collection of hymns.

For Jews, the Bible consists of Hebrew Scriptures, found in the first section of this book. For Christians, it consists of Hebrew Scriptures plus the New Testament, neither complete in itself the Hebrew Scriptures were written in preparation for the New Testament. Therefore, for Christians, the New Testament completes the Hebrew Scriptures (Old Testament).

The New Testament includes the Gospel of Jesus, his life and teachings, Acts of the Apostles (followers of Jesus) and Epistles (letters) written to and by early Christians. It tells of the beginnings of Christianity and founding of the earliest churches.

Most of the Hebrew Scriptures were written in Hebrew and New Testament books in Greek; but throughout the years, the Bible has been translated into *all* languages of the world.

Jews and Christians alike have treasured the Bible for many generations. Countless people have suffered or lost lives because of their belief in its teachings.

David Goldstein
James O'Hara
Kingsley Smith
E.B.R. Hirsh

Biblical Chronology

Years in history are shown in different ways: Christians use the terms B.C. and A.D. after the dates; Jews use B.C.E. and C.E.

B.C. means Before Christ

A.D. stands for the Latin *Anno Domini* which means The Year of our Lord

B.C.E. means Before the Common Era

C.E. means the Common Era

Before the Common Era or Before Christ, years are numbered from higher to lower: as 4500 to 1 B.C.E. (or B.C.) Years of the Common Era or A.D. increase in number and are written as from 1 C.E. (or A.D.) until the present time.

Many of the earliest dates are approximate.

The earliest stories of the Bible cannot be dated; the Period of the Patriarchs (Abraham, Isaac, Jacob and Joseph) is between 2000 and 1500 B.C.E.

Moses to David

The Exodus	1290 B.C.E. (B.C.)
Joshua and the Judges	1250-1150 B.C.E. (B.C.)
Samuel anoints Saul	1042 B.C.E. (B.C.)
David becomes king	1002 B.C.E. (B.C.)

Solomon to the Exile

Solomon becomes king	962 B.C.E. (B.C.)
Kingdom divided	922 B.C.E. (B.C.)
Fall of Israel	722 B.C.E. (B.C.)
Fall of Judah	586 B.C.E. (B.C.)

The Exile to the Apostle Paul

Proclamation of Cyrus	538 B.C.E. (B.C.)
Greek Conquest	333 B.C.E. (B.C.)
Revolt of the Maccabees	167 B.C.E. (B.C.)
Roman Conquest	63 B.C.E. (B.C.)
Crucifixion of Jesus	30 C.E. (A.D.)
Life and Journeys of the Apostle Paul	First Century C.E. (A.D.)

HEBREW SCRIPTURES

The Book of Genesis

A collection of stories from creation through the times of Abraham, Isaac, Jacob and Joseph.

Creation

Genesis 1-2

The First Day

In the beginning God created the heavens and earth. The earth was empty and without form. Darkness was everywhere, and in the darkness was the spirit of God.

Then God said: "Let there be light." And there was light.

God saw that the light was good, and He separated the light from the darkness. The light God called Day, the darkness He called Night.

There was evening and there was morning, the first day.

The Second Day

Then God said: "Let there be sky in the midst of the waters." And sky appeared, to separate the waters above from the waters below.

God called the sky Heaven.

There was evening and there was morning, the second day.

The Third Day

Then God said: "Let the waters under the heaven be gathered together and let dry land appear." And it was so.

God called the dry land Earth and the waters that were gathered together He called Seas.

And God said: "Let the earth make plants grow and trees and grass." The plants grew and

God saw that it was good.

There was evening and there was morning, the third day.

The Fourth Day

Then God said: "Let there be lights in the sky to divide day from night. Let them be for signs to count out the seasons and days and months and years. Let them shine and give light to the earth."

So there came into being two great lights: the greater light, the Sun, to rule the day; the lesser light, the Moon, to rule the night.

Stars appeared also, and God saw that it was good.

This was the fourth day.

The Fifth Day

Then God said: "Let there be great swarms of living creatures in the waters, and let birds fly above the earth in great numbers."

So God created whales and fishes and all kinds of living creatures in the waters, and He created birds to fly over the waters and over the earth.

God saw that it was good. He blessed the creatures and He said: "Be fruitful and multiply to fill the seas. The birds also shall multiply upon the earth."

There was evening and there was morning, the fifth day.

The Sixth Day

Then God said: "Let there be living creatures upon the earth, cattle and beasts and all kinds of creeping things." And it was so: cattle and beasts and creeping things appeared on earth.

Then God said: "Let man be made in our image to have power over the fish of the sea, the birds of the air, over the earth and over everything that moves on the earth." So God created man in His own image.

In the image of God were man and woman created. And He blessed them and He said: "Be fruitful and multiply. Fill the earth. You shall have power over all the fish, all the birds, and over every living thing on earth.

"And every plant and every tree which are on earth you shall have for food. To every bird, to every beast, to every living creature on earth I give the grass and the plants for food."

And God saw everything that He had made, and it was very good.

This was the sixth day.

The Seventh Day

Now the heavens and the earth were finished and they were filled with life. On the seventh day God rested from His work. And He saw that all He had done was good. God blessed the seventh day and made it holy because on that day He had rested.

This is how the earth and the heavens and every living thing were created by God.

When God had made man, a mist had gone up from the earth to water the surface of the earth. God formed man from the dust of earth and breathed into him the breath of life. And man became a living being.

God called the first man Adam because he had been formed of the earth.

The Garden of Eden

Genesis 2

God planted a garden in the east, in Eden. Out of the ground God made trees of every kind grow, both those that are good for food and those that are pleasant to see. In the middle of the garden was planted the tree of life and the tree of the knowledge of good and evil. A river flowed from Eden to water the garden.

God put the man whom he had formed into the Garden of Eden to care for it and guard it. And God commanded: "You may eat fruit from every tree in the garden except from the tree that gives the knowledge of good and evil. Do not eat of this tree for on the day that you do, you shall surely die."

Then God said: "It is not good for man to be alone. I will find a companion for him."

Adam

Genesis 2

God brought every bird of the air and beast of the earth to man for him to give each one a name. Thus all the birds, the beasts and all the creeping things were named. But for himself, man did not have a companion.

Then God put the man into a deep sleep and took one of his ribs, closing up the flesh without a scar. He made the rib into a companion for man.

Awakening, the man gave the creature a name: "She shall be called Woman because she was taken out of man. She is flesh of my flesh and bone of my bone. Therefore, a man shall leave his father and his mother when he marries and becomes one with his wife."

And the man and woman were naked, but they were not ashamed.

Driven from the Garden

Genesis 3

The serpent was the cleverest of all the beasts which the Lord God had made. And the serpent asked the woman: "Has God forbidden you to eat the fruit from any tree in the garden?"

The woman answered: "We may eat from all the trees except for the tree in the middle of the garden, for God has warned that if we eat that fruit or touch it, we will die."

"You will not die," said the serpent. "On the day you eat that fruit your eyes will be opened and you will become wise like God, knowing what is good and what is evil."

The woman saw that the tree was pleasant to look at and that its fruit looked good to eat. She wanted to be wise, so she reached out and took some of the forbidden fruit and ate it. She gave some to Adam and he ate it also.

At once their eyes were opened and they saw that they were naked. So they sewed fig leaves

4

together to make clothes, and they hid from God among the trees.

God called Adam. "Where are you?"

And Adam answered: "I knew you were in the garden, but I was afraid and I hid."

"Have you eaten fruit from the tree of knowledge? The fruit which I commanded you not to eat?"

"The woman you gave me to be my wife gave it to me," said Adam. "And I ate it."

Then God asked the woman: "What is this that you have done?"

She answered: "The serpent tricked me, and I ate the fruit."

To the serpent God said: "Because you have done this, you shall be cursed more than any other beast. You shall crawl on your belly in the dust all the days of your life. The woman shall be your enemy, and her children shall be the enemies of your children forever."

God turned to the woman. "I will multiply your suffering. You shall bring forth your children in pain. You shall depend on your husband for happiness, and he shall rule over you."

God said to Adam: "Because you listened to your wife and ate the forbidden fruit, you must leave the Garden of Eden. Always you will have to work to make the ground bring forth food.

"You shall earn your bread by the sweat of your brow until you return to earth, for of earth you were formed. Dust you are and to dust you shall return."

Then God made clothes of skin for Adam and his wife. And God said: "Behold, the man has become wise, knowing all things. If he would reach out and eat of the tree of life also, he would live forever."

God sent them out of the Garden of Eden. To the east of the garden He placed angels and a flaming sword that turned in every direction to guard the path to the tree of life.

Cain and Abel

Genesis 3-5

Adam named his wife Eve because she was the mother of all human beings. She gave birth to a son, Cain, and to a second son, Abel.

Cain became a planter, a tiller of the ground. Abel became a shepherd, a keeper of sheep.

One day Cain brought an offering to God: some of the plants that he had grown. Abel also

brought an offering: the choicest and fattest of all his lambs.

God was pleased with Abel and his offering. But with Cain and his offering God was not pleased.

Cain became angry and God asked: "Why are you angry? When you receive praise and things go well with you, you are happy. When you do not receive praise, when things do not go well, you are angry. Then you are tempted to do wrong, but you must master your anger."

Cain did not answer.

One day when the brothers were in the field together Cain rose up against his brother and killed him.

The Lord called to Cain: "Where is Abel?"

Cain answered: "I do not know. Am I my brother's keeper?"

"What have you done?" asked God. "The earth cries out, for you have killed your brother. From now on, even though you work and tend the ground, it will not yield food for you. You shall be a wanderer all the days of your life."

Then Cain said to God: "My punishment is more than I can bear. I will hide from you, and I will be a wanderer forever. Whoever finds me will surely kill me for what I have done."

But the Lord assured Cain that he would not be killed. He set a mark upon him so that he would be known and no one would kill him.

Then Cain moved to the east of Eden, to the land of Nod. There he married and had a son named Enoch. Cain built a city and named it after Enoch who had many children and grandchildren.

In the meantime, Eve had another son, Seth, who was much like his father, Adam, and he too had many children.

Adam and Eve had other sons and daughters who had children of their own. Thus many generations descended from Adam and Eve.

In the ninth generation Noah was born.

Noah's Ark

Genesis 6-9

In Noah's time, men had become wicked. They had become so evil that God was sorry he had created them.

Only Noah did what was right in God's eyes, for he was a righteous man, a man who walked

with God. Noah had three sons: Shem, Ham and Japheth.

God spoke to Noah, saying that because the earth was filled with violence he would destroy all men. In fact every living creature under heaven would be destroyed.

God said: "There will be a great flood. If you and your family wish to live, you must build an ark following the directions I will give you."

Then the Lord commanded Noah to make the ark like a great boat with a pointed roof and rooms inside. "It shall be made of gopher wood and have a window in it and a door. It shall have three decks and be covered with pitch to make it waterproof.

"When the flood comes, every creature on earth shall perish. But I shall make a promise, a covenant, with you. You shall enter the ark, you and your family.

"And you shall take with you two of every kind of living creature upon the earth. Birds and beasts and creeping things: two of every animal, one male and one female, you shall take. You shall also take every kind of food for you and the creatures which will be in the ark with you."

Noah and his sons did all that the Lord commanded. Finally the ark was finished. Noah and his family went into the ark, and the animals entered two by two.

Then it began to rain. Rain fell for forty days and forty nights. The waters rose above the earth, flooding everything. The waters rose higher and higher until even the mountains were covered.

Every living creature on earth was drowned: every bird, every beast, and every creeping thing, and every man, woman and child. Only Noah and his family and the creatures with him remained alive.

At last God caused a wind to blow over the earth. The rains stopped and the waters became quiet. Finally, after a hundred and fifty days the ark came to rest on the mountain of Ararat.

Slowly the waters went down. For almost six months Noah, his family, and the creatures with him stayed in the ark.

One day Noah opened the window and sent out a dove to look for land. But she could not find a tree to perch upon, so she flew back. Seven days passed and again the dove was sent out. This time she returned with a fresh green olive branch in her beak.

But Noah still waited another seven days to be sure that the waters had gone from the earth. This time the dove went out and did not return. Then Noah knew that there was dry land and that it would be safe to leave the ark.

God spoke to Noah: "Leave the ark, you and your family. And send out every living creature that is with you that they may multiply and raise their young upon the earth."

So Noah went out, he and his wife and his sons and his sons' wives. And every bird, every beast and every creeping thing left the ark.

Noah built an altar to God and made offerings to Him and thanked Him.

God was pleased and promised never again to cause a flood to cover the earth. And God promised that as long as the earth remains, there would always be summer and winter, heat and cold, day and night, seed-time and harvest-time.

God blessed Noah and his sons and said: "Go forth and have children so there will be people on the earth once more.

"Every living creature shall respect you. You shall be master over them and they will become food for you, just as I gave you the plants for food."

Then God made a rainbow appear in the sky as a sign of the covenant between Him and the peoples of the earth.

The Tower of Babel
Genesis 10-11

Noah's descendants increased greatly. They spoke only one language and had only one speech.

8

They journeyed eastward and came to the
Plain of Shimar. There they decided to build a
city and a great tower so high that it would
reach into heaven. "This way," they said, "we
will make a name for ourselves."

God saw the city and the tower. And He
said: "These are all one people and have one
language. If they do this thing, build a tower
into heaven, then there is nothing they cannot
do. I shall confuse their language so that they
will not understand each other's speech and
will be unable to finish their tower."

So the Lord caused the people to be scattered over the earth and each nation to have a
different language.

The name of that place was called Babel, for
it was there that the Lord made a babble of the
languages of the earth, that the speech of men
became confused.

So it was that Noah's descendants became
the nations of the earth.

The Call to Abram

Genesis 11

In the land of Haran lived a man named
Abram, a descendant of Shem, Noah's son. He
had moved to Haran from Ur of the Chaldees.

One day God called to Abram: "Leave your
country and your father's house and go to a
land that I will show you. I will make a great
nation of you and bless you and make your
name great. Through you all the families of the
earth shall be blessed."

So Abram took his wife Sarai and his
nephew Lot and all their goods and animals
and all the people of their household. And they
went into the land of Canaan.

At Shechem the Lord appeared to Abram,
saying: "This land I will give to your people."

There Abram built an altar to the Lord. At
Bethel, too, he built an altar and blessed the
name of the Lord.

Some time later, there was famine in the land
of Canaan, so Abram moved to Egypt with all
his household. When the famine was over, he
went back to Bethel where he had built his altar
to the Lord, and he settled there.

Abram and Lot

Genesis 13-14

Abram became very rich in cattle and silver
and gold, and Lot was also rich, having flocks

and herds and tents. Soon the land was not able to support them all in one place. Trouble and quarrelling began between the herdsmen of Abram and the herdsmen of Lot.

Abram said to Lot: "Let there be no trouble between you and me, or between your men and my men, for we are one family. Is not the whole land ours? Let us each go our separate ways. If you choose the left, I will go right. Or if you go right, I will go left."

Lot looked around and saw that the plain of Jordan was fertile and green in every direction. It was like the garden of the Lord and like parts of Egypt he had seen. So Lot chose the plain of Jordan and travelled east, pitching his tent near the city of Sodom.

Abram stayed in the land of Canaan. After Lot had left, God spoke to Abram: "Lift up your eyes; look north, south, east and west. All the land you see I give to you and your descendants forever. You can move throughout the land freely, for it is yours." So Abram moved his tent to Hebron, and there he built another altar and blessed the name of the Lord.

Now the kings of Sodom and Gomorrah, together with three other kings, began a war against nearby peoples. The kings of Sodom and Gomorrah and their followers were defeated. All their goods and all their people were captured. And Lot, Abram's nephew who lived near Sodom, was captured with them.

When Abram heard that Lot had been taken prisoner, he called his men together. They followed the enemy, and near Damascus they rescued Lot with all his goods and his people. And Lot returned to Sodom to live there once more.

God's Promise
Genesis 15

After these things, the word of God came to Abram saying: "Fear not, Abram; I am your shield and protector; your reward shall be great."

Abram asked: "Lord God, what reward will you give me? I am without children; my only heir is a trusted servant, Eliezer of Damascus."

The Lord answered: "You will have a son of your own to be your heir. Look toward heaven and count the stars if you can. Your descendants shall be as many." And Abram believed in the Lord.

Then the Lord made a promise to Abram: that this land would belong to his descendants.

"They will live in a land that is not theirs for many years, and be oppressed as slaves for four hundred years," said the Lord. "After that, they shall return. To them I promise this land, from the river of Egypt to the river Euphrates."

Abram and Hagar

Genesis 16

Abram and Sarai had been living in Canaan for ten years, and they still had no children. So Sarai sent her hand-maid, Hagar the Egyptian, to Abram to be his wife, for in those days it was the custom for a man to have more than one wife. Hagar had a son and his name was Ishmael. He grew up to be an unsettled youth and a wanderer.

The Covenant with Abraham

Genesis 17

When Abram was ninety-nine years old, the Lord appeared to him, saying: "I am God Almighty. Walk in My ways and do no wrong. I will make My covenant with you and your people, and they will increase."

Then Abram bowed before God, and God said: "My covenant is with you. Your name shall be Abraham, the father of many nations. I will keep My covenant with you and your descendants forever.

"Your children and your children's children shall prosper. They shall become nations and kings. And to you and to them I give all the land of Canaan forever. I will be their God as I am your God."

And God continued: "As for Sarai your wife, her name shall be Sarah. I will bless her and from her you shall have a son. With him and his children after him will I keep my covenant forever. Sarah shall be a mother of nations and of kings."

And Abraham believed in the Lord.

Abraham and the Visitors

Genesis 18

One day as Abraham sat at the door of his tent, three men appeared. They had been sent by the Lord. Abraham went to greet them and bowed before them, inviting them to stay and rest.

"Water and food will be brought so that you will be refreshed before continuing on your way," Abraham said. And it was done.

The men told Abraham that Sarah would have a son. Sarah, hearing this, laughed, for she and Abraham were old and beyond the time of having children.

But God spoke: "Why does Sarah think she is too old to have a child? Is there anything the Lord cannot do? At the appointed time, Sarah shall have a son. His name shall be Isaac which means laughter."

Abraham Questions God

Genesis 18

When the messengers of the Lord rose to leave his tent, Abraham walked with them a little way toward Sodom.

The Lord spoke: "Because the sins of the cities of Sodom and Gomorrah are very great, I will destroy them."

The men started on their way to Sodom, and Abraham stayed and spoke to the Lord, saying: "Will You really destroy the good, the righteous, along with the wicked? Suppose there are fifty good people in the city? Would You forgive and save the city for the sake of those fifty? Should not the Lord, the Judge of all the earth, act with justice?"

The Lord answered: "If I can find fifty, for their sake I will not destroy the city."

Then Abraham asked: "Suppose there are only forty-five? Or forty? Lord, do not be angry that I question You. But suppose there are only thirty? Or twenty? Or even only ten righteous people in the city?"

The Lord replied: "I will not destroy the city for the sake of ten who are righteous."

Then Abraham went home.

Sodom and Gomorrah

Genesis 19

Now Lot, Abraham's nephew, lived in Sodom. When the messengers of the Lord came near, he invited them in to eat and to rest from their journey.

The wicked people of Sodom came to Lot's house and surrounded it, demanding to see the strangers, to rob them and do them harm.

The messengers said to Lot: "If you have anyone in the city, your wife, your daughters or sons-in-law or any that you wish to save, get them out. Take them away with you, for the Lord is going to destroy this city. Flee for your life. Do not look behind you, or you too will be destroyed."

Lot took his family and left Sodom in great haste.

Then the Lord destroyed the cities of Sodom and Gomorrah as punishment for the wickedness of their people; not even ten righteous people could be found.

Lot's wife looked back, and she became a pillar of salt. But Lot and his daughters went on, unharmed.

In the morning, Abraham saw that there was smoke rising from the place where Sodom and Gomorrah had been. It was like smoke from a huge furnace.

Isaac and Ishmael

Genesis 21

The Lord did as he had promised, and Sarah had a son. His name was Isaac. He grew strong and healthy and brought much joy to his parents.

One day Sarah saw Ishmael, the son of Hagar and Abraham, playing with Isaac.

To Abraham Sarah said: "Send Hagar and her son away." And Abraham was displeased because Ishmael, too, was his son.

Then God spoke to Abraham: "Listen to Sarah your wife. And do not be dismayed. Your name shall be carried on through Isaac. But Ishmael, too, shall be the father of a people for he is also your son."

So Hagar and Ishmael set out and wandered in the wilderness of Beersheba. After a while they had no more water in the jugs they

carried. But God protected them and made a fountain appear so they could drink again. There Ishmael grew up and, when he was a young man, his mother took a wife for him from Egypt.

God Tests Abraham

Genesis 22

It happened that God decided to test Abraham. He called: "Abraham! Abraham!" And Abraham answered: "Here am I."

Then God said: "Take your son Isaac whom you love and go to Moriah. There offer him as a burnt offering at a place that I will show you."

So Abraham arose early in the morning. He took Isaac and two of his servants with him. They cut wood for the fire, saddled a donkey and set out.

On the third day they came near the place God had told Abraham about. "Stay here and wait," Abraham told the servants. "The boy and I will go and worship and return to you."

Abraham took the wood and the fire and a knife. And Isaac asked: "I see the wood and

the fire, but where is the lamb for the sacrifice?"

Abraham answered: "God will provide the lamb, my son."

When they came to the place of which God had told him, Abraham built an altar and placed the wood on it. He put Isaac on the wood. Then Abraham reached for his knife.

But the angel of the Lord called to him: "Abraham! Abraham!" and Abraham answered: "Here am I."

The angel commanded: "Do not lay your hand on the boy or do anything to him. Now I

know that you truly fear God, for you have not even held back your son, Isaac, whom you love."

Then Abraham looked around and saw, behind him, a ram caught in a thick bush by its horns. Abraham took the ram and placed it on the altar as a burnt offering in place of Isaac.

The angel of the Lord called Abraham once more and said: "Because you have done this and have not held back your beloved son, the Lord will bless you.

"Your descendants shall be as many as there are stars in the heaven and grains of sand on the seashore. And your descendants shall conquer their enemies. And they shall be blessed because of you."

So Abraham and Isaac returned to the servants and they went home again.

The Death of Sarah

Genesis 23

Sarah died in the land of Canaan and Abraham mourned for her and wept. Then he rose up and looked for a burying place for Sarah. He chose a cave east of Mamre (that is, Hebron) in the land of Canaan, and there Sarah was buried.

A Wife for Isaac

Genesis 24

Now Abraham was very old and the Lord had blessed him in all things. One day he said to his servant Eliezer, the one whom he trusted above all: "Give me your hand, and swear by the Lord, the God of heaven and earth, that you will not take a wife for Isaac from among the daughters of Canaanites. You must go back to my country and to my family to choose a wife for Isaac."

The servant answered: "Suppose the one that is chosen will not come here with me? Should I take Isaac back there?"

Abraham said: "No, do not take him there. The Lord God who brought me here from the land of my birth made a promise to me, saying: 'To your children and your children's children I will give this land!'

"The Lord will send His angel to show you the way. There you must choose a wife for Isaac. If she is not willing to follow you, you are free from your promise. But do not take Isaac there."

Eliezer gave his hand to Abraham and promised.

Then he took ten of his master's camels and some of his master's choice possessions as gifts. He travelled to Mesopotamia, to the city of Haran.

There he made the camels kneel down at the well outside the city. It was the time of evening when the women came out to draw water from the well for their households.

Eliezer prayed, saying: "O Lord, God of my master Abraham, make me successful today, for my master's sake. The daughters of the city are coming to the well. I will ask one to let down her pitcher so I may drink. Let her answer: 'Drink, and I will give your camels water also.' Let this girl be the one that You have chosen for Isaac. By this sign, O Lord, You will show Your love for my master."

Rebekah at the Well

Genesis 24

Soon Rebekah, the granddaughter of Abraham's brother Nahor, appeared. She was lovely to look at. She carried her pitcher on her shoulder and she filled it at the well.

Eliezer went toward her and asked: "May I have a little water from your pitcher?"

And she answered: "Drink, my lord." She lowered the pitcher and gave him a drink.

When he had finished drinking, she said: "I will get water for your camels also, until they have had enough." So she emptied her pitcher into the trough, and went back to get more water for the camels.

When the camels had finished drinking, Eliezer thanked her and gave her a ring and bracelets, asking: "Whose daughter are you? Is there room in your father's house for me to spend the night?"

Rebekah answered: "I am the daughter of Bethuel, the granddaughter of Nahor and Milcah. We have both food and room for you to stay with us."

When he heard this, Eliezer bowed his head and prayed: "Blessed be the Lord, the God of Abraham, who has shown His love and mercy for my master and led me to the house of my master's people."

Rebekah had a brother, Laban. When she went home and told her family about the stranger and Laban saw the ring and the

bracelets, he ran to the well to welcome Eliezer.

"Come home with me," he said. "We have room for you and for your men and your camels. There is food and water for all of you."

Eliezer went with him and said: "I will come, but I will not eat until I have told you why I am here. I am Abraham's servant. The Lord has blessed my master and he has become great. The Lord has given him cattle and camels, silver and gold, menservants and maidservants and a son, Isaac."

Then he told how Abraham had sent him to find a wife for Isaac and how the Lord had led him to Rebekah.

Laban and Bethuel answered: "This thing has been the work of the Lord. Here is Rebekah. Take her with you to be the wife of Isaac, your master's son. The Lord has spoken."

When he heard these words, Eliezer bowed his head in thanks to the Lord. Then he brought out the silver and gold and all the gifts that he had brought. He gave them to Rebekah and to her mother and her brother. And he and the men with him ate and drank and spent the night there.

In the morning Eliezer said: "Now you must send me back to my master."

So they called Rebekah and asked her: "Will you go with this man to become Isaac's wife?"

And she said: "I will go."

Rebekah's family blessed her and wished her well. Then Rebekah and her attendants and Abraham's servant and his men began their journey.

It happened that one evening Isaac went out walking in the fields. He looked up and in the distance he saw camels coming toward him. Rebekah, too, looked up and when she saw Isaac in the field ahead, she got down from her camel and covered herself with a veil.

Then Eliezer told Isaac all that had happened. And Isaac took Rebekah home. She became his wife and he loved her.

The Death of Abraham
Genesis 25

Abraham was a very old man when he died. Isaac and Ishmael, his sons, buried him in the cave in Canaan beside Sarah his wife.

Ishmael had many sons. Isaac and Rebekah had twins, Esau and Jacob.

Jacob and the Birthright
Genesis 25

Isaac prayed to the Lord for Rebekah to have children, and the Lord answered his prayer.

Rebekah had twins. The firstborn had reddish hair all over his body and was called Esau. His brother was born holding onto Esau's heel, and he was called Jacob.

Esau became an expert hunter, a man of the field. Jacob became a quiet man who spent much time in his tent. Isaac loved Esau and liked to eat the meat he hunted and prepared; Rebekah loved Jacob.

One day, when Jacob was cooking soup, Esau came in hungry from the fields and said: "Let me have some of that soup. I am very hungry."

Jacob answered: "Then sell me your birthright."

Now Esau, being older, was to inherit his father's belongings, but he said: "I am about to die of hunger. What good will an inheritance do me then?"

Jacob said: "All right. But swear to me first."

So Esau promised Jacob and sold his inheritance to him. Then Jacob gave Esau bread and soup. Esau ate and drank and went away.

So it was that Esau sold his birthright for a bowl of soup.

The Blessing

Genesis 27

When Isaac was old, his eyes became dim and he could barely see. He called Esau.

"I am an old man and may soon die. Take your bow and arrows, go out into the field and hunt for me. Then prepare the meat I like best, and bring it to me, so I can give you my blessing before I die."

Rebekah heard what Isaac said to Esau. When Esau went out to hunt, she told Jacob what she had heard.

"You, my son," she said, "must go quickly and bring two goats and I will prepare them just the way your father likes them. You will take the meat to him and he will bless you."

Jacob answered: "But my brother is a hairy man and my skin is smooth. He will feel my hand and know that I am not Esau."

But his mother said: "Just do as I say. Go and get the goats so that I can prepare them."

Then Jacob did as he was told, and his mother prepared the meat. She put Esau's best clothes on Jacob. With the hairy skins of the goats she covered Jacob's hands and the back of his neck. Then she gave him the meat and bread for his father.

Jacob went in to Isaac, saying: "Here is your food, Father."

"Who are you?" asked Isaac.

"I am Esau, your firstborn," answered Jacob. "I have done as you told me. Sit up and enjoy your food, then you can bless me."

"How is it that the meat is ready so soon?"

"Because the Lord your God helped me."

Then Isaac said: "Come near so I may touch you to see if you are really Esau."

Jacob went to his father who said: "The voice is Jacob's voice, but the hands are the hands of Esau."

The hands were hairy like Esau's hands, so Isaac seemed satisfied.

But then he asked again: "Are you really my son Esau?"

16

And Jacob answered: "I am."

He gave his father the meat and bread and he brought wine also.

"Now," Isaac said, "Come near and kiss me, my son." Jacob came near and Isaac smelled Esau's clothes and blessed him, saying:

"The smell of my son is like a field which the Lord has blessed. So may God give you the dew of heaven and the bounty of the earth, plenty of corn and wine. Let people serve you and nations bow to you. Be a leader of your people and let even your mother's sons bow down to you."

When Jacob had been blessed, he left his father.

Esau's Threat

Genesis 27

Esau came in from hunting, prepared the meat and took it to Isaac.

"Father," said Esau, "sit up and eat the food I have for you so you may bless me."

Isaac asked: "Who are you?"

"I am your son, your firstborn, Esau."

Isaac trembled and said: "It must have been Jacob who already brought meat to me. I ate it before you came, then I blessed him. And he must remain blessed."

Esau cried out in despair: "Bless me also, Father!"

Isaac said: "Your brother came and took away your blessing."

"But it was Jacob, and he tricked me. He took away my birthright, and now he has taken away my blessing! Have you no blessing for me? Have you only one blessing? Bless me also, Father!" And Esau wept.

Then Isaac answered him: "You shall live away from the bounty of earth and away from the dew of heaven. You shall live by your sword and you shall serve your brother. But when you finally break loose and have power, you will be free."

Esau hated Jacob because of the blessing. He thought the time of his father's death was near. Then he would kill his brother.

Jacob and the Covenant

Genesis 28

When Rebekah learned of Esau's threats, she called Jacob to her. "Your brother Esau is planning to kill you. Leave here at once. Go to Haran to my brother Laban. Stay with him un-

til your brother's anger is over and he forgets what you have done."

Then Isaac told Jacob: "Yes, go to Laban. But you must not marry any of the Canaanite women. Go to the house of your uncle Laban and marry one of the girls there.

"May God bless you and make you fruitful. May He give the blessing of my father Abraham to you and to your children and to your children's children. And may you take possession of this land which God promised to my father Abraham."

Then Isaac sent Jacob away.

When Esau saw that the Canaanite women did not please his father, he went to his uncle Ishmael to seek a wife.

Jacob's Dream

Genesis 28

Jacob left Beersheba and started toward Haran. At sunset he stopped for the night. Taking a stone from the ground, he put it under his head for a pillow and lay down to sleep.

Jacob had a dream. He dreamed that there was a ladder set on the ground and the top of it reached to heaven. And angels of the Lord were going up and down the ladder.

The Lord was above the ladder and spoke: "I am the Lord, the God of Abraham and the God of Isaac. The land on which you are lying I will give to you and your descendants. They shall be many and shall spread throughout the earth to the north, south, east and west. I will be with you and will protect you wherever you go, and I will bring you back to this land."

Then Jacob awoke and said: "Surely the Lord must be in this place."

He got up, took the stone he had used for a pillow and set it up as an altar. He called the place Bethel, the house of God.

Then Jacob made a vow: "If God is with me on my journey and if I return to my father's house safely, then the Lord will be my God and this stone will be God's house forever. And of whatever I have, I will give a tenth to the Lord."

Jacob and Rachel

Genesis 29-31

One day Jacob came to a well in the middle of a field. At the well men were watering their flocks.

Jacob asked the shepherds: "Where are you from?"

"From Haran," they answered.

"Do you know Laban, the son of Nahor?"

They said: "We know him and things are well with him. There is Rachel, his daughter, coming now with her sheep."

When Jacob saw Rachel, the daughter of Laban his uncle, he watered the flock for her. Then he kissed her and told her that he was Rebekah's son. When she heard this, she ran to tell her father.

Laban came quickly to meet Jacob, and embraced him and brought him to his house. Jacob stayed there a month and helped Laban with his sheep.

Now Laban had two daughters. The older one was Leah, the younger was Rachel.

Jacob loved Rachel, so he told Laban:

"I will work without pay for seven years for your daughter Rachel to become my wife."

Laban agreed. So Jacob served seven years, but they seemed to him only a few days because of his love for Rachel.

At the end of the seven years, Jacob said to Laban: "Now, let Rachel be my wife, for I have done as I promised."

So Laban prepared a wedding feast, but he arranged for Leah to be heavily veiled and he married Leah to Jacob instead of Rachel.

"What have you done to me!" cried Jacob. "Why have you deceived me?"

Laban answered: "Because in our country the firstborn daughter must be married before the younger one. But if you will agree to serve seven more years, I will give you Rachel, too, as a wife."

Jacob loved Rachel more than Leah, so he served Laban another seven years. Then Rachel, too, became his wife.

Leah gave Jacob many sons but Rachel had no children for a long time. Finally, the Lord blessed Rachel and she had a son and named him Joseph.

By then, Jacob had been with Laban twenty years, and he felt the time had come for him to go back to his own land.

But Laban and his sons did not want Jacob

to leave with his wives and his children and his flocks.

Then Jacob turned to God, and God said: "Go. Return to the land of your fathers and I will be with you."

So Jacob put his wives and children on camels and drove his cattle and his flocks before him. He took all his possessions and his servants to return to Canaan, the land of his father Isaac.

Jacob left quietly without telling Laban goodbye. Laban followed Jacob and asked: "Why did you leave without telling me, stealing away my daughters and grandchildren when I could have sent you away with a feast?"

There Laban and Jacob made a covenant, an agreement of friendship between them, and Jacob offered a sacrifice to God.

Then Laban kissed and blessed his daughters and his grandchildren and returned home.

Jacob becomes Israel

Genesis 32

Jacob continued on his way and sent messengers before him to find Esau. He had to pass through Esau's land to reach Canaan, and he was afraid of the threat Esau had made twenty years before.

The messengers returned and reported that Esau was on his way to meet Jacob with four hundred men. Jacob thought Esau was coming to attack him, so he divided his party into two camps so that, if Esau captured one, the other could escape.

Then Jacob prayed: "O Lord, God of my fathers Abraham and Isaac, I am surely not worthy of all the kindness You have shown to me. You promised to deal kindly with me, and now I pray for Your continued kindness so that my people and I might be safe."

Jacob divided his flocks and his herds, his cattle and goats and sheep and camels into several groups and put each group in charge of a manservant. He sent them ahead of him, one group at a time.

To each leader he said: "If you meet my brother Esau, tell him that these animals belong to his brother Jacob and that they are gifts to him from me."

Then Jacob sent his wives and children and maidservants across a nearby stream to spend the night in a safe place. And Jacob stayed alone, with his thoughts and fears.

Jacob Meets Esau

Genesis 33

The next morning Jacob saw Esau coming with his four hundred men. He went to meet Esau, bowing as he went. Esau ran to Jacob, embraced him and the two brothers wept.

"Who are all those with you?" asked Esau.

Jacob answered: "Those are the children whom God has graciously given me." The children and their mothers came forward and bowed before Esau.

"What did you mean by sending all the flocks and all the herds I met on the way?" asked Esau.

"They are for you, as gifts," answered Jacob.

"But I have enough, my brother. Keep what you have for yourself."

"No, I insist," said Jacob. "Take my presents because God has been good to me and I have enough."

"Just to see your face again is like a gift from the Lord," said Esau. But Jacob urged Esau, and Esau accepted.

They forgave each other, and again they embraced and wept.

Then they bid each other goodbye. Esau started his journey home. And Jacob went on his way slowly because of the children and the young animals with him. He stopped at Succoth and built a house for himself and booths for his cattle.

Then they journeyed to the city of Shechem

A stranger appeared and wrestled with him. They struggled all night.

In the morning the stranger said: "Your name shall no longer be Jacob, but Israel, for you have struggled with God and with man and you have won."

Then he blessed Jacob. And Jacob knew that he had been face to face with God.

in Canaan. Jacob made his camp there and built an altar to the Lord.

The Death of Isaac

Genesis 35-37

Jacob went to Hebron to see his father Isaac to tell him all that had happened. Isaac was very old and had lived a full life. When Isaac died, his sons Esau and Jacob came to Hebron and buried him.

Then Esau took his wives and his children and all the members of his household and his animals and lived in the hill country of Seir. And he had many descendants.

Jacob and his household stayed in the land of Canaan. Jacob had twelve sons and a daughter, Dinah. Jacob's sons were: Reuben, Simeon, Levi, Judah, Issachar, Zebulun, Dan, Naphtali, Gad, Asher, Joseph and Benjamin.

Joseph and His Brothers

Genesis 37

Jacob's twelve sons were shepherds and spent every day out in the fields with their flocks.

Now Jacob loved Joseph more than the others because he was the firstborn of Rachel. He made Joseph a long robe, striped and with sleeves.

When the brothers saw that their father loved Joseph the most, they were jealous of him.

One night Joseph had a dream and when he told it to his brothers, they were more jealous than ever and became angry.

He told them his dream, saying: "We were in the field tying bundles of wheat and my bundle stood upright and your bundles gathered around and bowed down to mine."

His brothers asked: "Does this mean that you will rule over us?" And they hated Joseph.

Then Joseph dreamed another dream and told his father: "In my dream the sun and the moon and eleven stars bowed down to me."

And his father asked: "What? Shall I and your mother and all your brothers come to bow ourselves before you?"

His brothers hated Joseph greatly, but his father remembered the dream.

One day the brothers had gone to feed the flocks without Joseph, so his father sent him out to join them. They saw him coming and began to plan against him.

"Here comes the dreamer," said one. "Let us kill him and throw him in an old well. We can say a wild animal killed him."

The oldest brother, Reuben, said: "Do not kill him, just throw him in." Reuben felt sorry for Joseph and planned to come and rescue him later.

When Joseph came near, they ripped off his coat and threw him into a well that had no water in it. Then they sat down to eat.

It happened that a caravan was coming that way with merchants and camels carrying goods to Egypt.

Judah saw the caravan and said: "It will do us no good to kill Joseph. We can sell him to those merchants and they will take him to Egypt. We will be rid of him then."

This satisfied them all, so they sold Joseph for twenty pieces of silver.

Reuben had not seen the others sell Joseph and when he came to rescue Joseph, he was frightened.

Now the brothers had killed a goat and had dipped Joseph's coat into the blood. They took the garment to their father and asked: "Is this Joseph's coat?"

Jacob saw it and said: "It is Joseph's coat. A wild beast must have killed him."

Then Jacob mourned his son and wept for many days and could not be comforted.

Potiphar's Wife

Genesis 39

In Egypt Joseph was sold to Potiphar, an officer of Pharaoh, the ruler of Egypt.

The Lord was with Joseph. He was well treated and lived in his master's house. He became the chief servant and had charge of all Potiphar's household.

Joseph was a handsome young man and Potiphar's wife loved him. But he was trusted by his master and would not love her. Though she spoke to him often, he would not listen.

One day, Potiphar's wife caught the sleeve of Joseph's robe and held it. But Joseph slipped out of the sleeve and out of the house, leaving his robe still in her hand.

When Potiphar came home, his wife showed him the robe saying that Joseph had been at fault and that she had grabbed his robe as he ran away. Potiphar believed his wife and became very angry.

He sent for Joseph and had him thrown into prison.

But the Lord was with Joseph and was kind to him. The keeper of the prison came to trust Joseph and put him in charge of the other prisoners.

Joseph in Prison

Genesis 40

It happened that Pharaoh's butler and his baker offended their master. In his anger, Pharaoh sent them to the prison where Joseph was kept. One night the butler and the baker each had a dream.

When Joseph came to them in the morning, they looked worried. "We each have dreamed a dream," they told Joseph, "and there is no one to tell us what our dreams mean."

"God interprets dreams," Joseph answered.

But the butler told his dream to Joseph, saying: "There was a vine before me with three branches of heavy clusters of ripe grapes. Pharaoh's cup was in my hand so I took the grapes and squeezed them into the cup and gave the cup to Pharaoh."

Joseph said: "In your dream the three branches are three days. In three days Pharaoh will release you from prison. He will give your job back and you will hand him his cup as you did before, when you were his butler.

"Only one thing I ask of you: remember me when you go to Pharaoh. Speak kindly of me so I may be set free from prison, for I have done nothing to deserve it."

Then the baker told his dream to Joseph: "There were three baskets on my head. In the top basket were baked goods for Pharaoh, but the birds came and ate out of the basket."

Joseph told him: "The three baskets are three days. Within three days Pharaoh will lift up your head — from you! He will hang you on a tree, and the birds will come to peck at you."

The third day was Pharaoh's birthday. There was a great feast. On that day Pharaoh ordered the butler back to his position in the household. And he hanged the baker, as Joseph had said. But the butler did not remember Joseph, so Joseph remained in prison.

Pharaoh's Dreams

Genesis 41

Two years passed and Pharaoh had two dreams which worried him.

In the first dream Pharaoh was standing by the river Nile and seven fine fat cows came out of the river into the meadow. Then seven other cows, thin and scrawny, came out of the river and ate up the seven fat cows.

In Pharaoh's second dream seven full ears of corn were growing on one stalk. Then seven skimpy ears of corn appeared and swallowed up the seven full ears.

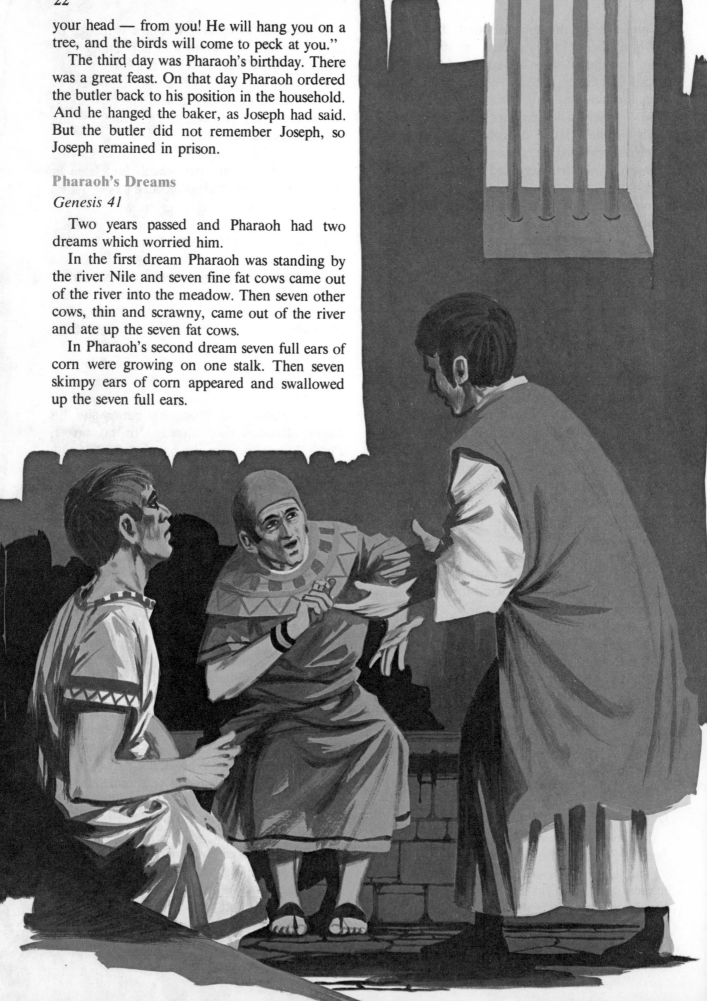

In the morning Pharaoh sent for all the magicians and wise men of Egypt. He told them his dreams, but no one could tell him their meaning.

Then the butler remembered Joseph and spoke to Pharaoh: "When the baker and I were in prison, we both had dreams. A young Hebrew was there with us and told us the meaning of our dreams, each one different. And the dreams came true just as he said."

So Pharaoh sent for Joseph and said to him: "No one here can tell me the meaning of my dreams. I hear that you understand dreams and can tell their meaning."

Joseph answered, saying: "It is not my power to understand dreams. God provides the meaning."

Pharaoh told Joseph his dreams of the seven thin cows eating the seven fat cows and of the seven thin ears of corn eating the seven full ears.

Then Joseph said: "In the two dreams God has shown you the future. The seven fat cows and the seven full ears are the same: they are seven good years. And the seven scrawny cows and the seven skimpy ears are the same: they are seven years of famine.

"There will come seven years of great plenty in the land of Egypt followed by seven years of famine. Then food will not grow and there will be hardship throughout the land. People will enjoy life and live well in the good years and will not prepare for the bad years."

Pharaoh looked worried and Joseph continued: "This thing is decided by God. Pharaoh should choose a wise man to govern the land and prepare for these things that will happen. Let some food of the good years be stored up and saved for the bad years so that the land and the people will not perish."

The plan seemed good and wise to Pharaoh. He wondered where he could find such a man, a man with the spirit of God.

Then Pharaoh looked at Joseph and said: "Since God has shown you all this, there is no one wiser than you. You shall rule, and all my people shall do as you command."

Pharaoh took off his ring and placed it on Joseph's finger. He gave Joseph fine clothes and a gold chain to wear around his neck. And he made people bow down to Joseph.

Joseph as Governor
Genesis 41

Joseph travelled throughout the land of Egypt. In the seven years of plenty, the earth brought forth food of all kinds. Because there was so much food, more even than could be used up, Joseph ordered some of it to be stored in the cities for the lean years ahead. In every city he stored food from the fields around it.

The seven years of plenty came to an end, and the seven years of famine began. There was hunger and poverty in every land but Egypt.

In Egypt there was still food. People from other lands came to Joseph for help because he was in charge of the storehouses.

Joseph's Brothers in Egypt
Genesis 42

In Canaan Jacob heard that there was food in Egypt. He called his sons together and said: "Go and buy grain for us that we may live." So ten of Joseph's brothers went to Egypt. The eleventh, Benjamin, was the youngest and stayed at home with his father.

Now, Joseph was governor over all the land. His brothers came and bowed down to him. He knew them but they did not know him. He treated them like strangers and spoke harshly to them.

"You have come as spies from Canaan," said Joseph.

"No," they said. "We have come to buy food. We are twelve brothers, the sons of a righteous man in Canaan. Our youngest brother is home with our father, and one is missing."

But Joseph wanted to test his brothers. He said: "You will not leave Egypt unless your youngest brother is brought to me." And he put them in prison for three days.

On the third day, Joseph spoke to them again: "Do as I say and save your lives. If you are men of truth and can be trusted, let one of you stay here in prison. The rest can take food to your households and bring your youngest brother back. Then I will believe you."

They looked at each other and were afraid. They talked together, saying: "This has happened to us because of what we did to our

brother Joseph. We had no mercy for him, and this is our punishment."

Joseph heard and, leaving them alone, he wept. Now he knew they still thought of him.

Then Joseph chose Simeon, the next-to-oldest brother, to stay in prison. He gave orders for the others to fill their bags with grain and in each man's bag he placed the money that had been paid for the grain. The nine brothers started home.

At the place where they stopped for the night, they opened the bags to feed their animals. They found the money and were afraid.

"What has God done to us?" they cried.

When they reached home, they told their father Jacob all that happened.

Jacob said: "You shall not take Benjamin to Egypt. Joseph is missing and you have left Simeon in prison. I have sorrow enough. You shall not do what is demanded of you!"

Benjamin Travels to Egypt

Genesis 43

Famine continued in the land of Canaan. Soon Jacob and his family had used up all the grain from Egypt. So Jacob called his sons together once more and said: "You must go to Egypt again to buy some grain."

Then Judah reminded him: "The governor of Egypt warned us, saying we can return only if Benjamin is with us."

"Why did you tell the man you had another brother?" asked Jacob.

They replied: "Because he questioned us about ourselves and about our father. Could we know he would ask us to bring our brother?"

Then Judah said: "We must go for grain so that we all may live, you and me and all our families. Send Benjamin with me. If he does not come back, I myself will bear the blame forever."

Jacob said: "If it must be so, do this: take the governor some presents. Whatever little we have, take the best. Take honey, nuts and spices. And take double the money, for you must give back the money that was with your grain.

"And take your brother Benjamin. May God Almighty be with you, so you may all come back, Simeon and Benjamin with you."

The brothers did as Jacob had told them. They went down to Egypt and came before Joseph.

Joseph Tests His Brothers

Genesis 43-44

When Joseph saw Benjamin with the others, he ordered his servant to prepare a feast. "These men will dine with me at noon," he said.

The brothers were afraid in such a fine house. They thought the governor would accuse them of stealing the money, but the servant told them not to be afraid. He brought Simeon to join them.

Joseph returned home and asked about their journey. And he asked: "Is your father well? Is he still alive?"

They bowed down to Joseph, answered him and gave him the gifts they had brought.

Joseph saw his youngest brother.

"May God be gracious to you," he said to Benjamin. Then he went to his room and wept. Afterwards he returned and ordered dinner to be served.

They ate and drank together. Joseph's servant filled the men's bags for the journey home.

Joseph had told him: "Fill the bags with as much as they can carry. Put every man's money in his bag as well. And in the youngest brother's bag, put my silver goblet."

The next morning, the brothers set out. When they had left the city, Joseph ordered his servant to follow them. "Ask them why they have done evil when I have done only good to them. Ask why they have stolen my silver goblet."

When the servant stopped them, he did as he was told.

"Why should the governor accuse us?" they asked. "We even brought back the money we found in our bags of grain the last time. If the goblet is found in any man's bag, let him die and the rest of us will offer ourselves to become slaves to the governor, for we have not done this thing!"

They opened their bags. And the goblet was found in Benjamin's.

With great sadness and fear, they went back to the city.

Joseph came out of his house and the brothers bowed down before him.

Joseph spoke harshly: "What have you done? You know that I cannot be deceived."

Judah answered: "What shall we say? How shall we clear ourselves? Now we will be slaves to you, all of us."

"No," said Joseph. "Only the man who had the goblet will be my slave. The rest of you will return to your father."

Then Judah spoke: "My Lord, hear me, I beg you. You asked us when we first came here if we had a father or a brother. And we answered you in truth. Then you said if we did not bring our brother, we could not come again. Our father did not want us to bring him here. If anything happens to Benjamin, our father will surely die. He has never stopped weeping for our missing brother Joseph.

"I myself have taken the responsibility for Benjamin. I told my father I would take the blame if harm came to him.

"Let me be your slave and let Benjamin go home with his brothers."

Joseph Reveals Himself

Genesis 45

Then Joseph could no longer control himself and ordered his servants to leave him alone with the brothers.

And Joseph said: "Come near me." And they came near.

And he said: "I am your brother Joseph, whom you sold into Egypt. It was not you who sent me to Egypt, but God. Do not be ashamed or angry with yourselves, for surely God sent me here to save lives. He has made me Pharaoh's governor to rule over Egypt."

His brothers were so amazed they could not speak.

Joseph continued: "Go, hurry home to our father and give him this message: that he shall travel to Egypt with you. Then you will all live in the land of Goshen where you will be near me. You, your children, your children's children and all your households and your

flocks and your herds, all will come here, for there are five years of famine still ahead of us."

Then they embraced each other, wept for joy and talked together.

Jacob and Joseph in Egypt

Genesis 45-47

Pharaoh heard about Joseph's brothers and was pleased. He said to Joseph: "Tell your brothers to load their animals for the journey home. Tell them to take wagons from Egypt to carry their wives and their little ones. Then they can bring your father and all their households to Egypt." So they went out of Egypt back to the land of Canaan.

And they told their father: "Joseph is still alive. He rules over the land of Egypt."

Jacob did not believe them. But when they told him all that Joseph had said, and he saw the wagons, he believed.

"Joseph, my son, is still alive," said Jacob. "Yes, I must go and see him before I die."

Then Jacob and his sons began their journey with all that they had. When they came to Beersheba they offered sacrifices to God.

In the night God spoke to Jacob: "I am the God of your fathers. Do not be afraid to go down to Egypt. There I will make of you a great nation. I will be with you and I will surely bring you back to Canaan."

Jacob sent Judah ahead to show the way to Goshen.

Joseph came in his chariot to meet his father. They embraced and wept for joy.

Joseph's father and his brothers and all their family, seventy altogether, settled with their goods and their flocks and their herds in the best pasture land of Goshen. And Joseph continued to manage the land of Egypt for Pharaoh.

The Death of Jacob

Genesis 47-50

Jacob lived in Goshen until he was a very old man. When he was about to die he called Joseph and said: "Do not bury me in Egypt, but take me back to Canaan to be buried with my fathers, Abraham and Isaac."

And he said: "God Almighty appeared to me in Canaan and blessed me. He said I and my descendants should be fruitful and multiply and become a company of nations. And he said the land of Canaan will be our everlasting possession."

Then he said to Joseph: "Bring me your two sons who were born in the land of Egypt. Bring them to me so I may bless them."

Joseph brought his sons, Manasseh and Ephraim.

Then Jacob died and was embalmed. When the days of mourning in Egypt were over, Joseph told Pharaoh his father's wish, and Pharaoh said: "Go to the land of Canaan and bury your father as he asked." So Jacob was buried with Abraham and Isaac in the land of Canaan.

The Death of Joseph

Genesis 50

Joseph lived a long life and saw even his grandchildren grow into manhood. Before he died, Joseph called together his brothers and his children and all his family and said: "God will one day bring you out of this land into the land which He promised to Abraham, to Isaac and to Jacob." Then Joseph died and was buried in Egypt.

Jacob, whom the Lord called Israel, blessed them, saying: "God of Abraham and Isaac, the God who has led me all my life and has delivered me from evil, bless these boys. May they carry my name, and let them grow into great peoples of the earth."

And he said: "By you Israel will always give blessings saying: 'God make you as Ephraim and as Manasseh.'"

To Joseph he said: "God will be with you and bring you again to the land of your fathers."

Jacob called all his twelve sons so he might tell them what would happen in the years to come. He told how twelve tribes would descend from the twelve brothers. He spoke to each one in turn. And he blessed each one. He said that Judah's tribe would one day be the one which all the others would praise.

The Book of Exodus

The history of the Israelites from slavery in Egypt through the wanderings in the wilderness to the building of the tabernacle to God by Moses.

Slavery in Egypt

Exodus 1

Joseph died and all his brothers and all of that generation. And their children and their children's children grew strong and prospered in Egypt.

Then there arose a new king over Egypt who had not known Joseph and the great work he had done. The new Pharaoh said to his people: "The children of Israel are too many and are becoming too powerful for us. If they would join our enemies or fight against us, we would surely be beaten."

So Pharaoh took away the freedom of the Israelites. The Egyptians forced the children of Israel to work for them and set taskmasters over them. They had them do heavy work in the fields and the cities. And they set them to work building the great cities of Pithom and Raamses.

The Egyptians made life hard for the Israelites and oppressed them. But still the Israelites grew in number. Pharaoh became fearful and commanded the people, saying: "Every Israelite son that is born shall be thrown into the river and drowned, but every daughter shall live."

The Birth of Moses

Exodus 2

At that time there was a woman of the family of Levi who had a baby son. She hid him until he was three months old. When she could no longer hide him at home, she made a basket of bulrushes, lined it and put the baby in it. Then she placed it at the water's edge, hiding it among the tall grasses that grew there. The baby's sister Miriam stayed nearby to see what would happen.

Pharaoh's daughter came to wash herself in the river. When she saw the basket, she sent one of her handmaidens to bring it to her.

The basket was opened and the baby cried.

Miriam came over and asked: "Shall I find a nurse to take care of the baby for you?"

Pharaoh's daughter answered: "Yes." Miriam brought her own mother, and Pharaoh's daughter said: "Take this child away and look after him, and I will pay you. He is truly a handsome child."

So the mother took her child home and cared for him. When he grew older he went to live with Pharaoh's daughter in the palace. She loved him and treated him as her own son. She named him Moses, meaning "to draw out," because she had taken him out of the water.

ing they cried out and God heard their cry. He remembered His covenant with Abraham, Isaac and Jacob.

The Burning Bush

Exodus 3

One day Moses was looking after the flocks of his father-in-law, Jethro, when he came to Horeb, the mountain of God.

There the voice of the Lord came to him.

Moses saw a bush on fire. He looked and saw that it was burning but it was not destroyed. He stood there and watched and wondered.

Moses heard a voice call from out of the middle of the bush: "Moses, Moses."

And Moses answered: "Here am I."

"Do not come any closer," said the voice. "Take off your shoes, for you are standing on holy ground."

And then: "I am the God of your fathers, the

Moses and Zipporah

Exodus 2

One day when Moses was a young man, he went out in the fields and watched the people at work. He saw an Egyptian beating an Israelite worker. So he killed the Egyptian and hid his body. Pharaoh heard of this and sent for Moses. But Moses had already left Egypt and had gone to live in Midian.

There he often sat before the well where shepherds came to water their flocks.

The priest of Midian had seven daughters and they brought their father's flock to that well. One day Moses saw them and helped them with the water. That day they went home early.

They told their father about the Egyptian who had helped them. He said: "Call the man that he might eat with us."

Moses ate with them and was happy to stay in their house. The priest Jethro gave Zipporah his daughter to Moses to be his wife. She had a son, and Moses called him Gershom which means "stranger," for Moses said: "I am a stranger in a strange land."

The king of Egypt died. But the children of Israel were still slaves and had to work even harder under the new Pharaoh. In their suffer-

God of Abraham, the God of Isaac, and the God of Jacob."

Then God said: "I have seen the hardship of My people in Egypt and I have heard their cries. I will deliver them from the Egyptians, and bring them out of Egypt to a land flowing with milk and honey.

"You must go to Pharaoh to plead with him. And you will lead the children of Israel out of Egypt."

Moses asked: "Who am I, that I should lead them?"

And God answered: "I will be with you, and when at last you have brought the people out of Egypt, you will worship on this mountain. They will listen to you."

"But," said Moses, "if I say that God has sent me, they will ask: 'What is His name?' How shall I answer them?"

God answered: "I am who I am. Tell the people: 'The Lord, the God of your fathers, the God of Abraham, Isaac and Jacob, has sent me.'

"This is My name forever, and this is how I am to be remembered for all generations.

"Now, you and the elders must go to Pharaoh and ask him to let the Israelites make a three day journey into the desert to sacrifice to the Lord."

Signs from God

Exodus 4

God said to Moses: "I know that the king of Egypt will not let the children of Israel go easily. So I will raise My hand and strike at Egypt. After that, Pharaoh will let you go."

Moses answered: "But they will not believe me."

God said: "Take the stick you are holding and throw it on the ground."

Moses did so and at once the stick became a snake.

"Now," commanded God, "reach out, and pick it up by the tail."

Moses did and it became a stick once more.

"When you do these things the people will believe you. They will believe that the Lord, the God of their fathers, the God of Abraham, Isaac and Jacob, has really appeared to you.

"Now put your hand inside your robe."

Moses did and when he brought it out, his hand was white and covered with sores.

"Put your hand inside your robe again," commanded God.

Moses did and brought it out clear and well once more.

Then God said: "If they do not believe the first sign or the second sign or listen to your voice, then you must take water from the river and pour it on the land. The water will become blood."

But still Moses doubted: "Lord, I do not speak well. I have a slow tongue."

God asked: "Who has made man's mouth? Is it not I, the Lord? Go, and I will be with you."

But Moses said: "Please, O Lord, send someone else."

Then God said: "Aaron is your brother. He can speak well. You shall speak to him and I will be with you both. He shall speak as a mouth for you, and you shall speak as a God for him. Now go and take the stick, the rod I have provided for you."

Moses Returns to Egypt

Exodus 4-5

Moses took the rod and the sheep and returned to his father-in-law. He said to Jethro: "The time has come for me to go back to my people in Egypt, to see if they are still alive."

Jethro bid him go in peace. So Moses took his wife and his son and returned to the land of Egypt.

Now, the Lord commanded Aaron: "Go into the wilderness to meet your brother Moses."

There Moses told Aaron all that the Lord had said to him and all that he was to do.

Then Moses and Aaron called together the elders of Israel and told them all the words and all the signs that the Lord had commanded.

The elders believed. They knew that the Lord had heard their cries. Then they bowed their heads and worshipped Him.

Moses and Aaron went before Pharaoh and spoke, saying: "Let my people go. The Lord, the God of Israel, has commanded that we hold a feast in the wilderness to worship him."

Pharaoh asked: "Who is this Lord that I should obey Him and let the Israelites go? I do not know your God, and I will not let your people go. Why take the people away from their work? Get back to work yourselves!"

And Pharaoh said to the taskmasters: "Make the people work harder. Make them gather their own straw to make bricks. And order them to make more bricks every day, so they will not have time to listen to foolish talk."

The taskmasters of Pharaoh did as they were told. They worked the Israelites until they collapsed, and still they were not satisfied.

Then the leaders of the children of Israel said to Moses and Aaron: "May the Lord punish you, for you have made trouble for us with Pharaoh. We can never work hard enough to satisfy him."

God Speaks to Moses

Exodus 5-7

Moses turned to the Lord, saying: "Why have you sent me? Since I went to Pharaoh, he has been harder on us than before."

God answered: "You shall see what I will do to Pharaoh. He himself will drive the children of Israel out of Egypt. For I am the Lord.

"I made myself known to Abraham, to Isaac and to Jacob. I made a promise to them, to give them and their descendants the land of Canaan."

And He said: "Tell the children of Israel that I am the Lord and I will free them from Egypt and take them out of slavery. I will bring them to the land I have promised."

Moses told all this to the children of Israel. But they did not listen because of all their suffering.

God spoke to Moses again: "Go to Pharaoh now and tell him to let all the people of Israel go." And God named all the families of the people of Israel to be set free.

"Speak to Pharaoh and tell him all that I command you. I will perform many signs and miracles, and still Pharaoh will not listen. But I

will stretch forth My hand again and again until finally Pharaoh will send you forth from Egypt. Then they shall know that I am the Lord."

Moses and Aaron went before Pharaoh and cast down the rod. At once it became a serpent.

Then Pharaoh called all his magicians and wise men to come before him. They each threw down a rod and they all became serpents. And Pharaoh would not let the people of Israel go.

God spoke to Moses: "Go to meet Pharaoh in the morning where he goes to the river. Take your rod with you. Tell him that you will strike the rod on the water and the water will turn to blood. Tell him the fish in the river will die, the water will smell foul and no one will be able to drink it."

God said to Aaron: "Then, stretch out the rod over all the rivers, streams, ponds, and pools of water in Egypt so they, too, will become blood."

Moses and Aaron did all that the Lord commanded. Even when he saw the water turn to blood, Pharaoh would not listen.

So God said to Moses: "Tell Aaron to reach out the rod and strike the dust of the earth so it will become lice throughout the land."

When the rod struck the dust, it became lice on all the people and all the animals of Egypt. Still Pharaoh would not listen.

Again God spoke to Moses: "Tell Pharaoh if he does not let My people go so they can worship Me, I will send swarms of flies upon Egypt. But I will separate his land from the land of Goshen where My people live. No flies will appear in Goshen, only in Egypt. Then he will see that I am the Lord over all the earth."

The Lord did as He had said. The land and the people and the animals of Egypt were covered with flies. But in Goshen there were no flies.

Again Pharaoh sent for Moses and Aaron. This time he said: "You and your people can sacrifice to your God, but sacrifice here in Egypt."

Moses answered: "We cannot worship before the Egyptians. They would not understand. According to God's command we must go three

The Ten Plagues

Exodus 8-11

Seven days passed and God said to Moses: "Go to Pharaoh again and tell him to let the children of Israel go. If he refuses, tell him that I will cause a plague of frogs to come to Egypt. Frogs will come from the river and will go into every house, every bed, every bowl and every oven. They will swarm everywhere. Tell Aaron to hold out the rod to make the frogs come forth."

Aaron and Moses did as God commanded, and the frogs came up and covered the land of Egypt.

Pharaoh called Moses and Aaron and said: "Go, pray to the Lord. Ask Him to take the frogs away and I will let the people go to make sacrifices to the Lord."

"It shall be done at once," said Moses. "Then you will know that there is none like the Lord our God."

Moses prayed. The frogs died and disappeared from the houses, the fields, the villages and the cities of Egypt.

But when Pharaoh saw that the frogs were gone, he changed his mind.

days into the wilderness and sacrifice."

Pharaoh said: "Very well. I will let you go into the wilderness. Go and speak to your God."

Moses left Pharaoh and prayed to God, and the Lord caused the flies to disappear.

Again Pharaoh hardened his heart and would not let the people go.

God called Moses, saying: "Tell Pharaoh if he does not let My people go, there will be a terrible plague on all the cattle, horses, camels, oxen and sheep of Egypt. I will separate the animals of the children of Israel from those of the people of Egypt."

The next day all the cattle and beasts of Egypt died. But not one of the animals of the children of Israel died. Pharaoh sent messengers to see it all, but still his heart was hardened.

God said to Moses and Aaron: "Now, you must take ashes from the ovens and furnaces and throw them into the air. They shall become fine dust and cause boils and sores upon every Egyptian."

They did as God commanded. The people were covered with boils and running sores. But still Pharaoh would not listen or change his mind.

Then God said to Moses: "Arise early in the morning and tell Pharaoh I will send all My plagues on him too, as well as on his servants and on his people. Then he will know there is none like Me in all the earth.

"If he still will not let My people go, I will cause terrible hail to fall from the sky and it will kill every man and animal in the field."

The people who feared the word of the Lord brought their families and their animals into their houses. The others left their children and their animals outside.

Moses pointed his rod toward the sky, and the Lord sent thunder and hail. And fire ran along the ground. The hail struck and killed every man, every animal and every plant and tree in the fields. Only in Goshen was there no hail and no fire.

Pharaoh sent for Moses and Aaron, and he said: "I have sinned. The Lord is just. Pray to

the Lord to stop the thunder and hail and fire, and I will let your people go."

But when the thunder and hail and fire stopped, he still would not let the children of Israel go as he had promised.

God spoke to Moses: "I have allowed these things to happen so that you can tell your son and your son's son what I have done in Egypt. Then they will know that I am the Lord. Go back to Pharaoh. And tell him all that I say."

Moses and Aaron went again to Pharaoh and said: "This is what the Lord, the God of the Hebrews, says: if you do not let our people go, tomorrow He will cause locusts in your land. They will completely cover the face of the earth so it cannot be seen. They will eat every plant in the land that is left after the hail and the fire. They will fill your palace and the houses of all your people."

When they had told Pharaoh this, they left him.

Pharaoh's servants said to him: "How long will these men make Egypt suffer? Let them go to worship their God."

So Pharaoh called Moses and Aaron back and said: "Go and worship your God. Who will go with you?"

Moses answered: "We will go with all our people, our young and our old, our sons and our daughters and our herds and our flocks, for we must worship the Lord as He has commanded us."

"No!" said Pharaoh. "I will never let all your people leave. Go, but take only the men you need to serve the Lord."

Moses and Aaron were sent away.

Then Moses stretched out his rod once more. And the Lord caused an east wind to blow over the land all that day and night.

In the morning the wind brought the locusts. Never had so many locusts been seen before. The whole land became darkened, and the locusts ate every plant and every leaf and every stalk and every fruit that the hail had left.

Not a plant remained throughout the whole land of Egypt.

Pharaoh ordered Moses and Aaron to come before him, and he said: "I have sinned against the Lord your God and against you. Forgive me and pray that this plague will be taken away."

So the Lord sent a west wind which took away all the locusts and blew them into the sea so that not one locust was left.

Still Pharaoh would not let the children of Israel go.

Then the Lord called to Moses: "Reach your hand toward the sky so that there will be a darkness over the land of Egypt, a darkness so thick that people will feel it."

Moses stretched out his hand. For three days there was complete darkness throughout Egypt. The Egyptians could not see each other or leave their houses. But all the children of Israel had light.

Pharaoh called Moses and said: "Now go and worship the Lord. Your children may go with you, but leave your herds and your flocks in Egypt."

Moses answered: "We must take our animals to offer sacrifices to the Lord our God."

But Pharaoh would not let them go.

The Lord spoke to Moses again, and Moses came before Pharaoh with the words of the Lord in his ears: "After this plague, Pharaoh will drive the children of Israel out of Egypt."

Moses told Pharaoh: "The Lord will bring one more plague upon Egypt: all the firstborn in the land shall die, from the firstborn even of Pharaoh to the firstborn of the servants and villagers and townspeople. Even the firstborn of the animals and birds shall die.

"But none of the children of Israel shall suffer, neither the people nor their animals. Then surely Pharaoh will see how the Lord has made a difference between the people of Egypt and the children of Israel."

The Passover
Exodus 12-13

The Lord spoke to Moses and Aaron, telling them what they must do: "This shall be the first month of the year for you. On the tenth day of the month, every Israelite shall take a lamb from his flocks, a lamb that is perfect, and kill it. And he shall take some of the blood and put it on the doorposts of his house. Then the people shall roast their lambs and eat in haste, with shoes on their feet and their belongings ready to go.

"For this is the Lord's passover: I will pass through the land of Egypt that night and kill all

Pharaoh called Moses and Aaron that night and said: "Go! Leave my land forever. Take all the people of Israel, the elders and the little ones, and take your flocks and your herds. Go and worship your God!"

The Egyptians urged the Israelites to leave and hurried them out of their houses. Thus they left the land of Egypt with all their possessions, and their dough before it was risen. And they baked unleavened cakes with the dough they had taken with them.

Then Moses said: "Remember this day, the day you came out of Egypt, out of the house of slavery. You shall keep this commandment every year: for seven days you shall eat unleavened bread because of what the Lord has done."

There were about six thousand men, not counting women and children, who left Egypt that night.

The people of Israel had lived in Egypt four hundred and thirty years.

Crossing the Reed Sea

Exodus 13-15

The Lord led Moses and the children of Israel out of the land of Egypt. To show the way, He sent before them a pillar of cloud by day and a pillar of fire by night.

Moses had with him the bones of Joseph who had died in Egypt many years before. For Joseph had said that the Lord would surely lead the people to the land which He had promised them.

When Pharaoh saw that all the Israelites had indeed left Egypt, he set out to bring them back into slavery.

Pharaoh took with him six hundred chariots and all his horsemen and his armies. He planned to capture the Israelites where they were camped near the Reed Sea.*

Now the people saw Pharaoh and his army coming after them and they cried out to Moses: "It would have been better for us to remain slaves than to die here in the wilderness!"

Moses answered: "Do not be afraid. The Lord will save us."

And the Lord said to Moses: "Tell the people to go forward. Hold up your rod and stretch your hand over the water to divide it.

the firstborn of the Egyptians. The blood will be a sign, so I will pass over the houses of the children of Israel and not allow death to strike them.

"And you shall keep this day as a feast day forever. You and your children and your children's children shall keep this day even after you come into the land which the Lord your God will give you."

Moses called the elders of Israel together and told them all that the Lord had said. And the people heard and bowed their heads and worshipped the Lord.

Then they did as the Lord had commanded them through Moses and Aaron.

At midnight the Lord struck down all the firstborn in the land of Egypt except the firstborn of the children of Israel. Then, a great cry of despair arose in the land, for in every house there was death.

*Reed Sea — According to modern scholars, this is the Reed Sea or Sea of Reeds, not the Red Sea.

You and the children of Israel will go through the sea on dry land. Then My power will be shown to them, and they will know that I am the Lord."

The pillar of cloud moved from in front to behind the Israelites, to be between them and the armies of Pharaoh.

Moses did as the Lord commanded. He stretched out his hand and a strong wind blew. And the sea was pushed back and divided.

Then the children of Israel with all their belongings walked into the middle of the sea.

They walked on dry land to the other side, for the waters separated, making a wall on the right and a wall on the left.

The Egyptians came after them, Pharaoh and his chariots and his armies.

Then the Lord said to Moses: "Stretch out your hand over the sea so the water will come back."

Moses raised his hand. The water rushed back, and all the Egyptians were drowned.

The people saw the great work of the Lord and they feared Him. They believed in the

Lord and in His servant Moses.

Then Moses and the people of Israel rejoiced, saying:
"The Lord is my strength and my salvation;
He is my God and I will praise Him,
My father's God and I will exalt Him;
In His greatness, He overthrows His enemy;
Who is like Thee, O Lord, among the mighty?
Who is like Thee, glorious in holiness,
Doing wonders?
The Lord will reign forever and ever."

Manna from Heaven

Exodus 15-16

Moses led the Israelites from the Reed Sea into the wilderness of Shur. For three days they found no water.

When they did find water, it was bitter and they could not drink it. They complained to Moses.

Moses called on the Lord, and the Lord showed him a tree. When Moses took a branch from the tree and threw it into the water, the water became sweet and the Israelites drank.

Then the Lord said: "If you will listen to the Lord your God and do what is right in His eyes, obey His commandments and keep His laws, I will lead you. I am the Lord your God."

They moved on and camped at Elim where there were twelve springs of water and seventy palm trees.

When they left there, they walked through the wilderness of Sin between Elim and Sinai. And they used up their supply of food.

The Israelites cried out against Moses and Aaron, saying: "It would have been better to die in Egypt where we had food. You have brought us into the desert to starve!"

Again God spoke to Moses: "I will rain food from heaven for you. In the evening the people shall eat meat, in the morning, bread. Then they shall know I am the Lord their God."

And He said: "The people shall gather a day's portion every day. But on the sixth day, they shall gather twice as much, for they shall not gather or prepare food on the seventh day. The seventh day is a day of rest, the holy Sabbath."

In the evening birds called quails flew over and dropped into the camp. In the morning dew covered the ground. When it had evaporated, the ground was covered with thin flakes, white like frost.

Moses said: "It is the bread God promised. Gather it and use it according to the commandments of the Lord."

And Moses told them all that God had said to keep the seventh day as a holy day.

The children of Israel called this food manna. And they ate it for forty years until

they came to the land of Canaan.

The Defeat of Amalek
Exodus 17

The people of Israel moved through the wilderness of Sin and pitched their camp at Rephidim. Again there was no water for them to drink.

Once more they found fault with Moses, saying: "Did you bring us out of Egypt to kill us with thirst?"

Then the Lord spoke to Moses: "Take your rod in your hand and strike the rock at Horeb. Water will come from it, so the people may drink."

Moses did as he had been commanded and there was enough water for everyone.

While they were at Rephidim, Amalek and his warlike tribe attacked the Israelite camp.

Moses called Joshua to become his captain and to gather men to fight the warriors of Amalek.

"And I will stand on the hill holding the rod of God in my hand," said Moses.

Joshua led his men against Amalek. Whenever Moses raised his hand, Israel won a battle; when he lowered his hand, Amalek won.

After awhile Moses' arms grew tired, but Aaron and Hur held up his hands, one on one side and one on the other.

The battle lasted all day but the hands of Moses were steady.

By the time the sun had set, Joshua and his men had defeated Amalek.

Moses Chooses Leaders

Exodus 18

Jethro, the priest of Midian, the father-in-law of Moses, heard all that God had done for Moses and for his people Israel. And he came into the desert to visit Moses.

Moses told him what the Lord had done to Pharaoh and the Egyptians, and Jethro blessed the name of the Lord.

The next day Moses held court and the people came before him all day long. They came with questions, with complaints, and with arguments. Moses gave judgment and told the people the ways of God.

Jethro watched and he said: "This is not good. It is too much for one man. You should choose men who are able and honest and who love God to help you rule the people and judge them.

"There should be rulers of hundreds and rulers of fifty and rulers of ten. Every important matter they could bring to you. Every small matter they could judge themselves. This way others will share responsibility with you."

Moses listened to his father-in-law and took his advice. He chose able men to be leaders of

the people. And it proved to be very good.

Then Jethro returned to his own land.

The Ten Commandments

Exodus 19-24

The children of Israel had been travelling three months when they came to the desert of Sinai. At the foot of the mountain of Sinai they pitched their tents.

Moses went up the mountain and God spoke to him, saying: "The children of Israel have seen what I did to the Egyptians and how I led them to this place.

"Tell them that if they listen to My voice and keep My covenant, they will become a kingdom of priests and holy people."

Moses came down and spoke the words of the Lord to the people.

And they said: "All that the Lord has said, we will do."

Then God said to Moses: "I will come to you in a thick cloud so the people will know when I speak to you.

"Go and bless them, and let them wash their clothes and prepare themselves for two days. On the third day I will appear to them."

On the morning of the third day there was lightning and thunder, and a thick cloud surrounded the mountain. A loud sound like a trumpet-blast was heard, and all the people trembled.

Mount Sinai was covered with smoke, and the smoke rose up as if from a great furnace. And the whole mountain shook violently.

The trumpet sound grew louder. Moses spoke and God answered with another great sound of thunder. Then the Lord called Moses to the top of the mountain, and Moses went up.

God spoke all these words to Moses, the words of the Ten Commandments:

"I am the Lord your God, who brought you out of the land of Egypt, out of the house of slavery.

"You shall have no other gods before Me. You shall not make for yourself any statue, or any likeness of anything that is in heaven above, or that is in the earth beneath, or that is in the water under the earth. You shall not bow down to them or serve them. For I, the Lord your God, am a jealous God, punishing the children of those who hate Me to the third and

fourth generation, and showing mercy to the thousandth generation of those that love Me and keep My commandments.

"You shall not take the name of the Lord your God in vain.

"Remember the Sabbath day to keep it holy. Six days you shall do all your work, but the seventh day is a holy Sabbath to the Lord your God; on that day you shall not do any kind of work, you, or your son, or your daughter or your manservant, or your maidservant, or your cattle, or the stranger that is within your gates. For in six days the Lord made heaven and earth, the sea, and all that is in them, and He rested on the seventh day and made it holy.

"Honour your father and your mother, that your days may be long in the land which the Lord your God gives to you.

"You shall not murder.

"You shall not commit adultery.

"You shall not steal.

"You shall not falsely accuse your neighbour.

"You shall not covet your neighbour's house, or your neighbour's wife or his manservant or his maidservant, or his animals or anything that is your neighbour's."

Now when the people saw the lightning and heard the thunder and the sound of the trumpet, they were afraid and stood a long way off while Moses went near the thick darkness.

There the Lord spoke to Moses at great length setting out many other laws which the people of Israel must understand and obey. And Moses told them to the people to be their guide in treating each other justly.

The people said: "Everything the Lord has said, we will do."

Then Moses built an altar to the Lord with twelve pillars for the twelve tribes of Israel. And the people made sacrifices to the Lord and worshipped Him.

The Ark of the Covenant

Exodus 24-27

Again God called Moses to come up on the mountain, saying: "There I will give you tablets of stone with the commandments written on them."

Moses and Joshua went to the mountain of the Lord and Moses told the elders: "Wait for

us here. Aaron and Hur are with you. If there is any dispute to be settled, they will handle it while I am gone."

Then Moses went up Mount Sinai and a great cloud covered it for six days.

On the seventh day God called to Moses from the cloud, and the sight was like a huge fire on top of the mountain.

Moses went into the cloud, and he stayed there for forty days and forty nights.

The Lord told Moses many things: "Tell all the people of Israel to bring offerings. From every man who gives willingly you shall take the offering.

"Tell them to bring gold, silver and brass, cloth of blue, purple and scarlet, fine linen, goats' hair, ramskins and goatskins, acacia wood, oil for lamps, spices, incense and stones and precious jewels.

"Let the people use all these things to build Me a sanctuary so I may live among them. Have them make it according to the directions that I will give you."

Then God told Moses how they were to build an ark of wood. He told them the size: the length, the width and the height. He said it should be covered with gold and have a gold ring at each corner for wooden rods to be slipped through so it could be carried.

"In the ark," said the Lord, "shall be kept My laws and commandments. On the ark shall be a seat of pure gold and two angels facing each other with their wings spread wide.

"The people shall make a table of acacia wood covered with gold and place gold rings at each corner. Rods shall be put through the rings so the table too may be carried.

"They shall make a candlestick of pure gold.

Six branches shall come out of it, three on one side and three on the other side so that altogether there will be seven lights. The candlestick shall be placed on the table.

"Also on the table shall be plates and bowls and dishes of pure gold. Every Sabbath there shall be loaves of bread to be eaten by the priests.

"And they shall make a tabernacle, a tent, and line it with many curtains of fine linen and blue, purple and scarlet cloth. It shall be covered with the skins of goats and of rams and of goats' hair.

"The ark shall be kept in the tent. A curtain shall be hung in front of the ark to separate the holy place from the most holy place.

"In front of the ark the table shall be kept. And an altar shall be built overlaid with bronze.

"Before the ark shall be a lamp, put there to burn continually. The people shall bring pure olive oil for the lamp. Aaron and his sons shall keep it burning forever."

For all these things the Lord gave Moses directions and measurements so the people would understand exactly how to build them.

The Consecration of Priests

Exodus 28-31

"Bring your brother Aaron and his sons to serve as priests," said the Lord. "They shall have holy garments made for them, both for beauty and for glory.

"Aaron shall be the high priest. He shall have a breastplate, an ephod, a robe, an embroidered coat, a turban and a sash."

Again, God gave Moses definite directions for each article to be made:

The breastplate must hang from chains of pure gold. It must be square and have precious stones set in it — twelve different jewels, one for each of the twelve tribes of Israel.

The ephod, a garment like an apron or cape to hang from the shoulders down the back,

must be made of gold, blue and scarlet cloth and fine linen.

There were directions from God, too, to make the robe like a shirt to go over the head. It must be blue with golden bells hanging from the hem so that all the people would hear and pay attention when the priest worshipped God in the tent.

Aaron's turban of fine linen must have a plate of pure gold attached to the front. On the forehead should be the words "Holy unto the Lord."

Then the embroidered coat was described: it should be designed in squares with fine needle-work of gold, blue and scarlet threads.

For Aaron's sons, too, the Lord told Moses how coats and caps should be made.

Then God said: "All these things shall be done because you have men of skill and in-telligence and talent who work well with their hands and are filled with the spirit of God.

"After all the garments have been made and the oil, incense and spices have been prepared, Aaron and his sons must be consecrated as priests to worship the Lord and make sacrifices for the people.

"First there must be seven days of con-secration to prepare the tent of worship, the ark and the holy altar. Aaron and his sons must be cleansed with water from a golden basin at the door of the tent. Then they will be consecrated and blessed to serve as priests for the people of Israel.

"And I will dwell among the people, to be their God. They shall know that I am the Lord who brought them out of the land of Egypt.

"They shall know, too, and remember, to keep the Sabbath as a sign between us as a covenant forever."

When the Lord had finished speaking, when He had told Moses all these things on Mount Sinai, He gave Moses two tablets of stone to take to the people at the foot of the mountain.

On the tablets were the ten commandments which had been inscribed by the finger of God.

The Golden Calf
Exodus 32-33

Moses had been on the mountain for forty days and forty nights.

When the people saw that Moses had been

gone for a long time, they gathered around Aaron.

"We do not know what has become of Moses," they said. "He brought us out of the land of Egypt to this place. Now he has disappeared and we need gods to lead us."

Aaron answered, "Take off your rings and the rings of your wives and daughters and bring them to me."

All the people did as he had ordered and Aaron melted the gold that they brought him. Then Aaron shaped it and engraved it and made it in the form of a golden calf.

"Let this be your god," he said. And he built an altar and declared the next day a feast day.

All the people rose up early the next morning and brought peace offerings and burnt offerings. Then they sat down to eat and drink together.

The Lord said to Moses: "Go down. Your people whom you brought out of Egypt have turned away from My commandments. They have made a golden calf and have worshipped it.

"I have watched these people. They are stubborn and I will destroy them."

But Moses pleaded with the Lord: "Why show anger against Your people whom You brought out of the land of Egypt? Should the Egyptians say that our God tricked us into leaving Egypt only to destroy us?

"Turn away Your anger, O Lord. Remember Abraham, Isaac and Israel. You promised to make a great nation of us and to give us this land forever."

So the Lord repented of the evil He had thought to do, to destroy the people.

Then Moses went down the mountain with the tablets. He heard the voices of the people singing. He came closer and saw the golden calf and the people dancing and shouting around it.

Then Moses blazed with anger and threw the tablets down, and they broke at the foot of the mountain.

Moses took the calf they had made, burned it in the fire and ground it into powder. He sprinkled it on the water and made the people drink the water.

Moses asked Aaron: "What did the people say to you that you let them do such a thing?"

Aaron answered: "Do not be so angry. You know the people. They said they needed gods to lead them. They did not know what had become of you. I told them to bring me their gold. Then I threw it into the fire and out came this golden calf."

The next day Moses spoke to the people: "You have sinned a great sin. I will go up to the Lord once more. Perhaps I can get His forgiveness for your sins."

So Moses turned to the Lord to beg forgiveness for his people.

The Lord punished the people with a plague because they had made the calf and worshipped it.

Then He told Moses to lead the people to the land He had promised.

"I will send an angel before you and I will appear in a cloud," said God, "but no man shall ever look upon My face."

After this, Moses went into the tent of worship every day. And the people bowed down and worshipped the Lord.

The Second Tablets

Exodus 34-40

Then the Lord said to Moses: "Bring two tablets of stone and I will write on them as I did on the first tablets which you have broken."

The next morning Moses went up Mount Sinai with the tablets.

God came in a cloud and said: "I am the Lord, the Lord God, merciful and gracious, patient, with goodness and truth; forgiving evil, wrongdoing and sin, but punishing the wicked, even their children and their children's children to the fourth generation."

Moses spoke: "If I have pleased you, O Lord, come among us. We are a stubborn people, but forgive us."

Then the Lord instructed Moses to write on the tablets the words of the covenant, the Ten Commandments.

And again Moses was with the Lord forty days and forty nights.

When Moses came down from Mount Sinai with the Tablets of the Law, his face glowed with a holy radiance. He talked to the people and told them the words of the Lord.

He gave them all the instructions and all the directions the Lord had given him for building the tabernacle as God's dwelling place. He told

The Book of Leviticus
The moral and ritual laws to be observed by Israel as God's "holy people."

Offerings and the Priesthood

Leviticus 1-10

The children of Israel remained camped at the foot of Mount Sinai for a long time. The tabernacle had been built and the priests had been consecrated to make sacrifices for the people and to lead them in worship. All this had been done according to the words of the Lord.

Then the Lord told Moses all the things the people must know: the commandments and laws they must learn and live by.

God told Moses all the duties of the priests and Levites, who were the descendants of the tribe of Levi.

There were directions for making sacrifices and offerings: thanksgiving offerings, peace offerings, and offerings to atone for sins.

And different kinds of sins were mentioned: disobeying God's laws; wrongs done to others; wrongs committed by rulers, judges, priests, and common people; and for wrongs done knowingly or unknowingly.

For each sin or wrongdoing, the necessary sacrifice was told by God to Moses. And Moses told the people all that God said to him.

Cleanliness

Leviticus 11-18

Next, the Lord gave Moses laws of cleanliness for the people to learn and obey.

These laws had to do with food and diet, diseases and healing, relations between men and women, and the general health and welfare of the people. Cleanliness and purity were mentioned together for: "A pure spirit," said the Lord, "can only be found in a clean body."

The Lord said: "For food, you shall distinguish between clean and unclean animals, between clean and unclean birds and between clean and unclean creatures of the sea. You shall not make your souls impure by eating that which I have named as unclean for you."

Then God spoke of the way animals should be slaughtered for food so that they might suffer

them about making the ark and the altar and all the holy garments for the priests.

All these things were built and prepared.

When Moses saw that everything was done according to God's instructions, he blessed the people and he caused the Tent of Meeting to be set up, with the ark and the table inside, and the altar at the door of the tent.

Then a cloud covered the tent and it was filled with the glory of the Lord throughout all their travels.

as little as possible and their blood be drawn off quickly.

Unclean persons, or those suffering from disease, were to be separated from the rest of the people:

"When a man has leprosy or running sores or boils, he shall be brought to the priest to be examined. The priest shall declare him clean or unclean."

Other laws of cleanliness and how to deal with them were explained in detail, together with directions for the priests.

Holiness
Leviticus 19-22

The Lord spoke to Moses about holiness, saying: "You and all the congregation of Israel shall be holy, for the Lord your God is holy.

"You shall keep the sabbaths, honour your father and your mother and not turn to false gods or worship idols. You shall not steal or deal falsely with people, lie to each other or swear in the name of the Lord. I am the Lord your God.

"When you harvest your land or your vineyard, you shall not strip away everything that is there or pick up what falls to the ground. These you shall leave for the poor and for the stranger. I am the Lord your God."

Then God added other rules: not to oppress one another; not to curse the deaf even though they cannot hear; not to put stumbling blocks before the blind because they cannot see; not to treat one people or one person differently from others, but to treat all justly; not to bear a grudge or seek revenge; to deal honestly in matters of business; in buying and selling, always to use honest weights and measurements.

God said: "Treat the stranger as you would one of your own, for you yourselves were strangers in the land of Egypt.

"You shall do all my laws and commandments. I am the Lord your God."

Festivals
Leviticus 23-24

The Lord said to Moses: "These are the feasts of the Lord which you shall observe, each at the proper time:

"On six days work shall be done, but the seventh day is a day of rest, a sabbath to the Lord.

"On the seventh day of the first month, toward evening, the Passover of the Lord shall begin, as an observance of the spring harvest and of freedom from slavery. For seven days you shall eat unleavened bread. The first day and the seventh shall be holy days on which you shall do no work.

"Seven weeks, that is fifty days, after the beginning of Passover shall be a harvest festival called Pentecost or the Feast of Weeks. On that day a grain-offering shall be made, a religious assembly shall be held and you shall do no work.

"The first day of the seventh month shall be Rosh Hashanah (New Year's day), a day of remembrance celebrated by the blowing of trumpets. On that day you shall remember the creation of the world and offer a sacrifice to the Lord, hold a religious assembly and do no work.

"On the tenth day of the seventh month is Yom Kippur, the Day of Atonement. This shall be the time of a holy assembly when you shall fast and offer a sacrifice to the Lord. And you shall not do any kind of work that day, for on that day atonement is made before the Lord your God. It is to be an everlasting law throughout all the generations to observe this day as a sabbath of complete rest.

"On the fifteenth day of this seventh month shall begin Succot, a seven day harvest festival to the Lord. The first day and the eighth day shall be days of solemn rest and of sacrifices to the Lord. It is the Feast of Booths: for seven days you shall live in booths as a reminder that the children of Israel lived in booths when I brought them out of the land of Egypt. I am the Lord your God."

And Moses told the people all that the Lord commanded about the festivals.

Punishment and Reward
Leviticus 24-27

The Lord said to Moses: "Tell the people of Israel that whoever curses God shall be responsible for his sin. He shall be put to death; all the congregation shall stone him. Even a stranger must obey this law. He need not worship the God of Israel, but he must not curse the name of the Lord, either.

"He who commits murder shall himself be put to death. He who kills a beast shall make it good. If a man causes another to be disfigured, the same shall be done to him: an eye for an eye, a tooth for a tooth, a fracture for a fracture —no more.

"The law shall be the same for the stranger as for the native-born. I am the Lord your God."

Moses continued telling the people all that the Lord spoke to him: about jubilee years, responsibilities toward servants, keeping vows and promises, and giving to the Lord.

"These are all My commandments," said the Lord. "You shall do them; then you shall live in peace and none shall make you afraid. I will be your God and you shall be My people. But if you do not do all these commandments, terror will come to you: plagues and enemies will overcome you, your cities will be laid waste, your land ruined, and you will be scattered among the nations.

"Then, if the people make amends for their sins, I will remember My covenant with Abraham, Isaac and Jacob. For their sake, I will remember the covenant and bring the people into a land flowing with milk and honey, the land that I have promised. I am the Lord."

The Book of Numbers
The continuing history of the Israelites from the wilderness of Sinai to the settlement in Moab.

Leaving Mount Sinai
Numbers 1-10

In the wilderness, at the beginning of the second year since leaving the land of Egypt, God commanded Moses to count all the children of Israel, to take a census. So, at the foot of Mount Sinai, Moses counted them all: men, women and children, according to the twelve tribes.

Altogether, there were six hundred thousand people at the beginning of the second year after leaving the land of Egypt.

Then the Lord reminded the priests to care for the tabernacle and to lead the people in worship and to bless them.

"And this shall be the priestly blessing to bless the children of Israel," said the Lord:

"The Lord bless you, and keep you;

"The Lord make His face to shine upon you and be gracious to you;

"The Lord lift up His countenance upon you and give you peace."

From that time on, whenever the children of Israel camped and set up the Tent of Meeting, the cloud of the Lord covered it. When the cloud rose above the Tent, the Israelites moved on.

Whatever the cloud indicated, the people did.

At the command of the Lord, they camped for a day or two days, for a month or even longer. And at the command of the Lord, they moved once more.

In the second month of the second year after they had left Egypt, the cloud rose above the tent. Then the people packed their belongings, gathered their families and their animals and set out from the wilderness of Sinai, with the ark of the covenant before them. Three days later the cloud came to rest in the wilderness of Paran. There they set up camp.

The Cry for Food

Numbers 11-12

At Paran the people began to complain that now all they had to eat was the manna that fell from heaven. "We remember the fish we had in Egypt. And the melons and the cucumbers and the vegetables," they said.

Moses heard and was displeased. And he said to the Lord: "Why have You placed all the responsibility for these people on me? To bring them to the land You promised them? Where will I find enough food for them? I cannot bear the burden alone! They complain every time things do not go well."

The Lord answered: "Gather together seventy of the elders in the Tent of Meeting. They will stand beside you, and I will talk with you there. And they will share the burden with you."

And He said: "As for the complaints, tell the people that they shall have meat, not one or two days, but every day for a month until they are bursting with it and begin to hate it."

Moses told the people, and sure enough, a wind brought thousands of birds from the sea and they fell outside the camp.

The people gathered the birds, cooked them and ate them, stuffing themselves with meat.

Then a plague came upon the people and many died because of their greed.

Forty Years

Numbers 13-15

The Lord spoke to Moses again in the wilderness of Paran, and said: "Send men to look over the land of Canaan, the land which I promised to the children of Israel."

Moses chose twelve men, one from each of the tribes and sent them.

"Go into the mountains and look over the land," said Moses. "See if the people are weak or strong, few or many. See what the land is like, whether it is good or bad. Find out about the cities, whether there are tents or strong buildings. See what kind of land there is, whether there are fields or forests, and what kind of plants grow there. And bring back some of the fruits of the land."

So the men went out to spy. They went throughout the land to look it over. And they were gone for forty days.

Then they came back and told all that they had seen. It was the season of the ripening of grapes, so they brought back ripe plump grapes and figs from the land of Canaan.

"Truly the land flows with milk and honey," they said. "But the people who live there are strong and the cities are large and have walls around them."

Then the people were afraid and cried out against Moses once again: "It would have been better if we had died in Egypt! Or in the wilderness! Have you brought us out of Egypt to be killed and our wives and children to be captured? These people will surely not let us enter their land. We should go back to Egypt!"

Then they said: "We need a leader who will take us back to Egypt."

Joshua and Caleb tried to calm the people, saying: "The land we saw is a good land. It is indeed a land flowing with milk and honey. If the Lord is pleased with us, He will lead us there safely.

"Stop questioning the Lord. The Lord is with us. Do not be afraid."

But the people would not listen.

Then the glory of the Lord appeared, and God spoke to Moses: "How long will these people complain against Me? How long will it be before they believe Me? I have shown them

signs, and brought them out of Egypt and sent food for them, and still they question.

"Now I will cause a plague to strike them, that not one of them shall come into the promised land."

But Moses spoke to the Lord, saying: "The Egyptians would surely hear of it. And if all the Israelites are destroyed, the nations would say it was because the Lord could not bring them into the land which He promised, and therefore He has killed them in the wilderness.

"Now O Lord, show the greatness of Your power. Show that the Lord is slow to anger, and full of love, forgiving sin, but not letting the guilty ones go free. Forgive the sins of these people according to the greatness of Your love."

The Lord answered: "I will forgive; I have forgiven. But none of the men who have seen My signs and who came out of Egypt and still do not believe in the Lord, none of these shall see the land that I have promised.

"Of them all, only Caleb and Joshua shall enter the land. The youths and the little ones shall go into Canaan. And even they shall be shepherds in the wilderness for forty years until the last of those who came out of Egypt shall have died.

"For forty years I shall withhold My promise that the children of Israel will enter the promised land."

Then it happened that the men who had been spies and who had made the people question Moses, died by a plague, all but Joshua and Caleb. The rest continued to travel from place to place for forty years.

The Lord said to Moses: "You must tell the people to make tassels on the corners of their garments. And on each corner shall be a blue cord so they will remember to do all My commandments. I am the Lord your God."

Korah's Rebellion

Numbers 16

Korah and two hundred and fifty others, leaders of the Israelites, came before Moses and Aaron. They said: "You have gone too far, always telling us what we must do. Why do you place yourselves above the rest of us? We are all holy, every one of us. God lives among us all."

Moses answered, saying: "In the morning the

Lord will show us who is really holy. Is it not enough that you, the elders and Levites have been chosen to do the work of the Lord, to be the keepers of the ark and to be near the presence of the Lord?"

The leaders answered: "Is it not enough that you have brought us to this place, to kill us in the wilderness? Must you make yourself a prince to rule over us? You have not led us to a land flowing with milk and honey, or given us fields and vineyards."

Moses became angry. He said: "Tomorrow you will come before the Lord and the Lord will appear to us all."

In the morning every man came before the Tent of Meeting with his incense. And the glory of the Lord appeared.

The Lord said to Moses: "Tell the congregation to get away from near the tents of the men who have rebelled."

Moses told them and he said: "Now you shall know that the Lord has sent me to do all these things, that I have not done them myself. The Lord will send a sign.

"If these men die like other men, the Lord has not sent me. But if the Lord causes the earth to swallow them up, then you will know that they have displeased Him, that the Lord He is God."

As Moses finished speaking, the ground split open. All Korah's followers and all their belongings were swallowed up in the earth, and they disappeared from sight forever.

Then the rest of the Israelites ran from that place crying out with fear, lest the earth swallow them also.

The Punishment of Moses

Numbers 20

The children of Israel continued their wandering until they came into the wilderness of Zin.

There Miriam, the sister of Moses and Aaron, died and was buried. It was a dry, barren place, and once again the people cried out against Moses:

"Why have you brought us to this place, to die? Why did you bring us out of Egypt? Surely this is not the promised land. There is no grain here, or figs or vines, not even water to drink."

Again the Lord spoke to Moses: "Take the rod and call the people together. Speak to the rock. Tell it to give water so the people may drink, they and their cattle."

Moses and Aaron gathered the people together before the rock. And Moses called: "Listen, all you who rebel. We will bring water out of this rock for you."

Then Moses, instead of speaking to the rock as he had been commanded, raised his hand and struck it with the rod. The water flowed. The people drank and so did their cattle.

Then the Lord spoke to Moses and Aaron: "Because you became angry and did not do as I commanded before the children of Israel, you shall not lead them into the land which I have promised."

Hostile Nations

Numbers 20

From his camp at Kadish, Moses sent messengers to the king of Edom, where Esau's descendants lived. He sent them to ask permission of the king to pass through the land.

"You know all the hardships we have had," said the messengers. "How we lived as slaves in Egypt, and when the Lord heard us He brought us out of the land of Egypt. And you know of our travels through the wilderness. Now we are at the border of your country and we ask if we may pass through.

"We will not go through your fields or your vineyards, or drink water from your wells or disturb your people in any way."

But the king answered: "You shall not pass through."

And he brought out a large army against the Israelites and refused to let them enter his land.

So the children of Israel were forced to turn away from the land of Edom. Instead, they travelled toward Mount Hor.

The Death of Aaron

Numbers 20

At Mount Hor, the Lord spoke to Moses: "Aaron shall not enter the land I have given to the people of Israel because you and he did not do as I commanded at the rock of Meribah.

"Now, take Aaron and Eleazar his son up to the mountain. And take Aaron's priestly robes and put them on Eleazar, for Aaron shall die there, at the top of the mountain."

Moses did as the Lord commanded. He

called Aaron and Eleazar and they went up the mountain. While the whole congregation waited, Moses put the robes of Aaron on Eleazar his son.

Aaron died at the top of the mountain and the children of Israel mourned his death for thirty days.

The Conquering Israelites

Numbers 21

From Mount Hor, Moses and the children of Israel went by way of the Red Sea, for they had to go around the land of Edom. And their wanderings took them many days for they stopped and camped along the way.

Every time they came to a new country, they sent messengers ahead to ask if they might pass through. Both the king of the Amorites and the king of Bashan refused.

The Amorites marched against the Israelites in the desert and attacked them. But the Israelites fought and won and settled there for a while.

Then the people of Bashan attacked. Again Israel won, taking over the land and staying there for some time.

The Blessings of Balaam

Numbers 22-24

The Israelites set out again. Then they camped east of the river Jordan on the plains of Moab.

Now Balak, king of the Moabites, had seen how the Israelites had defeated the Amorites and the people of Bashan, and he was afraid. He sent messengers to Balaam, a king to the north, asking him for help, for Balaam was believed to have very special powers.

Balak's messengers spoke to Balaam, saying: "A strong people has come out of Egypt and has camped beside me. It is said that your word is powerful, whether you give blessing or curse.

"Therefore come and curse this people, so I can turn them away."

But the Lord spoke to Balaam, saying: "The people whom Balak asks you to curse, you shall not curse. For they are blessed."

So Balaam refused to go with the Moabite messengers.

Then Balak sent princes to bring Balaam. They begged him, saying: "Just come and see these people, and see their strength."

So Balaam went with the princes, saying he would surely look, but that he would speak only the words of the Lord.

The two kings met and looked over the camps of the children of Israel. Balaam asked: "How can I curse whom God has not cursed?"

Balak insisted: "Come to Mount Pisgah and look over their camps. You can curse them from there."

At Mount Pisgah the Lord came to Balaam, and Balaam said: "God is not a man. He has given a blessing and I cannot call it back. The Lord is with the Israelites and lives among them. The people you see before you are the people of the Lord."

Balak took Balaam to still another place. And again the spirit of the Lord came to Balaam. He looked out over the camp of the children of Israel and he spoke, saying:

"How goodly are your tents, O Jacob,
And your dwelling places, O Israel —
Your kingdom shall be exalted;
God brought you forth from Egypt
And you shall destroy your enemies;
Blessed be all who bless you
And cursed be all that curse you."

Balak was furious and said: "I called you to curse these people, and you have blessed them."

And Balaam answered: "I cannot go against the commandments of the Lord, either to do good or evil. Before I leave, I will tell you what this people will do to your people."

Then Balaam told what the future would be: "A star will come from Jacob and strike the lands of Moab and of Seth, and will defeat the lands of Edom and Seir. The Israelites shall win and conquer all their enemies."

Then Balaam went back to his land and Balak, too, returned home.

The New Generations
Numbers 25-26

While Israel camped in that place near the Moabites, the people sinned. They made sacrifices to the Moabite gods.

The anger of the Lord was great, and a plague came upon the people and many died.

After the plague the Lord spoke to Moses and to Eleazar, the son of Aaron, saying: "Take a census of the people of Israel. Count all who are able to go to war." And it was done.

Now, among all the people who were counted at that time by Moses and Eleazar, there was not one who had been counted by Moses and Aaron at the foot of Sinai. Of all those, only Caleb and Joshua were left, for the Lord

had said that the others would die in the wilderness.

Then the Lord said: "The land of Canaan which I have promised you shall be divided according to the number of people with you. To a large tribe, there will go a large inheritance; to a smaller tribe, a smaller inheritance."

The Appointment of Joshua
Numbers 27-30

Then the Lord said to Moses: "Go up the mountain of Abarim and look into the land that I have given to the people of Israel. You will see it but you will not take My people there, because you rebelled against Me that day at the rock."

Then Moses asked the Lord to appoint a man in his place to lead the people into the promised land.

The Lord said: "Choose Joshua. He has the spirit of the Lord. Call him to stand before Eleazar the priest and the whole congregation. You shall lay your hands upon him and give him your authority and your blessing so all the people can see."

62

And God added: "Then you shall speak to the people of all my commandments." And Moses did so.

Moses called Joshua, laid his hands upon him, and gave him his commission and blessed him before all the congregation of Israel.

The Lord spoke to Moses again: "Now, you must go into battle against the Midianites and defeat them. You must gather your men into an army and you will be the victors."

In a short time this was done. After the defeat of the Midianites, the people brought offerings to the Lord and worshipped Him.

Then Moses spoke to the people as the Lord had commanded, telling them of all that the Lord had said and done.

Forty years earlier the people of Israel had gone out of the land of Egypt, and Moses had kept a record of all their travels. He had written down all the places where they had camped and all the lands through which they had travelled.

That day Moses reminded the whole congregation of Israel of the slavery in Egypt and of all the events of their journey and of all the hardships that their parents had endured, for none of those present had lived in the land of Egypt.

Moses spoke to them of all these things while they were camped in the plains of Moab by the Jordan river.

The Book of Deuteronomy

The words of Moses to the people concerning the laws and their observance; the death of Moses.

The Words of Moses

Deuteronomy 1-33

The words which Moses spoke to Israel were many. He told them all that had happened in the forty years since they had left the land of

Egypt. He reminded them of many things. Through it all, he spoke of God's love for Israel and urged them to obey and carry out the covenant between them and God. He repeated the ten commandments and said:

"These are the laws and commandments which the Lord your God commanded me to teach you. Do them, that all may go well with you in the land which the Lord promised you, the land flowing with milk and honey."

And Moses said: "Hear, O Israel: the Lord our God is one God. And you shall love the Lord your God with all your heart and with all your soul and with all your might.

"And these words which I command you this day shall you remember in your heart. You shall teach them to your children and speak of them when you sit in your house, when you walk by the way, when you lie down and when you rise up. And you shall write them upon the doorposts of your house and upon your gates.

"And when the Lord your God brings you into the land which He promised to Abraham, to Isaac and to Jacob, remember to serve Him and do all His commandments."

Moses spoke to the people of obedience to God. And he spoke of God's love, mercy and justice:

"The Lord your God is a merciful God. He will not fail you nor destroy you. He will not forget the covenant He swore to your fathers.

"The Lord your God asks only that you worship Him and walk in His ways, and love Him with all your heart and all your soul. And obey the rules and commandments which I command you this day, in the name of the Lord.

"I have set before you this day life and death, the blessing and the curse. Therefore, choose life so that you and your children may live and love the Lord your God.

"These commandments are not too hard for you or too difficult to do. Neither are they beyond the sea. But they should be in your heart, so you will do them.

"These commandments belong to us and our children and our children's children forever."

Then Moses said to the people: "Be strong and of good courage, for the Lord your God goes with you. He will not fail you nor forsake you."

The Death of Moses
Deuteronomy 34

After Moses had spoken all these words, he went up from the plains of Moab to the top of Mount Pisgah opposite Jericho. From there the Lord showed him all the land, saying:

"This is the land which I promised to Abraham, Isaac and Jacob, that I would give to their children. Now you have seen it with your own eyes, but you shall not go there."

So Moses, the servant of the Lord, died in the land of Moab, according to the word of the Lord. His burial place is in the valley of the land of Moab, yet no one knows the exact place.

The children of Israel wept for Moses for thirty days. Then they rose up from their weeping and they turned to Joshua.

So Joshua became their leader. He was full of wisdom for Moses had blessed him. The people of Israel listened to him and did as the Lord commanded.

The Book of Joshua
The story of the successor to Moses who led the Israelites in their conquest of the promised land.

Joshua and the Spies
Joshua 1-2

After the death of Moses, God spoke to Joshua: "Be strong and of good courage. I will be with you just as I was with Moses. You shall bring the people into the land that I have promised them."

Joshua believed in the Lord. He ordered his officers to tell the people to prepare to cross the river Jordan. Then they would take over the land.

He sent two men to spy on Jericho. They went into the city as travellers and stayed at the house of Rahab, a woman of Jericho.

The king of Jericho heard that spies were in the city and sent men to search for them.

But Rahab hid the spies on the roof of her house. She said, "I know the Lord has promised you this land, and most of my people are afraid of your people. We have heard how the Lord divided the Reed Sea for you and brought you through the wilderness.

"I will protect you from the searchers if you will promise to save my life and the lives of my family."

The men answered that they would indeed deal kindly with her if she would help them.

"In order for us to be sure to save you," they said, "you must bring your family to this house and keep them inside. Then tie a red cord to the window so we will know the house from a distance. Whoever is inside the house will be saved. But if anyone from here goes into the street, we cannot be responsible."

When the searchers had left the area, she let

the spies down from the window by a rope. They hid in the hills for three days until the men of Jericho had given up the search.

At the end of the three days the spies reported to Joshua that the people of Jericho had heard about the Israelites and feared them.

The Fall of Jericho
Joshua 6

The great gates of Jericho were shut tight because the people were afraid of the children of Israel. No one came into the city, and no one went out.

66

ark of the covenant to Jericho. And he told them to choose seven from among them to march before the ark blowing their trumpets.

"And before them," Joshua said, "will march all the men who are armed. The rest of us will surround the city in silence until I give the order to shout. Then when I give the signal, each of you will let out a mighty shout."

The armed men and the seven priests blowing trumpets took their places before the ark. They marched around the city once. Then they came back to camp. They did this every day for six days.

On the seventh day, they started early and circled the city seven times. The seventh time around, while the priests blew and the soldiers marched, Joshua cried: "The Lord has given us the city! Shout!"

Then all the people let out a mighty shout. And the walls of Jericho fell down flat, as the Lord had promised.

The people of Israel ran into the city and captured it. All who lived in Jericho were killed except Rahab and her household, because the spies she had helped had remembered their promise.

The City of Ai
Joshua 7-8

After the fall of Jericho, God spoke to Joshua again:

"Fear not and do not be dismayed. Take your people and go to the city of Ai. You shall do to that city and her king as you did to Jericho."

Again Joshua listened and did as the Lord commanded him.

This time he sent some of his men to lie in ambush west of the city.

"Wait there," he said. "I and the soldiers with me will attack the city from the north. When the people come out against us, we will run away from them. They will leave the city to pursue us; then you will enter the city and capture it."

Each group went its own way. The next morning Joshua and his men marched up close to the city. When the king of Ai saw this, he and his army went out to meet the Israelites, to drive them away. Joshua and his men pretended to be beaten, and ran away as if defeated. Not knowing that some of Joshua's troops were

The Lord spoke to Joshua where he was camped and told him all that he must do to capture the city.

The Lord said: "When you do all this, the walls of Jericho will fall down."

Joshua did as the Lord had said: he called the priests and told them to prepare to carry the

hiding behind the city, the king ordered all of his men to pursue the fleeing Israelites.

Then the troops who had been hiding entered the city, set it on fire and followed the soldiers of Ai, killing or capturing every one.

In this way the king of Ai and his people were defeated by the Israelites.

The Hivites

Joshua 9

The people of Gibeon had heard what Joshua and the Israelites had done to Jericho and Ai. Being rich and clever, the Gibeonites decided to make a treaty with Joshua to save their city.

They sent messengers to Joshua at Gilgal where he was camped, saying they had come from a far country. The messengers wore torn and dusty clothing, and carried stale bread and patched wineskins.

Joshua asked: "Who are you? And where are you from?"

"From a far country." they answered. "When we started out, this bread was taken fresh from the oven. Now it is dry and stale.

The skins which we filled with wine were new and now they are split. And our clothes and sandals have become old and dirty because of our long journey."

Joshua and his people looked at the men. They saw their clothes and food and believed them. They did not ask advice from the Lord. Joshua prepared a peace treaty, and swore an oath that the Israelites would not destroy the city of Gibeon.

However, within three days Joshua learned that the messengers were really Hivites from the

nearby city of Gibeon. He sent for their leaders and spoke with them, asking why they had tricked him.

The people of Gibeon answered: "We heard that the Lord promised Moses to give you this land and to destroy all the people living here. Therefore we were afraid, and we did this to save our lives and our city. We admit that we have tricked you. Now we are in your hands. We will do whatever you say, but we ask you to have mercy upon us."

Because Joshua had promised, he could not destroy the city or its people. Instead he said: "You and your people shall be our slaves forever. You shall become woodcutters and water carriers for the people of Israel and for the house of the Lord."

The Day the Sun Stood Still
Joshua 10-22

When other kings in the land of Canaan heard what had happened to the Hivites, they joined together to attack the city of Gibeon.

The Gibeonites sent a message to Joshua to come and save them.

Joshua turned to the Lord, and the Lord spoke, saying: "Do not be afraid. Your enemies shall be delivered into your hands. None of them shall be able to stand against you."

So Joshua called his men together. They set out from their camp at Gilgal and took the Canaanites by surprise. They killed many and others fled, with the Israelites close behind. As the Canaanites ran, the Lord caused hailstones to fall from heaven upon them, confusing and killing them as they ran.

Then Joshua spoke: "Sun, stand still above Gibeon, and Moon, in the valley of Ajalon."

The sun stood still and the moon stayed until the Israelites had defeated all their enemies. Never before had there been such a day, when the Lord listened to the voice of a man, for the Lord fought for Israel.

Joshua and his army of Israelites attacked and captured all the cities of their enemies. They left none standing, but destroyed them all.

Thus Joshua took the whole land according to all that the Lord had said to Moses. And, as the Lord had commanded, Joshua divided the land among the tribes of Israel, for each to have an inheritance.

Then, at last, the land had rest from war, and the Israelites began a new life in the promised land.

Joshua's Farewell
Joshua 23-24

For a long time, the people of Israel remained at peace with the people around them.

Joshua grew old and called together all the people of Israel and their elders and judges and officers. He said to them:

"You have seen all that the Lord has done to the nations because of you. The Lord your God has fought for you.

"You must be strong and do all that is written in the laws of Moses. Do not mix with the people nearby or serve their gods or worship them. But be faithful to the Lord your God, and do all His commandments. If you are disloyal to the Lord, know that He will no longer help you against your enemies. Then the anger of the Lord will be kindled against you, and you will no longer rule this land which the Lord has given you."

Then Joshua dismissed the people. Each group went to the land of its inheritance. And Joshua, the servant of the Lord, died and was buried in the land of his own inheritance in the hill country of Ephraim.

The Book of Judges
The history of the Israelites under various rulers until the time of Samuel.

Deborah
Judges 1-5

After the death of Joshua there was no strong leader to hold the tribes together. There arose a new generation of Israelites who did not live according to the commandments of the Lord.

Many of the people began to worship the gods of the people around them, and made sacrifices to those gods.

Each tribe struggled alone with the people who lived nearby. And each man did what was right in his own eyes.

From time to time, the Lord raised up judges in the tribes of Israel to lead the people and

save them from their enemies. For a short time, the tribe listened to a judge, and then there was peace.

But the people continued to do what was evil in the sight of the Lord and the Lord became angered. Then, their enemies became successful over them.

Jabin, the king of the Canaanites, and his commander, Sisera, defeated the Israelites and oppressed them for twenty years. Finally the people turned to the Lord for help.

At that time, one of the judges in Israel was a woman named Deborah.

She sent for Barak of the tribe of Naphtali. "The Lord commands that you gather ten thousand men and go to Mount Tabor," she said. "There Sisera and all his men will be delivered into your hands."

Barak answered: "I will go only if you go with me."

So Deborah agreed to go with him, saying: "But the glory of success will not be yours. The Lord will give Sisera into the hands of a woman."

The two armies met on Mount Tabor and Sisera was defeated. All of his men were killed, but Sisera fled on foot.

He came to Kedesh and stopped at the tent of one of his king's friends. The man's wife, Jael, invited him in, saying: "Come in, my lord. Do not be afraid."

Sisera entered and Jael made him lie down. She covered him and gave him milk to drink.

He fell asleep and while he slept, Jael killed him.

Then Deborah and Barak rejoiced and sang:

"Hear, O kings; listen O princes:
I will sing praises to the Lord, the
God of Israel.
The people chose new gods,
There was war in the gates;
And Israel had no leaders . . .
The people of the Lord
Marched to the gates, crying:
"Awake, awake, Deborah,
Arise, Barak,
Capture your oppressors, O Israel!
They marched against the warriors,
The Lord's people against the mighty.
They fought from heaven.
Blessed among women is Jael:
He asked water and she gave milk;
She struck Sisera a blow—
He sank and lay still at her feet;
Where he sank he fell down dead.
"So perish all Your enemies, O Lord.
Those who love You shall be as the sun,
Rising up and going forth in glory."

The children of Israel had conquered Jabin, king of Canaan. And the land was at peace for forty years.

Gideon

Judges 6-8

Again the children of Israel went back to evil ways. This time the Midianites defeated them and ruled over them for seven years. They drove the Israelites into the mountains where they found safety living in caves.

Once more the people called upon the Lord. And an angel of the Lord came and sat under an oak tree which belonged to Joash. His son, Gideon, was preparing wheat to hide from the Midianites.

The angel of the Lord appeared to Gideon, saying: "The Lord is with you, you are a man of great strength."

Gideon said: "If the Lord is still with us, why has all this happened? Where are the miracles of the Lord, that our fathers told us about? The Lord has surely forgotten us!"

The angel said: "With your strength, go and save Israel. I have chosen you, and I will be with you."

Gideon asked: "How can I save Israel? Show me a sign that you are sent by the Lord. Stay here and I will bring food for you!"

He went into the house and prepared some meat and broth and unleavened cakes. He brought them out and presented them to the angel.

Then the angel of the Lord commanded him to put the meat and cakes on a nearby rock and pour the broth over it.

Gideon did as he had been told. The angel stretched out the rod that was in his hand and touched the cakes. At once fire leaped out of the rock and consumed them, and the angel disappeared.

Gideon saw that this was indeed the work of the Lord, and he built an altar at that place, and worshipped there.

Then the Lord spoke to Gideon, saying: "I will be with you. You shall defeat the Midianites."

Gideon spoke to the Lord: "Give me a sign if You will indeed save Israel through me. I will put wool fleece on the floor and in the morning, if there is dew on the fleece only and the floor is dry, I will know that You mean for me to save Israel."

The next morning he looked: there was water on the fleece, but the floor was dry.

Still Gideon was not sure. "Do not be angry Lord, but give me one more sign. I will put fleece on the floor once again. This time, let the floor be wet with dew and the fleece be dry."

The next morning the fleece was dry and the floor was wet with dew.

Then Gideon believed. He gathered all his fighting men to go against the Midianites.

The Lord said to Gideon: "You have too many people with you. If I give you a victory over the Midianites, Israel will say: 'By our own power we defeated the Midianites!' Now send home any who are afraid."

Many did go back. But God said there were still too many men, so the number was reduced. Again and again the number was lowered until only three hundred men remained.

God spoke to Gideon that night: "Take your servant and creep down to the Midianite camp. Listen to what they are saying. Then you will be able to attack their camp.

Outside the Midianite camp Gideon and his

servant saw that there were great numbers of men and camels. When Gideon came near, he heard a man telling about a dream:

"I dreamed that a cake of barley fell into our camp. It struck a tent and knocked it over, turning it upside down and it lay on the ground."

His friend explained the dream, saying: "The cake is the sword of Gideon, coming into our camp. The Lord is giving him a victory over us and our armies and over all of Midian."

When Gideon heard this he bowed his head and worshipped God. Then he returned to his men saying: "Arise, the Lord has promised to deliver the army of Midian to us."

Then Gideon divided his men into three companies. He told each man to take a trumpet in one hand and a jar or pitcher with a flaming torch inside it in the other hand.

"Watch me," he told his men, "and do what I do. When I blow my trumpet, you must blow your trumpets and shout: 'For the Lord and for Gideon.' "

They set out and went down to the Midianite camp. There they blew their trumpets and broke the pitchers they were carrying. They waved their torches and shouted: "For the Lord and for Gideon!"

The Midianites awoke and took up their swords. But there was such noise and confusion on every side that in their panic they turned their swords on each other and fled. The men of Israel followed them and killed the Midianite leaders.

Then the men of Israel said to Gideon: "Be our ruler, and your son's son after you, for you have delivered us from Midian."

But Gideon refused to be king. He answered: "I will not rule over you, nor will my son. The Lord will rule over you. But I do have one request: give me all the gold you have taken from the enemy."

They gave the gold to Gideon gladly: earrings and ornaments and jewelled collars. He took it all to Ophrah where he lived and had a priestly garment made from it, a garment for the high priest to wear when worshipping the Lord.

After Midian was conquered by the children

of Israel, the country had peace for forty years, for as long as Gideon lived.

Abimelech

Judges 9

Gideon had many wives, and when he died he had seventy sons. One of them, Abimelech, went to his mother's family in Shechem and asked them:

"Do you want me to be the ruler now? Surely you do not want my brothers to rule over you."

The people agreed. They gave him money which he used to hire soldiers to kill his brothers. Only the youngest, Jotham, hid himself and was saved.

Then all of Shechem proclaimed Abimelech their king.

Jotham heard of this and went to the people of Shechem, saying: "My father fought for you and risked his life for you and defeated the Midianites. Now you have risen against him, killed his sons and made Abimelech your king.

"If you have done justice to Gideon, then rejoice with Abimelech and prosper. But if not, Shechem will surely destroy Abimelech and Abimelech will destroy Shechem."

Then Jotham left Shechem, for he was afraid of Abimelech.

After three years, some of the men of Shechem rose up against Abimelech, saying: "Who is he, that he should rule over us? He has become too powerful."

So they plotted against Abimelech and set out to defeat him.

But Abimelech called up his soldiers and destroyed many of those who marched against him. Just as he was about to charge a tower at Thebez, a woman hurled a huge stone down on his head, crushing his skull. Then Abimelech called one of his men, giving an order: "Kill me with your sword, so no one can say that I was destroyed by a woman."

On that day, many men of Shechem were destroyed and Abimelech with them. So it was that Jotham's prediction came true.

Samson

Judges 13-16

For a long time there was no single leader or ruler of Israel, and every man did what was right in his own eyes. Many of the Israelites turned to ways that were evil in the sight of the Lord. So for forty years they were enslaved by the Philistines.

Then there appeared a man of great strength who became a hero of Israel.

A man of the tribe of Dan, Manoah, had been married several years, and he and his wife had no children. One day an angel of the Lord appeared to them, saying:

"You will have a son, a son of great strength and he shall be dedicated to God. He must never cut his hair. He will begin to save Israel from the Philistines."

In time Manoah and his wife did have a son whom they named Samson. The boy grew strong and tall, and the Lord blessed him.

Many times Samson showed his strength. He

fought off animals when he tended his father's flocks. Once he even killed a lion with his bare hands. Several times he was captured and tormented by the Philistines, and each time he broke out of his bonds and killed all his captors.

The Philistines were continually looking for ways to destroy Samson for they were afraid of his great strength.

Now Samson loved a woman named Delilah. One day leaders of the Philistines came

to her and asked her to find out the secret of Samson's strength.

"He has broken out of the strongest ropes and chains," they said. "With his bare hands he took apart the gates of the city of Gaza, even ripping out the posts. If you tell us the secret of his power we will reward you handsomely with silver and gold."

Delilah thought about the reward the Philistines promised her. And she began asking Samson what made him so strong. She urged him and coaxed him and teased him about his strength, but he never gave her a direct answer.

Then she asked: "How can you say you love me and not tell me everything?"

Finally, he answered her, saying: "If I am shaved or if my hair is cut, my strength will leave me. And I will be like any other man."

Delilah sent for the Philistines.

That night Samson fell asleep with his head on her lap. She signalled for a man to come quickly, and he cut Samson's hair while he slept. The Philistines gave Delilah the reward and left.

Samson awakened and asked how such a thing could have happened.

"The Philistines came to us while you slept," answered Delilah.

Samson jumped up, saying: "I will go after them as I have done before and destroy them."

But this time Samson's strength failed him. He started out, but the Philistines were waiting. They seized him and bound him, and they put out his eyes. Then they threw him in prison where he was forced to work grinding grain.

While Samson was in prison, his hair began to grow.

The Philistines held a great feast to celebrate their victories over Samson and the Israelites. There was much rejoicing and eating and drinking for several days.

The hall was full of men and women. All the leaders of the Philistines were there. Altogether there were about three thousand people in that place.

Samson was brought from prison for them to look at him and make fun of him. He was their prisoner and he could not see.

Samson said to the men who were guarding him: "This must be a great hall; there are many people here. Let me feel the pillars that hold up the roof. They must be strong indeed."

Samson was led to the pillars and he stood between them, with his right hand on one and his left hand on the other.

And he called upon the Lord: "Lord God, remember me and strengthen me so I may have revenge on these people for all that they have done to me. And let me die with them."

Then Samson pushed against the pillars with all his might, and broke them into hundreds of pieces. The roof fell in, killing everyone in the great hall, even those who had gathered on the roof to watch.

So the Lord answered Samson. Then his family came and took his body to be buried in the land of his father Manoah.

The Book of Ruth

The story of a Moabite girl who married a Hebrew and of her faithfulness to her husband's people.

Ruth 1-4

In the time of the judges there was a famine in the land of Israel. So Elimelech, a man of Bethlehem, took his wife Naomi and his two sons to Moab to find food. And they settled there.

In Moab Elimelech died. And his sons grew

up and married Moabite girls: the name of one was Orpah, the other was Ruth.

After about ten years both of the sons died. Naomi heard that the famine was over in her land. Now, left without a husband or sons, she decided to go back to her own people.

Naomi called her daughters-in-law to her and said: "Go, return to your own families. You have been good to my sons and to me. But now you should go home and marry again. And I will return to Bethlehem."

They wept together and Orpah kissed Naomi goodbye.

But Ruth stayed with Naomi, saying: "Do not ask me to leave you. Wherever you go, I will go. Where you stay, I will stay. Your people will be my people, and your God will be my God."

When Naomi saw that she could not change Ruth's mind, she said no more and they set out together.

They came to Bethlehem at the harvest season, and Ruth went to work in the fields.

Now Naomi's husband had a wealthy cousin whose name was Boaz. And it happened that Ruth worked in his fields.

When Boaz learned that she was the daughter-in-law of Naomi, he welcomed her. And he made sure that she had enough grain to take home each day and enough to eat and drink.

Naomi spoke to Ruth again about the future, saying: "You should have a home and a life of your own. Go to Boaz and he will marry you. It is our custom for a widow who has no children to marry her husband's brother or cousin. That way the family will continue."

Ruth did as Naomi asked. She spoke to Boaz. But he told her there was a nearer cousin. "I will go to the gate before the elders and settle the matter," Boaz said.

So Boaz told the cousin that Naomi and Ruth had returned to Bethlehem to redeem the land of Elimelech and for Ruth to be married to her husband's nearest relative.

But the cousin had his own land and his own family, and could not marry Ruth. He took off his sandal and handed it to Boaz, for in those days this was the method of doing business. The elders were witnesses and gave Boaz their blessing, allowing him to marry Ruth in his cousin's place.

Then Boaz claimed the land of Elimelech and married Ruth. And Naomi found happiness through them.

Ruth and Boaz had a son named Obed, who had a son named Jesse, who was the father of David.

The Books of Samuel

The story of Samuel, the prophet-judge, and the unification of the twelve tribes under one king; the days of King Saul through the reign of King David.

God Calls Samuel

1 Samuel 1-3

There was a certain woman of the tribe of Dan, Hannah, who had no children. She prayed for a son, saying: "If I ever have a son, I will give him to serve the Lord all his life."

In due time she and Elkanah, her husband, had a son and they named him Samuel. And he grew to be a fine healthy child.

Every year Hannah and Elkanah went to the holy place at Shiloh to worship the Lord. When Samuel was still a young child, Hannah took him with her. She spoke to Eli, the high priest, and told him of her promise. Then she left Samuel with Eli and returned home with her husband. Each year when she came to Shiloh, Hannah brought the boy clothes she had made.

One night when Samuel and Eli had gone to bed, Samuel heard a voice call: "Samuel, Samuel."

Samuel answered: "Here I am," and he ran to Eli.

But Eli said: "I did not call you."

The boy went back to bed, and again he heard the voice: "Samuel, Samuel."

Samuel went to Eli again, saying: "Here I am. You called me?"

Again Eli answered: "No, I did not call you. Go back to sleep."

This happened a third time. Then Eli knew it was the voice of the Lord calling Samuel. So he said: "Go and lie down. If you hear the voice again, answer: "Speak, Lord.' "

Samuel went back to bed once more. And he waited.

The voice came again, calling: "Samuel, Samuel."

This time Samuel answered: "Speak, Lord. I am listening."

Then God spoke: "I am about to do something that will be a surprise to everyone. I will judge against Eli because his sons have become wicked and have mocked the Lord, and Eli did not restrain them. No amount of offerings or sacrifices will change what I intend to do."

Samuel heard all that God said and he was afraid to tell Eli.

But in the morning Eli asked Samuel:

"What was it that the Lord said to you? You must not hide it from me."

So Samuel told him, and Eli answered: "Let the Lord do what seems good to Him. The Lord He is God."

Samuel grew to manhood and served the Lord. Soon all the people of Israel came to know that Samuel was a prophet of the Lord. Every time that God appeared to him, Samuel told the words of God to the people.

Samuel became a prophet and teacher and judge for all of Israel.

War with the Philistines

1 Samuel 4-7

The Philistines gathered their armies and attacked Israel again, and things did not go well for the Israelites. Four thousand of their men were killed and the Philistines won many battles.

Then the elders decided to take the ark of the covenant from Shiloh and set it up in their camp. They thought it would help them defeat the Philistines.

When the Philistines heard about this, they were afraid. They said: "The Israelites have brought their God into camp. This is the same

God that made all the plagues happen in Egypt, and caused the sea to open."

But their leaders urged them, saying: "Go, be strong. Fight like men or you will become slaves to the Israelites."

So they went out and fought, and they defeated Israel. Thousands of the men of Israel were killed, including Eli's sons.

That day, too, the Philistines captured the ark of the covenant.

Eli was an old man by that time, and when he heard all that had happened, he collapsed and died.

The Philistines took the ark to their holy place. As soon as they set it up, the statue of their god Dagon fell over and was broken.

They moved the ark from city to city to find a place to keep it. But in every city, when the ark was brought in, the people who lived there became diseased and died. Then a great panic spread throughout the land, for the people were afraid.

The leaders and elders of the Philistines gathered together to decide what to do with the ark. It had brought them nothing but trouble, so they decided to get rid of it and return it to Israel with guilt offerings to the God of Israel.

They placed the ark on a cart pulled by two cows. And they followed it to the border of Israel.

There they watched as the people rejoiced to have the ark returned to them. The Israelites placed it in the house of Abinadab where his sons had charge of it.

After their defeat by the Philistines, the Israelites turned to Samuel for help and guidance.

Samuel spoke to them, saying: "If you return to the Lord and put away all wrongdoing, you may be saved. Serve the Lord with all your hearts and He will deliver us from the Philistines."

The people admitted that they had sinned, and they promised to change their ways and serve the Lord.

The next time the Philistines came to attack Israel, the Lord thundered with a mighty voice. This caused great confusion among the Philistines, and allowed Israel to defeat them and recapture all the cities they had lost.

Then there was peace in the land.

Israel Wants a King

1 Samuel 7-8

Samuel judged Israel all his life. His home was in Ramah, and there he built an altar to the Lord. But he was a judge of all Israel, so each year he travelled throughout the land judging the people in each city.

When he was an old man, Samuel made his sons judges. But they were not wise or just and did not keep the commandments of the Lord.

Then the elders came to Samuel and begged him to choose a king for them.

They said: "Give us a king to rule over us like all the other nations."

Samuel listened to the people and he warned them, saying: "You have put aside the Lord your God from being your king. If you have a king, he will take your children to work for him, to be his horsemen and to plow his fields, to become his captains and fight his wars. He will take your fields and your vineyards and your flocks. You would become his servants."

But the people refused to believe Samuel. They did not want to listen to his advice. They only wanted a king like all the other nations, a king to rule them and to unite them in battle.

Samuel spoke to God, and God said: "I have heard, and they shall have a king."

Samuel told them what God had said. Then he sent each man back to his own city.

Samuel and Saul

1 Samuel 9-10

At this time there was a man of the tribe of Benjamin who owned many flocks. He had a tall handsome son whose name was Saul.

One day Saul and a servant set out to look for some animals that had strayed. They went as far as the hills, and were just about to turn back, when the servant said: "I have heard that there is a man of God in the next city, and all that he says comes true. Maybe he can help us."

So they went to the city to find this man.

The day before, the voice of the Lord had come to Samuel, saying: "Tomorrow a man from the tribe of Benjamin will come to you. This is the man that you will make king of Israel. He will deliver Israel from the Philistines."

Now when Saul and the man with him came to the city, Samuel was on his way to the holy place to worship the Lord.

Saul asked him: "Can you tell me where I can find the seer, the man of God?"

Samuel answered: "I am that man. Come with me to worship the Lord. You can stop worrying about the lost animals; they are found."

Then he added: "As for you, you will lead the people of Israel."

Saul said: "But I am a Benjamite, a man from the smallest of all the tribes of Israel. And my family is the least important of all the families of Benjamin. Why have you said this?"

Samuel gave no answer. He took Saul with him, and together they worshipped the Lord.

Then Samuel invited Saul and his servant to eat with him. He placed Saul at the head of the table and gave him the choicest portions, saying: "The Lord has said you shall be anointed prince over all of Israel. You shall rule the people and save them from their enemies."

Then Samuel took some oil and poured it on Saul's head to anoint him.

"These will be the signs that I am speaking the truth," Samuel said. "On your way home you will meet two men who will tell you that the lost animals have been found. They will say that your father is no longer concerned about the animals, but about you, his son.

"Later, you will meet three men going to worship the Lord at Bethel. They will greet you and hand you loaves of bread which you must accept from them.

"Third, you will meet a group of prophets with harps, flutes and tambourines. Then the spirit of the Lord will come to you and you will become a changed man. Everyone who knows you will see the change."

Then Saul and his servant left Samuel and started for home. And all that Samuel had said came true. Saul's family saw the great change in him and wondered what had brought it about.

Saul told them that he had met a man of God who helped him find the lost animals. But he did not tell them that Samuel had anointed him.

Saul, First King of Israel

1 Samuel 10-14

Some time later, Samuel called all the people together and told them the words of the Lord: "The Lord, the God of Israel, brought you out of Egypt and saved you from the many kingdoms who tried to capture you. But you have turned aside from God and have asked for a king. You must come back to the ways of the Lord and keep His commandments. Then you will have your king."

The people came near and Samuel called Saul to stand before them. And Saul was taller than all the rest.

Samuel said: "This is the man the Lord has chosen to be king. There is no other like him in all the world."

All the people shouted: "Long live the king!"

Then Samuel told them all the rights and duties of the king, and wrote it all down for them. And he said: "The Lord has set a king over you. If you will walk in the ways of the Lord and serve Him, if both you and your king will do all the Lord's commandments, then things will go well with you.

"But if you go against the commandments of the Lord, and if you do evil in the sight of the Lord, then the Lord's anger will be against you."

The people listened. Then they offered sacrifices to the Lord and worshipped Him.

Saul became a man of strength and wisdom and a good king. He led the Israelites into battle many times against the Philistines and defeated them.

Saul's Disobedience

1 Samuel 15

The Israelites went into battle against the Amalekites to punish them for standing in their way when they had come out of Egypt. For the Lord had spoken to Samuel concerning the Amalekites.

The Lord had said: "Israel shall defeat the Amalekites. And when they are defeated, Saul and his men must kill all the people and their flocks and their herds, so that they will disappear from the face of the earth."

Samuel told all this to King Saul.

So Saul and his army went forth and defeated the Amalekites in battle and killed all the people. But they saved the choicest of the sheep and oxen and cattle.

When the Lord saw that Saul had not done according to His command, He was sorry He had made Saul king.

Saul came back from battle and told Samuel: "We have done what the Lord commanded. We have defeated the Amalekites."

Samuel asked: "Then what is the bleating of sheep and the noise of cows that I hear?"

Saul answered: "We brought them to sacrifice to the Lord."

Then Samuel spoke: "Would the Lord rather have sacrifices than obedience to His commandments? Surely, to obey and love the Lord your God is better than to make sacrifices.

"Rebellion and stubbornness are evil in the sight of the Lord. Because you have done this thing and not done the commandment of the Lord, your kingdom will not continue."

Saul bowed his head and said: "Truly, I have sinned. I have gone against the word of the Lord. I will go at once and worship Him and beg Him to forgive me."

But Samuel said: "You have rejected the word of the Lord, and now He has rejected you from being king over Israel."

Saul again admitted his wrongdoing and bowed down before Samuel. Then together the two men went to worship the Lord.

Afterwards, Samuel returned to his home in Ramah and grieved over Saul. Saul, too, returned home and was greatly troubled.

David is Anointed

1 Samuel 16

The Lord spoke to Samuel at Ramah, his home. And the Lord asked: "How long will you weep for Saul? I have rejected him as king of Israel, and I have chosen a new king.

"Go to Jesse in Bethlehem. Jesse is the grandson of Ruth and Boaz. One of his sons will be king."

Samuel did as the Lord commanded and went to Bethlehem. He called the people of the city together to come before him to be consecrated to the Lord. When they came, he looked at one man who was taller and more handsome than the rest.

But God said: "This is not the man. The Lord does not see as man sees. Man sees outward appearance only; the Lord looks into the heart."

Then the sons of Jesse came before Samuel, and Samuel asked: "Are these all your sons?"

"David, the youngest, is not here," answered Jesse. "He is out tending the sheep. But I will send for him if you wish."

When David arrived, the Lord spoke to Samuel, saying: "This is the one. Anoint him."

David was a handsome boy with beautiful eyes. And Samuel anointed him with oil in the

Saul's servants spoke to him and said: "An evil spirit is bothering you. Let us go out and find a musician who will play for you, soothe you and cheer you up."

"Find such a man and bring him to me," answered Saul.

Now the servants had heard that there was a shepherd who was a gifted musician. He was David, the son of Jesse. They sent for him and he came before Saul.

David played the lyre and sang. He raised Saul's spirits, and Saul grew to love him very much.

David and Goliath
1 Samuel 17

The Philistines again came to do battle with Israel. They gathered on a mountain above the valley of Elah on one side, and the Israelites stood on the slopes of the mountain on the other side.

Out of the Philistine camp came one of their heroes. He was Goliath, a great giant of a man. He was nearly ten feet tall and wore a bronze helmet and a bronze breastplate. He had metal protectors on his legs, and he carried a spear seven feet long.

Goliath bellowed across to the men of Israel: "Choose a man to come and fight. If he can kill me, we will become your servants. If I kill him, you will become our servants."

presence of his father and his brothers. And the spirit of the Lord was with David from that time on.

David Meets King Saul
1 Samuel 16

The spirit of the Lord had left Saul, and he was troubled; he was greatly disturbed. He had sinned after the battle with the Amalekites, and he was downhearted.

When King Saul and his people heard this, they made no move. None of the Israelites went out to fight with Goliath; they just waited.

Every day for forty days the Philistine giant shouted his challenge, but still no man of Israel came forward.

One day David came into the Israelite camp bringing supplies. When he heard Goliath call out, he said: "Send me. I will go and fight the Philistine."

Saul said: "You are only a youngster, and he is a great warrior."

But David answered: "I have looked after my father's sheep. If a bear or a lion came and seized a sheep, I would go out and kill the bear or lion with my slingshot. I could do the same thing to Goliath, for the Lord who has saved me from bears and lions will surely save me from Goliath."

David insisted, until at last Saul told David he could go, adding: "May the Lord be with you."

Then Saul ordered all manner of protection to be brought for David: a bronze helmet and

breastplate and clothes of mail, but David could hardly move in them, so he took them off.

Instead he picked up his shepherd's staff in one hand, and with the other he took five smooth stones from the brook. These he put in the shepherd's bag he wore on his shoulder. Then he took his sling and walked down into the valley to meet Goliath.

When Goliath saw David coming, he could not believe his eyes: a boy coming to fight a giant.

"Am I a dog," he called, "that you come to beat me with a stick?"

David answered: "I come to you in the name of the Lord, the God of Israel, whom you and your people have insulted. I will strike you down and cut off your head. Then all the world will know that there is a God in Israel. And they will know that the Lord does not depend on swords and spears."

David took a stone from his bag. As Goliath stepped forward, David shot the stone from his sling. It hit Goliath's forehead, and Goliath fell to the ground, dead.

David ran over to where Goliath had fallen. He drew the giant's sword and cut off his head just as he had said he would.

When the Philistines saw their hero dead, killed by a shepherd boy, they fled in panic. The men of Israel followed them and defeated the whole Philistine army.

Saul's Jealousy

1 Samuel 18

King Saul took David home with him, and all the people welcomed David and sang songs of praise to him. And Jonathan, Saul's son, came to love David as a brother. They made a covenant of friendship between them.

David became commander over the army of Israel and was successful wherever Saul sent him. The people continued to praise David and sang:

"Saul has killed thousands,
David, tens of thousands."

Saul became jealous of the love his people had for David. He knew the Lord was no longer with him, and he became troubled and ill-tempered as well as jealous.

Now Michal, Saul's daughter, loved David and told this to her father. In his jealousy, Saul devised a plan.

He called David to him and said he knew of the young people's love. Then David said: "But who am I to marry a king's daughter? I am poor and have no worthy gifts."

Saul answered that he would ask no gifts, only that David should kill a hundred Philistines in the front lines of battle. Then he could marry Michal. Saul thought David would be killed before he could kill this many men.

David set out, and in no time he had killed two hundred men; then he married Michal.

David's popularity grew and with it, Saul's jealousy. The king came to be afraid of David and of the power he thought David might have over him. When David was near, Saul was always uneasy. For this reason, David was sent out to fight every time the Philistines attacked.

Finally, Saul's fear became so intense that he began to plan to have David killed.

Jonathan heard of the plan and went to speak to his father about David.

Jonathan said: "David has not sinned against you. He has done only good for you and for all our people. You saw what he did to Goliath. He has led Israel in battle against the Philistines and won many battles. Why should you want to kill him? You must control yourself, Father."

Saul listened to Jonathan and promised not to harm David. And David continued to fight for Saul and to play the lyre for him as before.

One day Saul sat brooding, with his spear in his hand. David came before him holding his lyre, ready to sing. Saul suddenly threw his spear at David. But he missed.

In his fear and anger, Saul had forgotten his promise to Jonathan and his love for David. Now he became determined to have David killed. Later that day he sent messengers to David's house to kill him.

It was dark and Michal helped David escape through a window. Saul was furious and became increasingly depressed.

David went to Samuel and told him all that had happened. He stayed with Samuel and his followers for some time and worshipped the Lord with them.

David and Jonathan
1 Samuel 20

David sent for Jonathan to speak with him about Saul's anger. "What have I done that your father should want to kill me?" he asked.

Jonathan answered: "I will do all I can to save you. My father does nothing without telling me. I will ask him about you and let you

know what he says. Perhaps by now he is calmer.

"If he is determined to kill you, I will warn you so you can escape. But whatever happens, we will remain friends forever."

Again they made a covenant of friendship before the Lord.

Then Jonathan said: "In three days you must go to the great stone at Ezel and hide there. I will come out and shoot three arrows as if at a target, and I will have a young boy with me to pick up the arrows.

"If I say to him: 'The arrows are on this side,' you will know that all is well. And you can come back. But if I say 'Go, get the arrows I shot past you,' then you will know that you will have to go away. May the Lord be with us forever!"

Then Jonathan and David embraced, and Jonathan returned to his father.

The next day was the festival of the new moon. At the feast, David's place was empty. The first day Saul said nothing about David's absence.

But the next day Saul asked: "Where is David? Why is he not here with us?"

Jonathan answered: "He asked permission to go to his family in Bethlehem to celebrate the feast day there."

Then Saul became angry and shouted at Jonathan: "Now you, too, are against me! You have come under his spell, and you will not be safe as long as that son of Jesse lives! He deserves to die!"

Jonathan tried to calm his father. He asked: "Why should he die? What has he done?"

In answer, Saul threw his spear at Jonathan. Then Jonathan knew what he must do.

The next morning he went out to the great stone to meet David. He took a boy with him and said: "Run, and bring back the arrows that I will shoot."

Then he shot an arrow over the child's head beyond him. Jonathan called out, saying: "There, the arrow is past you. Hurry, do not waste a minute."

The boy ran, picked up the arrow and brought it back to his master. Jonathan handed the boy his bow and arrows, telling him to take them home for him. And he added: "I will return later."

The boy did as he was told, but he did not understand. Only Jonathan and David understood that the arrow had been a signal.

As soon as the boy had left, David and Jonathan embraced each other and wept.

Jonathan said: "Now you must go. And go in peace. The Lord will be between us and between our descendants forever."

Jonathan returned to the city and David left, a fugitive.

David's Wanderings
1 Samuel 21-22

After David had escaped from Saul's anger he was forced to move from place to place, for whenever Saul was not busy fighting the Philistines, his anger turned to David.

David fled to the priest of Nob and stayed with the prophets there. Because he had no weapons, they unwrapped the sword of Goliath which they had in their possession and gave it to him.

Then he went to the cave of Adullam. When his brothers and all his family heard that he was there, they came to see him. After a while, everyone that had trouble came to see him: those who were in debt, and those who were unhappy came to him. And they looked to him as their leader and listened to his advice.

Saul heard that David had the sword of Goliath. He heard that the people were going to David for advice and that priests were protecting him.

Saul spoke to his officers, saying: "Everyone has turned against me! Even you cannot find David for me. Why? Will David give you fields and vineyards? Can he make you captains and commanders? He can do nothing for you! Even my son stirs up trouble and has helped David escape. David must die!"

Then Saul sent for the priests that had helped David and had worshipped with him.

"Why are you determined to kill David?" they asked. "He has served you well. You trusted him. And he is your son-in-law."

Saul was angered at their words. He ordered his guards to kill the priests, but they were afraid and would not kill priests of the Lord.

But one man stepped forward and killed them. Eighty-four priests he killed, and then he went to Nob where David had stayed for a while. There he killed every man, woman and child.

When David heard this, he bowed his head before the Lord, saying: "I am to blame for all those deaths." And he mourned them.

Again and again, Saul tried to destroy David.

Saul and David at Engedi
1 Samuel 24-25

David went to the wilderness of Engedi. There he lived in a cave with his followers.

One day when Saul was returning from the wars against the Philistines, he happened to come to that very cave.

David's men wanted to rise up and kill Saul. But David stopped them, saying: "We must not lift our hands against him, for he was anointed by the Lord."

So David controlled his men and kept them there. And he followed Saul out of the cave and called to him: "My lord, the king."

Saul looked back, surprised. David bowed to him and asked: "My lord, why do you believe that I want to harm you? You yourself can see that I could easily have captured you in that cave. But I did not, and I would not. I cannot kill you and I am not against you. May the Lord hear my words."

Saul heard David and he wept. Then he said: "You are more righteous than I. You have shown only kindness to me, yet I have done

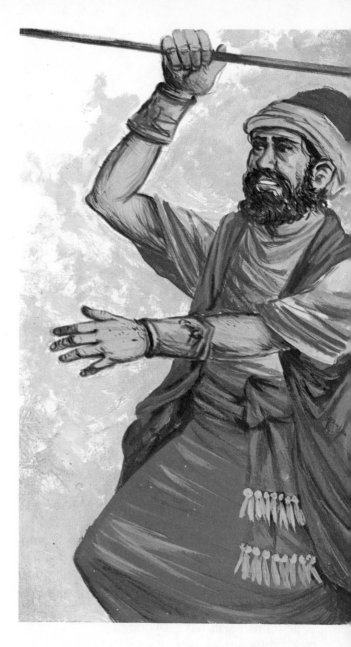

evil to you. You will be king of Israel one day and all this land will be yours. Only, promise me that you will not destroy my children and my children's children because of what I have done to you."

David promised. And Saul returned home.

Soon after this, Samuel died. They buried him where he lived, in Ramah, and all of Israel mourned for him.

David and Abigail
1 Samuel 25

David continued to move throughout the land. He went to the wilderness of Paran, near Maon. In Maon there lived a very rich man named Nabal, who had many goats and sheep and great vineyards.

Nabal was ill-mannered and evil. But his wife, Abigail, was wise and beautiful.

David learned that Nabal's men were shearing the sheep. He called ten of his young men, and said: "Go to Nabal and greet him in my name. Tell him that we wish him well and that we have not harmed his shepherds or his flocks in the fields. Ask him to think well of us and to send us whatever food he can."

David's men went to Nabal, but he was gruff with them. "Who is this David?" he asked. "Many slaves run away from their masters. Why should I give them my bread and wine and meat?" Then he turned away, offering them nothing.

David became angry and was ready to march against Nabal.

One of Nabal's men told Abigail what had happened, saying: "Nabal insulted them. They were friendly toward us and we spent time together in the fields. Your husband was most unreasonable to them, and now they will march against us."

Then Abigail gathered together loaves of bread, bottles of wine, roasted sheep and grain, raisins and cakes to take to David and his men. She loaded all these supplies on donkeys and sent men ahead with them. She followed, not telling her husband about her plans.

When Abigail came to David's camp, she bowed before him and said: "Let me speak. I beg you to listen to my words. Pay no attention to Nabal for he is a fool. Please do not seek vengeance because of him. Instead, accept the things that I have brought."

David answered: "Blessed be the Lord, the God of Israel, for sending you here this day. You have saved me from bloodshed and from seeking revenge."

David accepted the gifts Abigail had brought. And he said: "Go home in peace. I will do as you have asked. Your household will be spared."

Abigail returned home. Nabal was holding a great feast, like a king, and he was drunk. Abigail waited until the next day to tell him what she had done. He became very angry and his heart hardened.

About ten days later Nabal died.

Then David sent messengers to ask Abigail to be his wife. King Saul had given Michal to be the wife of another in David's absence.

Abigail took five maidservants with her, and went to David and became his wife.

David in Saul's Camp

1 Samuel 26-27

Once again Saul's jealousy flared up, and he set out to seek David in the wilderness.

David learned where Saul was camped. Taking one of his men with him, he entered Saul's camp at night.

They went to Saul's tent. There was King Saul, sound asleep, his spear stuck in the ground beside him. Abner, his captain, was next to him, and they were surrounded by their men, all asleep.

The man with David whispered: "Let me kill him with his own spear. It will only take one stroke."

But David held him back, saying: "Do not destroy him. His time will come. He will go into battle and the Lord will strike him down."

Quickly and quietly, David took Saul's spear and a jug of water from beside him, and they left the camp. No one saw them. No one awoke. They were overcome by a deep sleep from the Lord.

Then David stood on a hill opposite Saul's camp. And he shouted: "Abner! Abner, answer me!"

Abner answered: "Who is calling?"

David called back: "You are supposed to be so trustworthy! You have not stood watch over your king! Someone came in to murder him. See, here are his spear and his jug of water. You deserve to die for not protecting him."

Saul heard and asked: "Is that David's voice?"

David answered: "It is my voice, my lord. Why do you continue to chase after me? What have I done to you? You make me run from you like a hunted animal!"

Saul's heart softened once again. He said: "I have done wrong. Come back to us. I will stop chasing you. I promise that I will change my ways."

David called back: "Send one of your men for your spear. As your life was spared this time, so may mine be spared. May the Lord deliver me from trouble."

Saul spoke once more: "You will be blessed. And you will surely succeed in whatever you do." Then he returned to his men and they went home.

But David could not be sure of Saul. He still was afraid that one day the king would kill him. So he did not go back to the royal palace. Instead he went to live in the land of the Philistines who at that time were at peace with Israel.

The Woman of Endor

1 Samuel 28

The Philistines gathered to wage war on Israel once more. King Saul ordered the armies of Israel to come together, and they camped at Gilboa.

When he saw the strength of the Philistines, he called on the Lord, but the Lord did not answer him, and Saul became afraid.

Then Saul asked his men to find a magician or a medium who would give him advice.

Sometime before this, he had ordered all the magicians and mediums out of the land, so his men hesitated. But Saul insisted. Finally, they told him of such a woman at Endor.

Saul disguised himself and travelled to Endor with two of his men. He came to the woman's house and said: "I have come to ask you to call up a spirit for me: I will tell you his name."

"But the king has ordered all mediums and witches out of the land," she said. "I cannot do such a thing."

Saul asked again and said he would reward her for her help.

"Is this a trick?" she asked.

Saul assured her that it was not a trick and that no punishment would come to her.

Then he said: "Call up the spirit of Samuel for me."

She looked at Saul again, more closely. Then she screamed and bowed before him. "You are King Saul, and you have deceived me," she exclaimed.

But he calmed her fears and promised that she would not be harmed.

Then she called the spirit of Samuel. And she said: "Now I see a spirit, an old man covered with a robe."

Saul bowed his head for he knew it was the spirit of Samuel. And he said: "I am deeply troubled. The Philistines are preparing to attack us. God has turned away from me and does not answer me. Now I call on you to tell me what to do."

The voice of Samuel answered: "Why ask me? The Lord has left you. He has surely done as He has said: He has taken the kingdom from you and given it to David. This time tomorrow you and your sons will be with me, and the army of Israel will be in the hands of the Philistines."

These words of Samuel filled Saul with fear. He had not even the strength to get up because of his fear and because he had not eaten for several days.

The woman saw Saul's great fear and his weakness. She spoke to him, saying: "I listened to you even though I feared for my life. Now you must listen to me: eat and gain strength to go back to your men."

At first Saul refused, but she persuaded him to eat. So she prepared food for Saul and the men who had come with him. They ate; then they rose up and left Endor that night.

The Death of Saul

1 Samuel 29-31

Once again, the Philistines prepared to attack the Israelites.

Some of the Philistine commanders were worried because David had come to live in their land and was new in their camp. They knew David had been the trusted servant of Saul, and they knew about his reputation as a fierce warrior.

It was true that David had been helping them fight their enemies. But fighting against his own people might be different. So he was ordered to leave the scene of battle and go back to the city that the Philistines had given him.

Then the Philistines attacked the army of Israel at Mount Gilboa. Many men of Israel were killed in battle, including Jonathan and his brothers. And King Saul was wounded.

Saul called to the man who was his guard: "Draw your sword and kill me before the Philistines capture me. That would bring even greater dishonour to my name."

But the man dared not kill his king. So Saul took his own sword and fell upon it, killing himself. When the man saw that Saul was dead, he, too, killed himself with his own sword.

So they died: Saul and his sons and many men of Israel, all on one day at Mount Gilboa.

The Philistines found the body of the dead king. They cut off Saul's head and carried it throughout the land to proclaim their victory. And they hung the bodies of Saul and his sons on the wall at Bethshan.

When the men of nearby Jabesh heard this, they went at night to cut down the bodies. And they brought them back to Israel and buried them. Then they fasted for seven days.

David's Lament

2 Samuel 1

One man who had escaped from the Philistines at Gilboa went to David in his Philistine city and told him all that had happened. David and his men mourned for Saul and Jonathan and all those who had been killed. They wept, and David chanted:

"The glory of Israel has been slain
on the high places;
How are the mighty fallen!
Let there be no dew or rain
Upon the mountain of Gilboa,
For there the shield of the mighty
was taken away.
Saul and Jonathan were lovely and
beloved;
In their death they were not divided.
They were swifter than eagles,
Stronger than lions.
How are the mighty fallen,
And the weapons of war destroyed."

ened. David became well-liked by everyone, for he ruled well and was just in all his decisions.

Finally all the tribes of Israel came to David at Hebron to ask him to be king over them, saying: "When Saul was king, you led our armies. And the Lord spoke to you saying that you would rule us. Now the time has come for you to become king over all of Israel!"

So a covenant was made before the Lord, and David became king over the whole nation.

David was thirty years old when he began to reign, and he reigned for forty years. He reigned over Judah at Hebron for seven years; then he reigned over all of Israel at Jerusalem for thirty-three years.

The Capture of Jerusalem
2 Samuel 5-8, 1 Chronicles 11-16

While ruling from Hebron, David gathered his best soldiers together to capture the city of Jerusalem from the Jebusites. He took the city, moved into it and called it "The City of David." And he built a wall around it.

David and his armies grew stronger in all they attempted, for the Lord was with him and had established him king over Israel.

In time David even defeated the Philistines in battle. And he won over the Moabites and the Syrians and all the other enemies of Israel.

Again David called together the men of Israel, this time to bring the ark of the Lord to Jerusalem. It had been at the house of Abinadab in Judah since the early Philistine wars.

When they came before the ark, David and his followers rejoiced. They sang and danced, and played their harps and lyres and tambourines and cymbals. And trumpets were sounded.

Then they brought the ark to Jerusalem and set it up in the tent David had ordered to be ready for it. There he made offerings before the Lord and blessed the people in the name of the Lord. And each one received a loaf of bread, a portion of meat and a raisin cake. On that day a psalm of thanksgiving was sung:

"O give thanks to the Lord, call His name;
Make known His deeds to the peoples!
Sing to Him, sing praises to Him;
Tell of all His wondrous works . . .
Sing to the Lord, all the earth!"

David Made King
2 Samuel 2-5, 1 Chronicles 11

After the death of King Saul, David mourned and called upon the Lord. And the Lord told David to go to Hebron in Judah.

So David took his family and all the men who were with him and all their households to Hebron. There the people of Judah made David their king.

Some of the descendants of Saul and a few of his commanders who had escaped from the Philistines did not want David to be their king. But as time went on, their power was weak-

Now King David was established in Jerusalem as the ruler of all Israel. And he ruled his people with justice before the Lord.

Jonathan's Son

2 Samuel 9

One day David asked if there were any surviving children or grandchildren of Saul's family. Because of his love and friendship for Jonathan, he sent messengers to find out.

An elderly servant of Saul's heard about the search and came before David, saying: "Jonathan had a son who is lame and he still lives. I have been caring for him."

So David asked the servant to bring Jonathan's son to him. The boy arrived and bowed down before David.

"Do not be afraid," said the king. "I have called you here to show you kindness for your father's sake. He and I were as close as brothers and we made a covenant of friendship between us.

"I will restore to you the lands of your father. And you and your faithful servant and his family will come to Jerusalem to live. Here you will never want for anything and you will become part of my household."

So Jonathan's lame son came to Jerusalem to live with King David as part of the royal household.

David and Bathsheba

2 Samuel 11-12

One evening in the spring of the year David was walking on the roof of his palace. He happened to look down and he saw a beautiful young woman. She was so lovely that he sent his servants to find out who she was.

"She is Bathsheba, the wife of Uriah the Hittite," he was told. David invited her to the palace and he fell in love with her.

After Bathsheba had returned home, David sent a letter to Joab, the commander of his armies. In the letter he wrote: "Uriah is a good soldier. Be sure he is in the front lines of battle."

Joab obeyed the orders of the king. While besieging an enemy city, Joab sent Uriah to a place in the front lines near the city wall. Men stormed out of the city and killed hundreds of the Israelites. And Uriah was among those killed in battle on that day.

Bathsheba mourned for her husband. When the time of mourning was over, David sent for her.

She came to live in the palace as his wife, and in time she had a son.

The thing that David had done displeased the Lord. So He sent the prophet Nathan to David. And Nathan told David a story:

"There were two men living in the same city. One was poor and the other was very rich. The rich man had many flocks; the poor man had only one lamb. He fed it and protected it and cared for it.

"A stranger came to the rich man hungry and in need. Now the rich man did not prepare one of his own animals for the stranger; instead he took the poor man's only lamb."

David heard and became angry, saying: "The man who would do such a thing deserves to die and pay back the poor man for his lamb several times over, for he had no pity."

Nathan said: "You are the man."

David understood, and he was ashamed, and he said: "Truly, I have sinned against the Lord."

Nathan continued: "The Lord has made you ruler over all of Israel. Why have you done wrong in the sight of the Lord? You killed Uriah in battle just as surely as if you had killed him yourself, and you took his wife to be your wife.

"The Lord does not want your death. You shall not die. But great sorrow will come to you. The child who is born to you and Bathsheba will die."

Then Nathan left King David and went home.

Soon the child became ill. And David prayed to God and fasted for a week. On the seventh day the child died.

Then David arose, changed his clothes and ate, for he said: "While the child was still living, I prayed to the Lord and I fasted. Now that he is dead, I cannot bring him back."

So David went to Bathsheba and comforted her.

In due time they had another son whose name was Solomon. And the Lord loved Solomon.

Absalom
2 Samuel 13-19

David had many wives, as was the custom in those days, and he had many children. Ab-

salom was the most handsome of all his sons, tall and slender with thick wavy hair.

Amnon, the oldest son, had committed a crime against Absalom's sister, Tamar. In revenge, Absalom had ordered his servant to kill Amnon.

Then, because of his father's anger, Absalom left Jerusalem to live with his mother's family in a distant town. He stayed away for three years.

Even after he came back to Jerusalem, it was two more years before Absalom saw his father. Finally he came before King David and bowed before him, and David kissed Absalom as a sign of forgiveness.

Now, Absalom had chariots and horses and several men who were his servants. He would stand by the gate of the city near the place of judgement. Whenever anyone came with a case for the king to decide, Absalom would say:

"Your cause is just. If I were judge, I would be sure to rule wisely and you would receive justice."

In this way, Absalom became loved and trusted by many people. And the number of people who loved him continued to increase.

One day Absalom decided to go to Hebron, for he had a plan.

Absalom sent messages to all the tribes of Israel, saying: "The time will come when you will say Absalom is king at Hebron."

The men who went with Absalom knew nothing of his plot. But David heard about it and he called together the commanders of his army to go out and find Absalom to put an end to his plan.

David divided his troops into three armies

and prepared to go with them himself. But the commanders said: "You must stay behind where you will be safe. You are worth ten thousand of us."

So David stayed. But he called after the troops: "For my sake, deal gently with Absalom." And all the people heard their king.

David's army met Absalom's men in the Forest of Ephraim. There Absalom's men were defeated, and many were killed.

It happened that Absalom was riding into battle on a mule. As he rode under the branches of an oak tree, his thick hair got caught. He was pulled off the mule, and the animal trotted away. There Absalom hung, between heaven and earth.

David's men saw this and told Joab, who asked: "You saw him? Why did you not strike him down? I would have given you a reward."

One of the men answered: "Even if I received a thousand pieces of silver, I would not have done it. The king ordered us not to harm Absalom, for his sake."

But Joab strode off to where Absalom was hanging. He took three spears and plunged them into Absalom's heart, killing him. Then his men cut Absalom down and threw him into a pit in the forest. And they placed a mound of stones over it.

Then Joab blew his trumpet and all the fighting stopped.

Now David was at the gate of the city waiting for news of the battle. A watchman called that he saw messengers running toward the city, so David went to meet them.

David asked: "Is Absalom safe?"

The messenger answered: "The Lord has had revenge on all who rose up against you. May all your enemies meet the same fate."

Then the king knew that Absalom was dead.

He went to his room and wept and mourned for Absalom. And he said: "Absalom, my son. Would that I had died instead of you! Absalom, my son, my son!"

David Praises the Lord

2 Samuel 21-22

So the victory of Joab and the army was turned into weeping and mourning. And the soldiers came back into the city, not as victors, but as if they had been defeated.

Then Joab spoke to David, saying: "You have made the soldiers that fought to protect you feel as if they had wronged you. You seem to show love for those who hate you and hate to those who love you. You must speak to your people."

So King David rose up and went to receive his people. Then they knew that once again he was their leader, king over all of Israel.

The Philistines attacked again, but David defeated them in battle.

After that, David raised his voice in praise to the Lord, saying:

"The Lord is my rock and my fortress,
In Him do I trust;
I call upon the Lord,
And I am saved from my enemies."

The Books of Kings

The story of the kingdom of Israel from the death of King David through the reign of King Solomon and the years of the division of the kingdom into two parts: Judah and Israel.

References to the Books of Chronicles which tell much the same story are included here.

The Books of the Prophets and their teachings are woven into the historical background of this section. The Prophets spoke to the people interpreting the past, giving instructions for the present and revealing what would happen in the future. Their appeal was always for righteousness and justice, stressing God's power, love and mercy.

Solomon becomes King

1 Kings 1-2, 1 Chronicles 28-29

Now King David was an old man and growing weak. Bathsheba, his wife, and Nathan, the prophet, were at his side. He sent for his son Solomon.

Then he ordered Zadok the priest, Nathan the prophet and other elders of the people to take Solomon to Gihon, there to anoint him with oil and proclaim him king.

They did as their king commanded: they put Solomon on David's mule and anointed him. Then they blew the trumpet and all the people shouted: "Long live King Solomon!"

King David, hearing this, bowed his head before the Lord, saying: "Blessed be the Lord, the God of Israel, who has granted one of my sons to rule over Israel. And has allowed me to see this day."

The time for David's death came near, and he spoke to Solomon, charging him to walk in the ways of the Lord, saying: "Be strong, and of good courage. Keep the commandments of the Lord and you will prosper. Then the Lord will fulfil the promise that if my children live according to His ways and are wise and just, they will continue to be kings of Israel."

And David charged Solomon to build a house for the Lord, saying: "I had wanted to build the Lord's house, but the word of the Lord came to me saying that I had shed too much blood and waged great wars. Therefore it is your duty to build the house of the Lord, and all the leaders will help you."

And David told Solomon all the plans he had made for the building.

Then he blessed the Lord, saying:

"Blessed art Thou, O Lord, God of Israel, for ever and ever."

King David died and was buried in Jerusalem. And Solomon sat on the throne of David his father and ruled over all the people of Israel, and he prospered.

The Wisdom of Solomon
1 Kings 3-4

Solomon loved the Lord and served Him well.

And the Lord appeared to Solomon in a dream, saying, "Ask of me whatever you will."

Solomon answered: "You have made me king in place of my father. I am still young in the ways of ruling a great people. I ask, O Lord, that I may have an understanding heart and mind so that I may know good from evil, right from wrong. Then I can govern my people wisely."

God was pleased and answered: "Because you have asked for this and not for great riches or death for your enemies, your wish shall be granted. You shall have wisdom and understanding. And I will also give what you have not asked: both honour and riches."

Then Solomon awoke and made offerings to the Lord and worshipped Him.

One day two women came before King Solomon. One of the women said: "My king, this woman and I live in the same house. I had a child in that house, and three days later she also had a baby. We were alone in the house, just we two and our babies.

"Her baby died in the night and she took my baby from beside me and put her dead baby in my baby's place. When I got up in the morning to feed my child, I knew what she had done. The dead baby is not mine. My child is still living."

Then the other woman said: "No, the living is my son; the dead one is yours!"

The first woman said: "The living one is mine."

The king thought, and then he said: "Bring me a sword. We will divide the living child in two, so each woman will have a half."

Then the mother of the living child who loved him dearly, said: "Oh no, do not kill the child. Give it to her so it may live!"

But the other said: "The baby shall belong to neither of us. Divide it!"

Then the king spoke: "Give the first woman the baby. She is surely the mother."

And it was done.

All the people of Israel heard of the king's judgement in this case, and in many others. They came to respect him, and they saw that the wisdom of God was with him.

Solomon's wisdom was greater than any other man's, and his fame spread far and wide. People came from all the nations to gain understanding from him.

Solomon wrote three thousand proverbs, and

the songs he wrote numbered a thousand and five.

Building the Temple

1 Kings 5-9, 2 Chronicles 2-5

Now that there was peace in the land, Solomon prepared to build the Lord's house as his father King David had commanded.

In the fourth year of Solomon's reign the building was begun. It was now four hundred and eighty years since the children of Israel had come out of the land of Egypt.

Cedar and cypress trees were imported from Lebanon. Stones were brought from the hill country. The finest olive wood was sent for.

Fabrics and fine linen were made. Precious stones were cut, and spices were ground for use in the Temple.

Many thousands of men were put to work preparing the timber and the stones and bringing them to Jerusalem. Craftsmen of all kinds were busy, also: woodcutters, masons, carpenters, metalworkers, weavers, and artisans.

Inside the Temple there was no noise of hammer or axe, for all the materials were measured and made ready before being brought to the building site. There they were put into place and fitted together.

It took seven years to build the Temple.

When it was finished, the house of the Lord was ninety feet long, thirty feet wide, and forty-five feet high.

The wood for the inside of the building was carved and overlaid with gold. The altar was covered with pure gold.

In the innermost part, the Holy of Holies, were carved two angels, each fifteen feet high. They, too, were covered with pure gold.

Inside the Temple were ten golden lamp stands and lamps.

All the bowls and candlesticks and lamps and basins that belonged to the house of the Lord were made of pure gold also.

When the Temple was ready, Solomon called all the leaders of Israel to gather in Jerusalem to bring the ark to the Temple. It was the time of the autumn festival.

The priests carried the ark of the Lord into the Temple to its proper place. In the ark were the tablets of stone which Moses had put there.

When the ark was in place, a great cloud filled the Temple, for the glory of the Lord was there.

Solomon spoke to the Lord, saying:
"I have built You a great Temple, O Lord,
A place to dwell in forever.
There is no God like You
In heaven above or in earth beneath."

Then the king prayed to the Lord. And he blessed all the people, saying: "Blessed be the Lord, the God of Israel, who has given rest to His people Israel, and who has kept the promise He made with our fathers when He brought them out of the land of Egypt."

There was great rejoicing and thanksgiving. The sound of trumpets, flutes, cymbals, harps and lyres was heard. And the people sang: "Praise the Lord for He is good, His mercy endures forever."

All the people offered sacrifices to the Lord and worshipped Him there at the dedication of the Temple. They held a feast for seven days. Then they went home filled with joy because of all the good that had come to Israel.

Once again God appeared to Solomon and said: "I have heard your prayer and your blessing. If you keep My commandments, your

throne will be established over Israel forever. But if you or your children turn away from the ways of the Lord, the people of Israel will be sent out of this land and out of the Temple. And the house of the Lord will become a pile of ruins."

Solomon's Riches
1 Kings 9

After the Temple of the Lord was finished, Solomon built a palace for himself. This took thirteen years to build. Then he built a hall of justice and a palace for the Pharaoh's daughter who was one of his wives. All these buildings were built of fine wood and stone.

Many men were kept busy with buildings for the king. And they built a fleet of ships for him and cities on the Reed Sea.

The king gathered together horsemen and fine chariots. And he had shields and breast-plates made and a throne of ivory overlaid with heavy gold.

So Solomon had more wealth and wisdom than all the kings on earth.

The Queen of Sheba

1 Kings 10

The Queen of Sheba heard of Solomon's great wealth and wisdom. She travelled to Jerusalem to see him. She asked him many difficult questions to test him. And she brought many attendants with her, and camels carrying spices and gold and precious stones.

Solomon answered all her questions. None were too hard for him, and he gave her good advice.

When the Queen of Sheba had seen the great wisdom of Solomon and the palace he had built and all his riches, she was surprised and impressed, saying:

"Everything I heard about you is true. But I hardly believed it until I came here and saw it

for myself. In fact, your wisdom and wealth are greater than I could ever have imagined.

"Those who come to you for your wisdom are fortunate indeed. Blessed be the Lord who has made you king over Israel."

King Solomon gave her many fine gifts of great value. Then the Queen of Sheba and all her servants left Israel and returned to their own land.

Solomon's Wrongdoing

I Kings 11

King Solomon married many foreign women. They were the daughters of the kings of all the countries he had made treaties with, for such was the custom in those days. This Solomon did even though the Lord had said through Moses that the people of Israel must not marry foreigners.

"Foreign wives will surely turn the hearts of their husbands to foreign gods," the Lord had said.

Solomon's wives did worship their own gods. And Solomon built places of worship for them.

When he grew old, the king's wives even influenced him to worship their gods with them, so that he did not remain true to the Lord. And the Lord became angry, and He said:

"Since you have not kept the covenant and the commandments of the Lord, the kingdom shall be taken from your family. Not from you but from your son will I take the kingdom, and I will give it to your servant."

So the Lord made enemies rise up against Solomon, and there was trouble in the land at the end of Solomon's reign.

Two Kingdoms

I Kings 11-16

Solomon had a servant, Jeroboam, who was a hard worker and had great ability. The king had placed him in charge of all his construction workers.

One day the prophet Ahijah spoke to Jeroboam, saying: "Because Solomon has not kept the commandments of the Lord, his kingdom shall be taken from him. Then you will become king over ten of the twelve tribes of Israel, and the king's son will rule the rest from Jerusalem."

Solomon, hearing of this, sought to kill Jeroboam, who then fled to Egypt.

Not long after this, King Solomon died. He had reigned in Jerusalem for forty years. And Rehoboam, his son, became king.

Now God did as He had promised.

The people came to the new king, and they said: "Your father worked us very hard. We built his palaces and his public buildings, and his cities and ships, and we built the Temple to the Lord. Now we ask you to make life easier for us."

The elders advised Rehoboam to listen to the people and make their lives easier so they would serve him willingly. But Rehoboam did not take their advice. Instead he threatened to make the people work even harder than before.

When the people heard this, they rebelled against the king. Only the two tribes of Judah and Benjamin remained loyal to him and to the house of David. The other ten tribes of Israel called Jeroboam to be their king.

So it was that Rehoboam ruled the southern kingdom of Judah, and Jeroboam ruled the northern kingdom of Israel.

Jeroboam was afraid that the people would want to go to Jerusalem to worship the Lord and make sacrifices there. If they went to Jerusalem, he was afraid they would come under the influence of Rehoboam.

So Jeroboam made golden calves to become gods for his people. He built altars for them and holy places, and he appointed priests.

All this displeased the Lord and led to the disappearance of the house of Jeroboam from the face of the earth.

Rehoboam ruled Judah for seventeen years, and Jeroboam ruled Israel for twenty-two years. There was continuous trouble between the two.

After they died, many kings ruled in each kingdom. The kings had great power over the people and did evil in the sight of the Lord.

Then there arose spokesmen for the oppressed people. They interpreted the commandments of the Lord, telling the people what the Lord expected them to do. These were the great prophets.

The Prophet Elijah

I Kings 16-17

Ahab became king over Israel and his capital was the hill city of Samaria. He married Jezebel, daughter of a king, and he built an altar and a temple for her god Baal. Then he, too, began to worship Baal. And he displeased the Lord more than all the kings who had gone before him.

The prophet Elijah came to Samaria and spoke to Ahab, telling him of his wrongdoing and that God was displeased. And he said: "There will be a great drought in the land. There will be no rain or dew and all the rivers will dry up."

The Lord told Elijah to leave Samaria and go to live by a brook where there was water. The Lord sent ravens to feed him, and he stayed there until the brook dried up.

Healing the Widow's Son

I Kings 17

Then the Lord sent Elijah to the city of Zarephath where he was told he would meet a woman who would look after him.

When Elijah arrived at the city, he met a woman gathering sticks. She gave him some water. Then he asked for some bread.

"I have nothing baked," she answered. "And only a very little meal and oil at home, enough to make a little bread. My son and I will eat it today and after that, we will starve."

Elijah said to her: "Do not worry. Go and do as you have planned, but bring me a taste of the bread first. The Lord has spoken. Neither your barrel of meal nor your jar of oil will be empty until rain comes to the land."

The woman did as Elijah said. And she and her son and Elijah had enough food for many days.

Some time later the woman's son became ill and he even stopped breathing. Elijah went to the boy, lifted him up and prayed to the Lord, saying: "O Lord, spare this child's life. Do not bring sorrow to this good woman by killing her son."

The Lord listened to Elijah's prayer, and the child began to breathe again. And he sat up.

Then the mother said: "Now I know you are truly a man of God and that you speak the word of the Lord."

Elijah and the Power of God

I Kings 18

In the third year of the drought the Lord sent Elijah back to King Ahab.

The drought had caused famine in the land. People were starving and there was no grass for the animals to eat. There was great fear and suffering everywhere. Queen Jezebel had ordered all the prophets of the Lord put to death, and now only a few remained alive, hiding in caves.

Elijah did as the Lord had commanded, and appeared once more before King Ahab. "You have returned, you troubler of Israel!" said the king.

Elijah answered: "I have not caused the famine. You and your family are the trouble-makers because you have turned away from the Lord and are worshipping the false Baal."

And he said: "Now call together all the people of Israel and all the prophets of Baal and have them meet at Mount Carmel. And I will speak to them there."

This was done.

At Mount Carmel, Elijah spoke before all the people, saying: "How long will you be divided and have two separate beliefs? If the Lord is the true God, follow Him. If Baal is true, then follow him."

Elijah went on: "I am the only prophet of the Lord here, but there are four hundred and fifty prophets of Baal. Let us get two bulls to sacrifice. Let the prophets of Baal choose one and cut it up and lay it on a pile of wood with no fire under it. I will prepare the other the same way.

"Then the prophets of Baal will call on their god, and I will call on the Lord. The one that answers with fire will be the true God."

The people agreed to this plan. In the morning, the prophets of Baal prepared a bull for sacrifice and placed it on a pile of wood. Then they called on Baal to send fire. They called and danced and shouted, but there was no voice or answer or any sign of fire.

At noon Elijah mocked them, saying: "Call louder. Maybe your god has gone out or is sleeping."

So they called and shouted and danced themselves into a frenzy until evening. Still there was no answer or sign from Baal.

Then Elijah said: "Come closer. Now I will prepare the second bull."

And all the people watched Elijah set up an altar to the Lord. He built up a pile of wood. And he prepared the bull and placed it on the wood.

Then he told the people to bring barrels full of water to pour on the wood and on the cut-up bull and on the ground around the altar. This they did until there was so much water that it made puddles on the ground around the altar.

It was time for the evening sacrifice. Elijah called upon the Lord, saying: "O Lord, God of Abraham, Isaac and Jacob, show us that You are God and that I have done all these things at Your command. Hear me and send fire so

these people will know that You are God. Then You will win back the hearts of Your people."

When Elijah finished speaking, there was fire. In a cloud of smoke the fire appeared and burned the offering, the wood and even the dust. And it dried up the water that was on the ground around the altar.

When the people saw this, they fell to the ground and cried out: "The Lord, He is God! The Lord, He is God!"

After this, the rains came and the drought and famine were over.

Elijah and Elisha
1 Kings 19

King Ahab told his wife Jezebel all that Elijah had done. She sent a messenger to Elijah saying that she would have him put to death at once, for she still did not believe in the Lord.

Elijah fled into the wilderness and sat down under a juniper tree.

An angel of the Lord came to him and told him to travel to Horeb (Sinai), the mountain of the Lord, and that the Lord would speak to him there.

Elijah arrived at the mountain to await the coming of the Lord. First a great wind blew. But the Lord did not appear in the wind. After the wind, there was an earthquake, but the Lord was not in the earthquake. After the earthquake, there came a fire, but the Lord was not in the fire either.

Then, after the fire came still a small voice saying: "What are you doing here, Elijah?"

Elijah answered: "I have worked for the Lord, but the Israelites have thrown down the altars of the Lord. They no longer walk in His ways. They have killed the prophets until I am the only one left, and now they plan to kill me."

The Lord spoke again to Elijah saying: "Go to Damascus. There you will find Elisha who will go with you and will be a prophet after you."

Again Elijah did as the Lord commanded. In Damascus he found Elisha working in his father's field. Elijah threw his robe over Elisha as a sign that he had been chosen to be a prophet. So Elisha made a sacrifice to the Lord. Then he told his family goodbye and followed Elijah.

Ahab and the Vineyard

1 Kings 21-22

There was a man, Naboth, who had a vineyard next to the palace of King Ahab in the land of Israel. And the king wanted Naboth's land for himself for a garden. He offered to give Naboth another vineyard or to pay him for his property.

But Naboth answered, saying: "The Lord has given me this inheritance and I will not give it away."

Ahab became angry. He grew sullen and displeased and even refused to eat. Jezebel, his wife, asked what the trouble was. He told her about the vineyard, and she said:

"Are you not the king? Cheer up, you shall have Naboth's vineyard."

Then Jezebel wrote letters to the elders of the city, telling them to call all the people together on a certain day. She signed the letters with King Ahab's seal.

"On that day," she wrote, "call Naboth before the people. Two men will step up and say that he has spoken out against God and against the king. Then, as is the custom for such a crime, you must order the people to stone Naboth to death outside the city near the brook."

The elders did as the letters had commanded them.

When Naboth was dead they sent a message to the palace. Jezebel told Ahab that Naboth had died and urged him to go out and take possession of Naboth's land. So the king took the vineyard for himself.

Now, the word of the Lord came to Elijah, saying: "Go to King Ahab and tell him that he has sinned. Tell him that evil will come to him, that his blood will flow as surely as the blood of Naboth has flowed. Tell him that Jezebel, too, shall die and her body shall not be buried."

So Elijah went to Ahab and the king, afraid, asked: "You have already found me out?"

Then Elijah told him all that the Lord had said, and King Ahab fasted and repented and prayed to the Lord.

After this, there was peace in the land for three years.

But then war broke out between Israel and her enemies. Ahab was killed in battle while riding in his chariot. And he was buried at the brook where Naboth had been stoned to death.

Ahaziah, the son of Ahab, ruled Israel after him and continued to do evil in the sight of the Lord. At the same time Jehoshaphat ruled Judah. He made peace with Israel and walked in the way of the Lord, doing all His commandments.

Elijah Disappears in a Whirlwind

2 Kings 2

Elisha followed Elijah throughout the kingdom and was loyal to him. When Elijah knew that the Lord was about to take him up to heaven, Elijah said to Elisha: "The Lord has commanded me to go to Bethel. You must stay here."

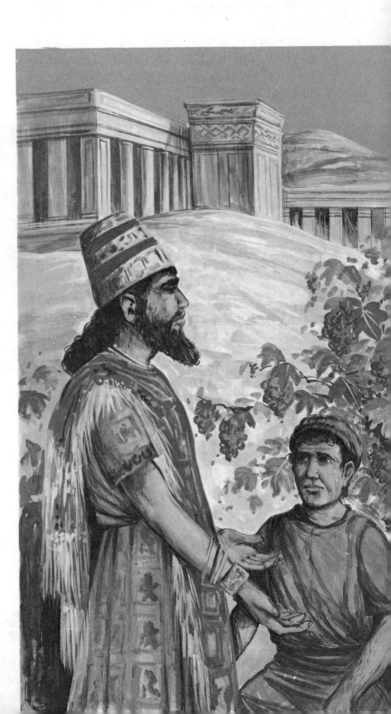

Elisha answered: "As surely as the Lord lives and you live, I will not leave you."

So they travelled together from Gilgal to Bethel. There Elijah spoke to Elisha again, saying: "Now I will leave you. The Lord has commanded me to go to Jericho. You must stay here."

Again Elisha answered: "As surely as the Lord lives and you live, I will not leave you."

So together they travelled to Jericho. And fifty of their followers came after them.

At Jericho, Elijah once more said: "You must stay here. The Lord has commanded that I go to the banks of the river Jordan. You must stay here."

And once more Elisha answered: "As surely as the Lord lives and your soul lives, I will not leave you."

So the two went on, followed by the fifty, until they came to the river Jordan. There Elijah took off his cape, folded it and threw it out in front of him.

At the place where the cape struck the water, the river divided, making a path. Elijah and Elisha walked across on dry land. Their followers stayed behind.

Then it happened, as the two walked on together, that a chariot of fire and horses of fire appeared and separated them. And Elijah was whisked into heaven in a whirlwind.

Elisha stood there for a moment. Then he picked up Elijah's cape and went back to the river. He struck the water as Elijah had done and the waters separated. Elisha crossed over.

When the followers of the prophets saw this, they said: "Surely the spirit of Elijah is with him." So they went to meet Elisha and bowed down before him.

Elisha and the Widow
2 Kings 4

Elisha won the love of the people. He was

kind and always eager to help the poor and the sick. He was helpful to all people and brought the spirit of the Lord to them.

Once a widow came to Elisha saying: "My husband is dead, and a creditor has come to take my children to be his slaves, for I have nothing at all to pay him with. I have only one jar of oil."

Elisha said: "Go and borrow jars and bowls and all kinds of empty containers. Then shut yourself up in your house and pour some of your oil into each one. When one container is full, put it aside, and fill the next."

The woman did as Elisha had said. Her sons brought containers to her one at a time and she poured the oil, enough to fill every jar and every bowl that her sons brought to her.

Then she went back to the man of God, and he said: "Now, sell enough oil to pay your debts. Then you and your sons will live on the rest."

Naaman the Leper

2 Kings 5

During a time of peace between Israel and Syria, Naaman was captain of the Syrian army. He was a great man and a famous warrior, but he was a leper.

Now the Syrians had raided Israel and had carried away a young girl who became a servant of Naaman's wife. She told her mistress about a prophet of the Lord in Samaria who could cure Naaman.

When the king heard about this, he called Naaman, saying: "Go to Israel, and I will send a letter with you."

Naaman set out with the letter. And he took many gifts with him: silver and gold and festive garments.

With his horses and chariot and all his gifts, Naaman arrived at the door of Elisha's house.

And Elisha said: "Go and wash in the river Jordan seven times. Then your body will be clean and well."

Naaman was angry, saying: "I expected him to come out and call on the name of the Lord and lay his hands on the place and cure the leprosy. Are not the rivers of Damascus better than the waters of Israel? Have I come all this distance to wash in a river?"

Then one of his servants spoke to him: "If the prophet had asked you to do a difficult thing, would you not have done it? But he has asked a simple thing: to wash and be clean."

So Naaman went to the river Jordan and dipped himself in the water seven times as Elisha had commanded him. And his skin became clean and fresh as a child's.

Then Naaman returned to the man of God and stood before him. And he said: "Now I know that there is no God in all the earth except in Israel. Accept my gifts for I am grateful for what you have done."

But Elisha would accept nothing from Naaman. Instead he blessed Naaman and sent him home. And Naaman took with him some of the earth of Israel and said he would worship no god but the Lord.

Elisha and his Servant

2 Kings 5

Now Gehazi, the servant of Elisha, thought to himself: "My master has refused gifts from the Syrian. He has brought many gifts with him, so I will get something for myself."

So Gehazi followed Naaman, and Naaman stopped his chariot and asked: "Is anything the matter?"

Gehazi answered: "All is well, but my master has sent me to ask for some silver and garments for two young men, the sons of prophets."

Naaman gladly packed some silver and clothing into two bags for Gehazi. Then he went on his way.

Elisha sent for Gehazi and asked: "Where have you been?"

And Gehazi answered: "Nowhere."

Then Elisha spoke: "I was with you in spirit when you followed Naaman. Was this the time to accept gifts from him?

"Because of what you have done, the leprosy of Naaman shall pass to you and your descendants."

Gehazi bowed down before Elisha and when he went away from him he was a leper, with skin as white as snow.

Jehu, King of Israel

2 Kings 8-9

Now Elisha set out to fulfil the prophesy of Elijah: that the house of Ahab would be destroyed because of their worship of Baal.

Jehu went back to his men and they asked: "What was that about?"

When Jehu told them what the young man had said, they rose up, blew their trumpets and proclaimed: "Jehu is king!"

Then Jehu set out for Jezreel. It happened at that time that both the king of Israel and the king of Judah were in the city of Jezreel.

Joram, the king of Israel, had been wounded in battle near Jezreel, and Ahaziah, his cousin and the king of Judah, had come to visit him.

As Jehu approached the city, the two kings set out to do battle with him, each in his own chariot. They met outside the city near the place which had once been the vineyard of Naboth.

Jehu drew his bow and his arrow struck

At this time the kings who ruled Israel and Judah were both descended from the house of Ahab, the king who had done evil in the sight of the Lord; he had married Jezebel and had worshipped Baal.

Elisha sent for one of his followers and said: "Go and find Jehu, the son of Jehoshaphat. Take him to an inner room. When you are alone together, take the vial of oil which I will give you and anoint him with it. Tell him that the Lord has declared him to be king of Israel. Then leave immediately."

The young man took the vial of oil and set out. He found Jehu sitting with other officers and he said: "Captain, I have a message for you."

So Jehu and the young man went into the house together.

There the young man poured oil on the head of Jehu saying: "The Lord, the God of Israel, has said you shall be anointed king of Israel. And you shall destroy the house of Ahab."

Then he hurried away.

Joram, killing him at once. When Ahaziah saw this, he turned his chariot to flee. But Jehu pursued him and killed him also.

So it was that Jehu killed both the king of Israel and the king of Judah in one day.

Jezebel and Jehu

2 Kings 9-10

Jezebel heard that Jehu was on his way into the city. She painted her face and fixed her hair and leaned out, mocking him from her window.

Jehu called up to her servants who were standing beside her: "Whoever is on my side, throw her down!"

Two of her servants pushed her out of the window so that she crashed to the ground. Her blood spattered on the walls and horses trampled over her.

Jehu went on to refresh himself, and he said to his men: "Go now and bury Queen Jezebel; after all, she was the daughter of a king."

But when they went to find her, there was little left; dogs had eaten her flesh. Thus the prophecy of Elijah was fulfilled.

Jehu continued to destroy the descendants of Ahab by having seventy of Ahab's sons killed. And the men who had been Ahab's leaders and commanders and trusted servants were also put to death.

After this, all the people of Israel who had worshipped Baal were brought into the temple of Baal. There, they were killed by Jehu and his men. The temple, too, was destroyed, and the worship of Baal was wiped out of the land of Israel.

Jehu reigned over Israel for twenty-eight years. When he died, he was buried in Samaria, the capital.

Athaliah and Joash

2 Kings 11-12

After the death of Ahaziah king of Judah, his mother Athaliah, who was the daughter of Jezebel and herself a worshipper of Baal, destroyed the rest of the royal family so that she could become queen. And she rebuilt the temple of Baal.

The wife of the high priest had rescued Joash, the infant son of the slain king. She hid him in the house of the Lord for six years while Athaliah reigned as queen.

In the seventh year of Athaliah's reign, the high priest planned a revolt. He called together captains of the guard and leaders of the people to guard the Temple. Then he brought out the little prince and placed the royal crown on his head. The boy was anointed with oil and proclaimed king over Judah.

Then all the people clapped their hands with joy and shouted: "Long live the King!"

When Athaliah heard the cheers, she went to the Temple of the Lord. There she saw the young king standing by a pillar and all the people rejoicing to the sound of trumpets.

Athaliah shouted: "Treason! Treason!"

The high priest ordered his men to take her out of the Temple, saying: "She must be slain, but not in the house of the Lord."

So they followed her and seized her on the road to the palace, and there she was killed.

Then the high priest made a covenant between the Lord and the king and the people, that they would return to the ways of the Lord. The people went out and destroyed the altars of Baal and the great temple of Baal as well.

The boy Joash went from the house of the Lord to the palace. There he reigned as king of Judah for forty years. He did right in the sight of the Lord and ruled his people well.

The Death of Elisha

2 Kings 13

Elisha became ill while Joash was king of Judah. And Joash went to Elisha and wept at his bedside.

Elisha said to the king: "Take a bow and arrow and put your hand on the bow."

Joash did so, and Elisha said: "Open the window to the east."

The king opened the window. And Elisha said: "Shoot!" And the king shot an arrow out of the window to the east.

"This is the arrow of the Lord's victory," said Elisha, "the arrow of deliverance from Syria. You shall fight the Syrians and defeat them. Now take the arrows and strike the ground."

Joash struck the ground three times with the arrows.

Elisha became angry and said: "You should have struck the ground five or six times or more. Then you would surely have struck down Syria and ended her power. Now you will defeat Syria only three times."

This was Elisha's last prophecy, for he died soon afterwards and was buried.

Jeroboam II

2 Kings 14-16

Just as Elisha had prophesied, Israel won three battles against Syria.

Then, during the reign of Jeroboam II, the great-grandson of Jehu, Israel prospered. New territory was conquered, and Israel grew in wealth and power.

The merchants of Israel traded with nearby countries and grew rich, but the masses of the people lived in poverty and were continuously in debt. Many were sold, or sold themselves, into slavery. And their land was taken away from them.

The wealthy had power as well as riches. Judges took bribes, and there was little justice in the land.

The Prophet Amos

Amos 5, 6, 8, 9

At this time, the prophet Amos preached his sermons. He spoke out against the lack of justice and the excesses of the rich. He urged the people to live by the commandments of the Lord, saying:

"Seek good and not evil that you may
live;
And the Lord, the God of hosts, will
be with you.
Take away your peace offerings and
the noise of your songs . . .
Let justice well up like waters
And righteousness like a mighty stream.
Woe to those who are at ease
and lie on beds of ivory . . .
Who sing idle songs, and drink wine
in bowls, and anoint themselves
with oils . . ."

Amos was the first of the prophets to forecast the fall of the Hebrew nations. He pleaded with the people to change their ways to prevent the punishment that would surely come. He continually warned:

"The days will come, says the Lord,
When there will be famine in the land;
Not a famine of bread or a thirst for water,
But of hearing the word of the Lord.

The people shall wander from sea to sea;
They shall run to and fro
To seek the word of the Lord,
And they shall not find it.
The eyes of the Lord are on the sinful
   kingdom
And it will be destroyed . . ."

But the people refused to change their ways.

After the wave of prosperity in the time of Jeroboam II, Israel steadily became weaker. A succession of kings ruled the kingdom and turned further away from God's commandments. These kings were more concerned about their own comfort than about ruling their people with justice.

There were plots and murders and assassinations in the land.

Then, King Hoshea came to the throne, ruling Israel from Samaria.

King Hoshea and Hosea the Prophet

2 Kings 17, Hosea 13-14

King Hoshea was to be the last king of Israel.

During his reign, the prophet Hosea spoke to the people of their wrongdoing. He tried to persuade the king to live according to God's commandments, and he warned of disaster. He spoke of the power of Assyria to destroy Israel.

At the same time, Hosea held out hope. He pleaded with the people to change their ways. Then, he said, the Lord would forgive them and they would be saved through His love and mercy.

Hosea likened God's forgiveness of Israel to his own forgiveness of his unfaithful wife, Gomer. The unfaithful had gone astray, he said, and then would return to be forgiven and welcomed back. Hosea preached:

"Return, O Israel, to the Lord your God;
You have fallen because of your sins;
Israel will fall by the sword,
Assyria will destroy us;
Return to the Lord,
Ask Him to accept all that is good . . .
Those that return to the Lord shall
   prosper,
They shall grow and blossom . . .
The ways of the Lord are right,
And the righteous shall walk in them."

Israel did not heed the words of Hosea. Instead, the people continued to worship idols, sacrificing to the gods of nature and to the gods of the people around them. They believed in magic and witchcraft and even sacrificed their children as burnt offerings.

The priests, too, did evil in the sight of the Lord. They turned away from teaching God's commandments.

While all this corruption and evil was taking place within Israel, Assyria had become a great power.

The End of Israel

2 Kings 17

In the seventh year of King Hoshea's reign, the Assyrians marched against Israel and besieged Samaria, the capital. After nearly three years, the city was captured by Shalmaneser, the great Assyrian king.

The Israelites were marched away and scattered throughout the Assyrian Empire, and many Assyrians were moved into the land of Israel to rule over it.

Since that time, the people of Israel who were taken away have been called "the ten lost tribes."

The Assyrian victory caused the kingdom of Israel to end. Then, only the Hebrew kingdom of Judah was left.

Hezekiah, King of Judah

2 Kings 18-20, Micah 3, 4, 6

When the kingdom of Israel was destroyed, Hezekiah was king of Judah. He was a good king and lived according to God's commandments. The Lord was with him and he prospered.

Hezekiah ordered the Temple to be repaired and purified, for his father Ahaz had removed much of the gold and silver and other treasures from the Temple. These he had used to pay tribute to Syria and Egypt, nations which threatened his land. When the Temple was ready, it was the Passover season, the Feast of Unleavened Bread.

King Hezekiah sent messengers throughout the land to call the people to come to Jerusalem to celebrate. For seven days there was great rejoicing and sacrificing in the Temple.

At that time, the prophet Micah was speaking the words of the Lord, reminding the people of their responsibilities. He spoke to them, saying:

"How should we come before the Lord:
With burnt offerings, or calves, or rams,
Or vials of oil?
It has been told us what is good and
what the Lord requires of us:
Only to do justly, to love mercy,
And to walk humbly with our God."

And like the prophets before him, Micah foretold coming disaster:

"Jerusalem shall become a heap of
rubble
And the people shall be carried
away . . ."

But he also spoke of hope, of a time when there would be justice and peace once again:

"When the word of the Lord is established
on the earth . . .
And every man can live in his own land,
And none shall make him afraid."

By this time, a new king, Sennacherib, reigned over Assyria. He saw that Judah was prosperous so he gathered his armies together to march against it.

Now Hezekiah was afraid and paid tribute to Assyria to ward off attack. He did what his father had done: he took gold and silver from the Temple and from the royal treasuries and sent them to the Assyrian king.

The commander-in-chief of Assyria's armies entered Jerusalem. He shouted to the people in the streets: "Don't listen to your king! He says the Lord will save you. Did the Lord save Israel?"

Then Hezekiah went to the Temple and he called on the Lord, saying: "O Lord, God of Israel, God of all the kingdoms on earth, save us from the power of Assyria. Then, all the world will know that the Lord our God is the only God."

The prophet Isaiah spoke the words of the Lord to Hezekiah: "Do not fear the Assyrians, for they shall not enter the city or besiege it or capture the city of Jerusalem."

That night a plague overcame the Assyrian army where they camped, and thousands died. Sennacherib ordered the rest of his men to return to their own country, to the city of Nineveh. So the threat of danger from Assyria was turned aside.

Soon after this, the king of a new power, Babylon, sent messengers to visit King Hezekiah, bringing him gifts. Hezekiah welcomed the visitors and showed them all his treasures.

Isaiah the prophet warned Hezekiah, saying: "Hear the word of the Lord: Babylon will be a great power. The day will come when all that you have stored up will be taken to Babylon. Then Jerusalem will be destroyed and even your sons will be taken away."

But Hezekiah was not concerned, for there was peace and prosperity in the land.

The Prophet Isaiah
2 Kings 19-20, Isaiah 1,2,6,7,9,11

At this time, one of the greatest of all the prophets was preaching. He was Isaiah: prophet, statesman and advisor to the kings of Judah for about forty years.

As a young man Isaiah had had a vision. He had seen the Lord sitting on a high throne, and the train of His robe filled the Temple. Above the Lord were angels who called back and forth to one another: "Holy, holy, holy is the Lord of hosts; the whole earth is full of His glory."

Isaiah trembled for he thought himself unworthy to have seen the Lord.

Then, in his vision, one of the angels took a glowing coal from the altar and touched Isaiah's lips. In this way he became the Lord's spokesman.

Like the other prophets, Isaiah spoke of the wrongs of the people and of injustice in the land. He had seen the fall of Israel and thought it was a warning to the people of Judah.

He had learned much from the teachings of Amos and Hosea. Like them, he reminded the people of what the Lord expected of them: not sacrifice, but holiness and justice:

"Listen to God's teaching—
He has had enough of burnt offerings;
Make yourself clean,
End evil-doing, learn to do good . . .
Seek injustice, stop oppression,
check violence . . .

Isaiah gave advice to the kings of Judah, although often his words were not heeded. He believed that Judah should remain free from all alliances and pay bribes to no one, not to Assyria or Egypt.

He forecast the deliverance of his people if they would follow the ways of the Lord. Though he predicted that Jerusalem would be destroyed, he believed that eventually a better and happier world would come.

"The Lord will give a sign: a young woman shall bear a son, and his name shall be Immanuel."

Isaiah had said to Ahaz, father of King Hezekiah:

> "To us a child is born, a son given;
> Government will be on his shoulders;
> His name shall be called:
> 'Wonderful-counsellor-is-God-the-
>   mighty-everlasting-Father-ruler-of-
>   peace.'
> Of the width of his kingdom,
> Of peace and justice and righteousness
> There will be no end . . ."

All of Isaiah's teachings came from his strong belief in the holiness of God. His faith was so strong that, even in the warlike world in which he lived, he dreamed of a Golden Age.

The Golden Age would be a time when all wrongdoing would disappear. And it would be a time of universal peace, when:

> "It shall come to pass . . .
> That the people shall beat their
>   swords into plowshares
> And their spears into pruning hooks;
> Nation shall not lift sword
>   against nation,
> And they shall not learn war any
>   more."

In the Golden Age of which Isaiah spoke, a remnant of the people of Israel would return to the city of Jerusalem, which he called Zion. "Then," he said, "out of Zion shall go forth the law, and the word of the Lord from Jerusalem."

Manasseh and Amon

2 Kings 21

After King Hezekiah's death, his son Manasseh ruled Judah for fifty-five years.

Hezekiah had ordered all the altars to Baal and other gods to be destroyed. Manasseh had them rebuilt. He even had pagan altars and idols placed in the house of the Lord.

Manasseh himself worshipped idols and practised witchcraft and child sacrifice. He persecuted the prophets of the Lord and had them put to death. And Isaiah died, or was put to death, at this time.

Prophets spoke out against the evil ways of the people. They warned of God's anger if they would not mend their ways, saying: "Because of all the evil in the land, Judah and Jerusalem shall be wiped off the face of the earth. And the people shall be captured by their enemies from the north."

But Manasseh did not change. He caused much bloodshed and committed evils of every kind.

When Manasseh died, his son Amon ruled. His reign lasted only two years, then he was killed by his own servants. He, too, had worshipped idols and encouraged evil in the land.

King Josiah

2 Kings 22-23, Jeremiah 1-2

Josiah, the son of Amon, became king of Judah when he was eight years old. As he grew into manhood, he did what was right in the sight of the Lord.

In the eighteenth year of Josiah's reign, he sent his scribe to the house of the Lord to arrange to have it repaired.

When Shaphan the scribe went to the Temple, the high priest said to him: "I have found the book of the law; take it to the king."

When Josiah saw the words of the book he was afraid, for he knew his fathers had not obeyed the Lord's commandments. He sent for

all the priests and the prophets and the elders to meet together before the Temple.

There, the king read to them all the words of the book that was found in the Temple. And he made a covenant that day before the Lord: to keep the commandments and to walk in the ways of the Lord.

The people, too, agreed to the covenant.

Then Josiah commanded the destruction of all the idols and altars built to Baal and the other false gods. He ordered the holy places of these gods to be destroyed. And he denounced the priests of the false gods. All the witches and magicians were banished from Judah.

All these things Josiah did in order to glorify the name of the Lord.

There had never been a king like Josiah. He was the first who turned to the Lord with all his heart, all his soul and all his might. And no king who came after him followed his example.

The prophet Jeremiah spoke out in those days as did other prophets: Zephaniah, Nahum and Habakkuk. They warned the people, saying: "The time will come when Judah will be destroyed. And Jerusalem, too, shall fall."

By this time Babylon had become a great nation. The Babylonians defeated Assyria and captured Nineveh, the Assyrian capital.

Jeremiah warned Josiah of the danger of becoming involved with surrounding nations.

But when the king of Egypt marched against Assyria, Josiah called out his army. He feared an attack by Egypt, and went to meet the Egyptians.

In the valley of Megiddo, Josiah met the Egyptian army, and there he was killed in battle. His body was taken back to Jerusalem and buried there.

Now Egypt had power over Judah.

Judah Ruled by Egypt and Babylon

2 Kings 23-24

After the death of King Josiah, his son Jehoahaz ruled for three months. Then Pharaoh, the king of Egypt, carried him off to Egypt and placed another of Josiah's sons on the throne.

Pharaoh demanded tribute from the land of Judah, and the new king taxed his people to pay the tribute to Egypt.

Then Nebuchadnezzar, the king of Babylon, defeated Egypt. He captured all the lands of Egypt between the Nile and the Euphrates rivers. When Egypt fell, he ruled over Judah.

The king of Judah rebelled against Nebuchadnezzar. As a result, bands of Moabites and Syrians and other peoples were sent against Judah by Nebuchadnezzar to subdue the land and its people.

The armies of Babylon besieged the city of Jerusalem and captured it. Nebuchadnezzar carried away the king of Judah and all his family, his princes, his servants and his officials. He also removed the treasures from the house of the Lord and from the king's storehouses.

The princes and merchants and craftsmen and soldiers were taken to Babylon. Altogether, ten thousand captives were taken.

King Zedekiah and the Prophet Jeremiah

2 Kings 24-25, Jeremiah 1-8

The king of Babylonia proclaimed a new

king in Judah. He was Zedekiah, another of Josiah's sons.

Zedekiah reigned for eleven years.

In the fourth year of his reign, the prophet Jeremiah spoke to the king, saying: "Submit to the king of Babylon. Serve him and live."

Jeremiah preached to the people, saying: "Change your ways. Acknowledge your wrongdoing. Return to the Lord and you will be returned to Jerusalem to possess it again in the presence of the Lord.

"Otherwise, the anger and wrath of the Lord will be poured out and the land will become a waste. A great army from the north will bring terror, and you will be scattered among the nations of the earth."

But Zedekiah did not take Jeremiah's advice. Instead, Jeremiah was thrown into prison and the king rebelled against the rule of Nebuchadnezzar. Then the king of Babylon came to Judah, and Jerusalem was besieged and surrounded once more.

Again Zedekiah asked Jeremiah's advice. Jeremiah answered, saying: "If you surrender to the king of Babylon, your life will be spared and the city will be saved. If you do not surrender, the city shall surely be destroyed, and you shall be captured."

But, once again the king did not take Jeremiah's advice. The prophet was sent back to prison and was kept there until the day Jerusalem was captured.

The Fall of Jerusalem
2 Kings 25

For almost two years the Babylonian army besieged Jerusalem until there was no food left in the city, and there was famine throughout the land.

One night the king and his family and some of his officers tried to escape through the walls of the city. But the Babylonians pursued them and captured them in the plains of Jericho.

King Zedekiah was taken to Babylon. There, his sons were put to death before his eyes. Then he was blinded and put in chains.

Meanwhile the armies of Nebuchadnezzar entered Jerusalem. They burned the house of the Lord, the magnificent Temple that Solomon had built. The bronze pillars of the Temple and all the gold and silver that was there were carried away.

The king's palace was also burned and all the buildings in the city were set on fire. And the walls around the city were broken down.

The high priest and all the priests of the Lord and the gatekeepers were taken before the king of Babylon and put to death.

Then the people in the city and in the land of Judah were carried into exile in the lands of Babylon. Only a few of the very poorest people were left to work in the fields and tend the vineyards of Judah.

So the city of Jerusalem was destroyed and the kingdom of Judah came to an end.

Sorrow and Hope

Jeremiah 8, 29-31, Lamentations 1,5

Jeremiah wept at the destruction of Judah, saying:

"My grief is beyond healing,
My heart is sick within me;
I mourn and am dismayed . . ."

And the Book of Lamentations speaks of the fall of Jerusalem:

"How lonely sits the city
That once was full of people . . .
She was great among the nations;
A princess among cities,
She has become a servant . . .
She weeps bitterly at night,
Tears are on her cheeks . . .
Her friends have dealt treacherously
    with her,
They have become her enemies . . .
She stretches forth her hand,
But there is none to comfort her."

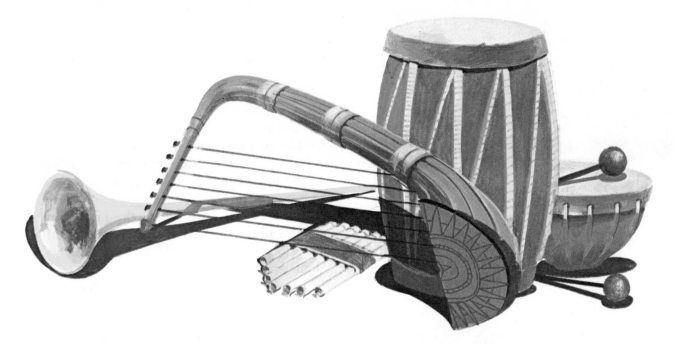

In his sorrow, Jeremiah called on the Lord, saying: "Restore us, O Lord: renew our days as of old. Can it be that we are rejected forever?"

Then the word of the Lord came to Jeremiah, so that even in his grief he wrote and spoke of hope. He sent letters to the people and their elders and priests in exile.

He told them to live good lives in Babylon. He wrote: "Plant gardens, take wives and have children. Pray to the Lord, and seek the welfare of the place where you live.

"There is hope for the future. Babylon shall be destroyed. After seventy years, the Lord's promise will be fufilled and you shall return. Then there will be a new covenant with the Lord. And the city of Jerusalem shall be rebuilt."

The Book of Daniel

A story of faith which marks the transition from Biblical Judaism to concepts of rabbinic Judaism and early Christianity.

Daniel in Captivity

Daniel 1

When Nebuchadnezzar, king of Babylon, destroyed Jerusalem and the kingdom of Judah, he took many of the people captive. And they settled in his lands.

One day the king ordered the chief of his household to bring before him some of the youths of Judah. He wanted boys who were handsome and bright, clever and quick to learn.

They were to be taught the language and the wisdom of Babylon. And they were to be fed a daily portion of the king's food and wine. Then, at the end of three years, they would be ready to enter the king's service.

The servant did as the king commanded.

Among those he chose from the Israelites were Daniel, Hananiah, Mishael and Azariah. And he gave them each a new name.

Daniel became Belteshazzar, Hananiah became Shadrach, Mishael became Meshach, and Azariah's new name was Abednego.

Daniel decided that he would not eat the king's food or drink his wine, for this was not the food of his people. So he asked the king's servant to allow him and his friends to eat only vegetables and to drink only water.

The servant was afraid to disobey the king's orders, but Daniel said: "Test us for ten days. Then compare the way we look with the appearance of those who eat the king's food."

The servant did as Daniel asked. At the end of ten days, Daniel and his friends looked healthier than those who ate the king's rich food, so vegetables and water were ordered for them all.

As for the four youths from Judah, God blessed them with knowledge and skill and

wisdom. And Daniel had the special ability to understand and interpret dreams.

When the three years had passed, all the young men were brought before the king. There they were tested. Everything the king asked, the four were ten times better able to answer than all the magicians and astrologers in the kingdom.

Nebuchadnezzar's Dream

Daniel 2

The king of Babylon had a dream that troubled him. He sent for all the magicians and astrologers and wise men in Babylon to interpret his dream.

They said: "Tell us the dream, and we will tell its meaning."

Nebuchadnezzar answered: "Tell me both the dream and its meaning. Then you will receive great rewards. But if you cannot, you will be torn limb from limb."

They said again: "Tell us the dream and we will tell its meaning."

But the king insisted: "Tell me the dream, then I will know that you can give its meaning."

The magicians and astrologers said that this had never been asked of them before. "No man can tell another's dream," they said. "Only the gods know men's dreams."

Nebuchadnezzar became angry and ordered all the magicians and wise men in Babylon to be put to death.

When Daniel heard about the king's anger and his order, he asked to be brought before the king. The king agreed and set a time for Daniel to appear before him.

In a vision that night, the mystery of the king's dream was made known to Daniel. And Daniel blessed the name of the Lord, saying: "To Thee, O Lord, I give thanks, for You have given me strength and wisdom."

Daniel appeared before the king at the appointed time. The king asked: "Can you tell me the dream and its meaning?"

Daniel answered: "No man can know another man's dream. Only the Lord God reveals mysteries. Through your dream He has shown you the future."

Daniel continued: "In your dream you saw a great statue. The head was gold, the chest and arms were silver, the stomach and the thighs were bronze, and the legs were iron. The feet were part iron and part clay.

"Then you saw a stone come near to the statue. It struck the feet of the statue and broke them into pieces. Then all the rest of the statue was broken into pieces: the iron, bronze, silver and gold. And the wind blew all the pieces away, so that not a piece was left.

"Then the stone that had destroyed the statue grew. It became a great mountain and filled the earth."

Nebuchadnezzar listened carefully.

"That was the dream," said Daniel. "Now for the meaning: You, a great, powerful and glorious king, are the head of gold. After you, there will come another kingdom, not as mighty. Then there will be a third kingdom, the bronze part of the figure; then a fourth kingdom as strong as iron, that will crush the others. But just as the feet were part iron and part clay, so will that kingdom be divided.

"Then the God of heaven will establish a

kingdom that will break all the others into pieces. And this kingdom of God will stand forever.

"Through your dream God has made the future known to you."

When Daniel had finished speaking, Nebuchadnezzar bowed before him, and said: "Surely, your God is the God of gods and the Lord of kings."

Then he gave Daniel many gifts and made him ruler over the whole province of Babylon and chief of all its wise men. But Daniel wished to remain at court, so the king appointed Shadrach, Meshach and Abednego to rule the province. And Daniel, whose name was now Belteshazzar, stayed at court.

The Golden Statue

Daniel 3

King Nebuchadnezzar ordered a great golden statue to be formed. It was ninety feet tall and nine feet wide.

When it was finished, he sent for all the officers, governors, judges and treasurers and all the rulers of the provinces to come before the statue. And all the people came.

Then the messenger of the king announced: "At the moment that the sound of music is heard, everyone must bow down and worship the golden statue. Whoever does not will be thrown into a fiery furnace."

Immediately, there was a great noise of horns and flutes and harps and lyres and tambourines and all kinds of musical instruments. And the people bowed down before the golden statue.

Now, certain men of the kingdom came before the king, saying: "There are men of

Judah who do not bow down to your golden idol. They are the rulers of Babylon: Shadrach, Meshach and Abednego."

The king was furious and commanded that the three be brought before him.

He asked them: "Is it true that you do not bow down to the golden statue? If you agree to worship the statue, all will be well with you. But if you do not, you will be thrown into a fiery furnace to burn. What god will save you then?"

They answered: "Our God will save us from the fire. We cannot serve your gods or bow down to your golden idol."

Nebuchadnezzar blazed with anger and commanded that the furnace be heated seven times hotter than usual. And he ordered the strongest of his guards to bind and tie Shadrach, Meshach and Abednego and cast them into the fire.

Now the furnace was hotter than ever; and

the flames were very high.

As the three men were pushed into the flames, the guards who pushed them were burned by the fire. But Shadrach, Meshach and Abednego were not hurt. They stood in the midst of the flames. Even their clothes were not burned.

Nebuchadnezzar could not believe his eyes. He asked his advisors: "Were not three men tied and bound and cast into the fire?"

They answered: "Yes."

And the king said: "But I see four men not tied or bound, standing in the flames unhurt by the fire. The fourth looks like an angel."

Then Nebuchadnezzar called to the men to come out of the fire.

They did. And all who were there saw that the men were not hurt. Their hair was not even burned; they did not even smell of fire.

Then Nebuchadnezzar said: "Blessed be the God of Shadrach, Meshach and Abednego. He sent His angel to deliver these men who trust Him and serve Him. They risked their lives rather than serve any other god.

"Therefore, if anyone in the kingdom speaks against this God, he will be cut to pieces and his property destroyed."

And Shadrach, Meshach and Abednego were promoted to even higher offices by the king.

The Handwriting on the Wall

Daniel 5

After the death of Nebuchadnezzar, his son Belshazzar became king of Babylon.

The new king gave a great feast for a thousand people. And he ordered his servants to bring out the vessels of gold and silver that his father had brought from the house of the Lord in Jerusalem.

When the cups and bowls were brought, the king and his wives and lords and officers drank from them. And they drank to their gods and praised them.

At that very moment a hand appeared and wrote a message on the wall of the king's palace.

The king saw the hand, and he grew pale. He became frightened and he trembled.

Then he ordered all the magicians and astrologers and wise men of the kingdom to come at once, saying: "Whoever reads this writing and tells me its meaning shall become the third ruler of this kingdom. And he shall have a gold chain and fine clothes."

All the wise men came, but none could read the writing or tell its meaning.

Then the queen spoke, telling the king about Daniel, an exile from Judah, whom his father had made master of all the magicians and wise men.

"Send for Daniel, whom your father named Belteshazzar. He will know the meaning of this message."

Daniel came before the king. And the king spoke to him, saying: "I have been told that you can tell what dreams mean and that you have great wisdom. If you can read this writing and tell me its meaning, you will have fine clothes and a golden chain and you shall rule in the kingdom."

Daniel answered: "Keep your gifts for yourself. But I will read the words to you and tell their meaning: Almighty God gave your father greatness and all peoples feared him. And he had power.

"But when he was overcome with pride, his glory was taken from him and his mind became like that of a beast, and his body was wet as if with the morning dew. Then he learned that God rules all men.

"Now, you have known all this, but you have not lived according to your knowledge. You brought bowls and cups from the house of the Lord and praised other gods with wine from them. But you have not praised God, the God of life.

"The hand you saw was sent from Him, and these are the words that are written:

MENE. MENE. TEKEL. UPHARSIN."

Then Daniel told Belshazzar the meaning: "MENE, God has numbered the days of your kingdom; MENE, He has counted them; TEKEL, you have been weighed and have been judged lacking by God; PARSIN (or UPHARSIN), your kingdom will be divided and will be given to the Medes or the Persians."

Belshazzar listened carefully to all Daniel said. Then he commanded princely robes to be brought. Daniel was dressed in purple with a gold chain around his neck. And he was proclaimed the third ruler in the kingdom.

That very night the king was killed and Darius the Mede became ruler over Babylon.

Daniel in the Lions' Den

Daniel 6

Darius appointed one hundred and twenty princes to rule over the land and three presidents to rule over the princes. Daniel was one of the presidents, but the king planned to make him ruler over all the rest because of his wisdom and loyalty.

The princes and other rulers of the people became jealous of Daniel. But they could find no fault with him, except that he was faithful in worshipping his God.

Then they came before Darius and asked that he establish a new law, saying: "You are the king over us. All the people must understand this. Whoever asks anything of another for thirty days except you, whether it be asked of god or man, shall be thrown into a den of lions. This you should sign into law."

The statement was written down and the king signed it so that it became law.

Daniel learned of this new law. Nevertheless, he went into his house as he had always done, with his windows open toward Jerusalem, and he worshipped God.

The men who had plotted against Daniel found him praying and immediately reported him to the king.

"Have you not signed a law forbidding anyone to ask anything of another except your majesty?" they asked.

The king answered: "It is true. The law stands."

Then they told him that Daniel, whom he trusted, had not obeyed the law, but continued to pray to his God.

When the king heard this, he was greatly troubled. He tried to find a way to spare Daniel, for he admired and trusted him.

But the rulers insisted that the law be carried out. So the king commanded that Daniel be thrown into the lions' den, saying: "May your God deliver you."

Then the place where the lions were kept was closed up with Daniel inside.

The king went to his palace and fasted. But he could not sleep; he kept thinking of Daniel.

Early the next morning he hurried to the lions' den. He called Daniel and, to his great joy, Daniel answered.

The king was relieved and asked: "Has your God, whom you worship so faithfully, saved you from the lions?"

Daniel answered: "God sent His angel and shut the lions' mouths. They could not open their mouths to harm me, because I am innocent before the Lord. And I have done you no wrong either, O King."

The king rejoiced. He commanded that Daniel be set free and that all those who had accused Daniel be thrown into the lions' den, and their wives and children with them. The lions quickly tore them to pieces.

Then King Darius wrote to all nations and to all people and in every language: "May peace be with you! I set this law before you: that in all my royal kingdom men must fear the God of Daniel, for He is the living God. He will endure forever. And His kingdom will never be destroyed."

Daniel's Visions

Daniel 7-12

Daniel had four dreams or visions which troubled him greatly. When he awoke from each one, he wrote it down.

In the first dream he saw four beasts arise out of the sea: the first was like a lion with eagle's wings, the second was like a bear with three ribs between its teeth, the third was like a leopard with four heads and four wings on its back, the fourth was even more terrible and stronger than the others and had ten horns.

Then thrones appeared, and, as he looked:
"One that was old sat on a throne,
 his clothing white as snow . . .
A stream of fire came before him
 and a thousand thousands stood
 before him, serving him.
A court sat in judgement,
 and books were opened . . .
Behold, one appeared like the son of man
 and was presented to the ancient one.
To him was given power and glory
 that all peoples and nations
 should serve him,
So that his dominion shall not pass
 away and his kingdom shall not be
 destroyed."

After each of Daniel's visions, the angel Gabriel came to him.

"Your dreams are of the end of days," said Gabriel. "The beasts are kings that will rise to power only to be destroyed by a greater king.

But even he shall be broken, though not by a human hand.

"All of your visions are true, but they will happen a long time from now.

"Then, there must be an end to sin and the people must atone for their wrongdoings.

"At that time Michael, the guardian angel of Israel, shall arise and your people shall be delivered. That is, everyone whose name is written in the book shall be saved.

"Many who sleep in the dust will awake to everlasting life, and others to everlasting punishment. Those who are wise will understand and will turn others to righteousness. You, Daniel, shall rest and stand again at the end of days."

The Book of Esther

The story of a queen who saved her people from persecution.

King Ahasuerus

Esther 1

After Persia had conquered Babylon, the Jews remained in exile and there was peace for a number of years. Then, in the reign of King Ahasuerus, trouble arose for the Jews of Persia.

King Ahasuerus ruled in the fortified city of Shushan. At that time Persia included one hundred and twenty-seven provinces, from India to Ethiopia.

In the third year of the reign of Ahasuerus, he gave a series of banquets for the princes and officials of Persia and Media. He showed them all his riches and his royal treasures.

On the seventh day of the great celebration, when the king had been drinking wine, he commanded his attendants to bring in Vashti, the queen, to show off her beauty. But Queen Vashti refused to come at the king's command, and he became very angry.

Then King Ahasuerus asked his advisors: "What shall be done to Vashti, according to the law?"

And they answered: "The queen has wronged the king and all the people in the land. Vashti shall no longer be queen."

Esther and Mordecai

Esther 2

The advisors suggested that the king choose a new queen, saying: "Let the most beautiful young maidens from all the provinces be brought to Shushan. And let the one who pleases the king most, become queen."

At the royal palace there was a Jew named Mordecai, whose ancestors had been exiled from Jerusalem to Babylon. He had a cousin, Esther, whom he had adopted and looked after as his own daughter. And Esther was very beautiful. She was one of the young maidens brought to the palace to appear before the king. But she told no one who she was or about her people, for Mordecai had told her not to tell.

At last the time came for Esther to go before the king. Immediately he loved her more than all the others.

Then King Ahasuerus made Esther queen instead of Vashti, and placed the royal crown on her head. There was a great feast and all the king's princes came to honour the new queen.

Soon after this, Mordecai overheard two of the king's servants plotting to kill their ruler. Mordecai told Esther and she told the king. As a result, the two servants were put to death. And the incident was written down in the book of the king's records.

Haman's Plot

Esther 3

Haman was the king's chief minister. He had authority over all the other princes and advisors of the king. And the king commanded that everyone bow down to Haman; only Mordecai would not.

When Haman saw that Mordecai did not bow down, he became very angry. He had been told that Mordecai was a Jew, and he decided not to punish Mordecai alone, but to destroy all the Jews of the kingdom.

Haman went to King Ahasuerus, and said: "There is a certain people in your kingdom who do not obey the king's laws. Therefore an order should be given to destroy them."

The king agreed and gave his ring to Haman as a sign of power to carry out the order. Then letters were sent to all the cities and provinces to destroy the Jews, young and old, including women and children.

Mordecai's Appeal

Esther 4

When Mordecai heard of the king's order, he mourned and wept for his people. And he sent Esther a message to go to the king and plead for her people. But Esther was afraid because it was forbidden for anyone to go before the king unless sent for.

Then Mordecai sent another message to Esther, saying: "Even you cannot escape the king's order. If you keep silent, surely help will come from another. But perhaps you have become queen at this time for this special purpose: to save your people."

Esther answered: "Gather together all the Jews of Shushan to fast and pray. I too will fast and pray. Then I will go before the king, even though he has not sent for me. And if I perish, I perish."

Queen Esther

Esther 5

Three days later, Queen Esther put on her royal robes and entered the inner court. The king was on his throne facing the door. When he saw Queen Esther, his heart went out to her. He raised his hand and nodded as a sign that she could come forward.

The king said: "Whatever you wish, Queen Esther, shall be granted to you, even to half of my kingdom."

Esther answered: "I wish only for the king and Haman to come to a feast that I have prepared."

The king said: "Tell Haman to come at once to grant the queen's wish."

So the king and Haman went to feast with Queen Esther. Again that night, the king asked Esther: "If there is anything you wish, it shall be granted, even to half my kingdom."

Esther answered: "My request is, if the king agrees, for the king and Haman to come here to a banquet again tomorrow night."

The king agreed.

Haman left the queen's house joyful and happy. When he passed Mordecai in the gate and Mordecai did not bow down to him, he became angry, but controlled his temper and went home.

There he told his wife and friends of all his riches and good fortune and how the king trusted him. And he added: "I was alone with

128

the king and queen at a private banquet. Tomorrow I am invited again. But I can never be completely happy as long as Mordecai the Jew sits in the king's gate."

His wife and friends advised him to have a gallows built to hang Mordecai. "Then you will be content," they said.

Immediately Haman ordered the gallows to be built.

The King's Reward
Esther 6

It happened on that same night that King Ahasuerus could not sleep. He ordered the book of records to be brought and read to him. When he heard about Mordecai and the two servants who had plotted to kill their king, he asked: "How has Mordecai been rewarded?"

Before the servants could answer, Haman arrived to consult the king about hanging Mordecai.

The king asked Haman: "What shall be given to the man whom the king wishes to reward?"

Haman, thinking the king wished to reward him, answered: "As a reward, let the royal coat and crown be brought and the king's horse. Then, let this man ride through the city wearing the royal finery so that all the people will know that he is the most trusted of all the king's men."

Then the king said: "All shall be done as you have suggested. Bring the coat, the crown and the horse. And bring Mordecai before me, for he is the man the king wishes to honour."

So Mordecai was dressed in the royal garments and placed on the king's horse. As he rode through the city streets, it was proclaimed that this is what happens to the man whom the king wishes to reward above all others.

Then Haman returned home in anger and in shame. While he was talking with his wife, the king sent for him to go to the queen's banquet.

A Great Celebration
Esther 7-9

King Ahasuerus and Haman went in to feast with Queen Esther for the second time.

Again the king told the queen: "Whatever you wish shall be granted, even to half of my kingdom."

Queen Esther answered: "If it please the king, let my life and the lives of my people be spared. For it has been ordered that I and my people are to be destroyed."

The king asked: "Who has done this? Who dares to give such an order?"

Esther answered: "An enemy of my people: none other than this man Haman, whom you trust."

Haman shrank in terror, and he trembled, for the king became exceedingly angry.

Then a servant of the king said: "Your majesty, in the courtyard there is a gallows, seventy-five feet high, which Haman had built to hang Mordecai."

At once the king ordered: "Hang Haman on the gallows."

So Haman was hanged on the gallows that he had built for Mordecai. And the king's anger subsided.

Then Mordecai was made chief advisor to the king. He was dressed in royal robes and given a golden crown. And King Ahasuerus gave Mordecai his ring to sign a proclamation to all the people, a proclamation to prevent the killing of the Jews.

Mordecai wrote to all the princes and sealed the letters with the king's ring. He sent the letters by messengers on the fastest horses in the kingdom to cancel the order to destroy the Jews.

On that day, the thirteenth day of the month of Adar, a time of mourning and despair became a time of thanksgiving for all the Jews of Persia.

The Prophets of the Exile
The story of the Jews in exile and their return to Jerusalem as seen through books of the Prophets.

The Prophet Ezekiel
Ezekiel 14-16, 20-22, 18, 36

For many years after the fall of Jerusalem, the Jews lived in exile in Babylon. They continued to practise their religion and to worship their God. And they were encouraged by prophets who continually reminded them that their God was the God of all nations.

The prophets of the exile preached hope, and foretold a return to Jerusalem. The prophet

Jeremiah wrote to the people in exile. The prophet Ezekiel himself was exiled to Babylon.

Ezekiel had begun to preach before the fall of Jerusalem. In those days he was filled with a sense of doom and foretold the exile.

In Babylon he preached that Jerusalem fell, not because God was weak, but because the people had turned away from His ways. In exile, Ezekiel changed his tone to one of comfort and hope.

He led his people in worship and spoke of the individual's responsibility for his own actions, saying: "The one who sins shall be destroyed. A son shall not suffer for the wrongdoing of his father, nor a father for the wrongdoing of his son. But the righteousness of the righteous and the wickedness of the wicked shall depend on the one who does it."

Then Ezekiel forecast the return to Jerusalem. God spoke to him in visions, and he told the words of God to the people, saying:

"I will gather you from among the nations and bring you back to your own land. Your cities will be rebuilt and your land will prosper. You will have a new heart and a new spirit, and will do all My commandments. You will be My people, and I will be your God."

Isaiah of the Exile
Isaiah 40, 43, 52-54

Near the end of the years of exile, another great prophet preached of the return to Jerusalem; he is called the Second Isaiah or Isaiah of the Exile.

He spoke to the people, saying: "Be comforted, tell Jerusalem that her days of service are over, that her punishment has been paid, that a voice cries:

'In the wilderness, prepare the way of the Lord,
Make a highway in the desert;
Every valley shall be raised up,
Every mountain and hill made low,
And uneven ground shall be
smoothed . . .
Then the glory of the Lord will be
revealed
And all people will see it together.
Get up on a high mountain,
Lift your voice with strength,
And behold your God . . .
Fear not, for the Lord is with you . . .

Your children will come from the east
and west,
The north and south;
They will come from the ends of the earth.
All your children shall turn to the Lord
And great shall be their peace.' "

Isaiah wrote, too, of the suffering of the Hebrews in exile, of a "suffering servant" bearing the sins of many. According to Isaiah, the Lord says:

". . . Israel, my servant,
Jacob, whom I have chosen
The children of Abraham:
I have called you from the ends of the
earth, saying you are My servant;
Fear not, for I am with you . . .
I will strengthen you, I will uphold
you . . .
Behold My servant,
My chosen in whom My heart delights.
I have put My Spirit upon him,
He will bring justice to the nations . . .
He will not fail or be discouraged
until justice is established . . .
The coastlands wait for his law . . .
How beautiful upon the mountains
are the feet of him who brings glad
tidings . . .
My servant shall prosper and be exalted,
He shall surprise many nations.
He was rejected and despised by men;
a man of grief and sorrow,
He was despised and we did not respect
him.
He has carried our griefs and our sorrows,
He was afflicted and smitten by God.
He was wounded for our sins,
With his wounds we are healed.
The Lord has laid on him the iniquity of
us all.
He was oppressed,
but he opened not his mouth . . .
Like a lamb led to slaughter,
he opened not his mouth . . .
They made his grave with the wicked,
With a rich man is he in death.
Although he performed no violence
and had no deceit on his mouth . . .
He poured out his soul to death
and was counted among the sinful.
He bore the sin of many
and interceded for those who sinned."

The Return to Jerusalem

The story of the return told in the Books of the Prophets and Chronicles.

The Proclamation of Cyrus
Ezra 1-2, 2 Chronicles 36

The Jews had been in exile about fifty years when Cyrus the Great became king of Persia. His armies conquered Babylon and its empire

He issued a proclamation throughout all his lands: "The Lord God has charged me to build Him a house in Jerusalem, in Judah. Whoever belongs to the people of the Lord shall go up to Jerusalem to build the house of the Lord, the God of Israel. And let each one, wherever he lives, be helped by the people in that place. Let the survivors be given silver and gold, animals and goods and offerings for the house of the Lord in Jerusalem.

"May the Lord be with all who go."

The elders, priests and Levites led the people in rejoicing. They hurriedly gathered their belongings to go to Jerusalem to rebuild the Temple of the Lord. They were given silver and gold and horses, mules and camels to take with them.

King Cyrus gave them the bowls and cups and all the vessels that Nebuchadnezzar had brought from the house of the Lord years before. These were to be returned to Jerusalem.

More than fifty thousand people journeyed to Jerusalem: men, women and children, menservants and maidservants.

Rebuilding the Temple
Ezra 3-6

Seven months after their return, the Israelites gathered in Jerusalem. The priests built an altar to the Lord, and they worshipped the Lord according to all His commandments, keeping the feast days and making offerings.

In the second year of their return they began work on the rebuilding of the Temple. When the foundation was laid, priests with trumpets and Levites with cymbals praised the Lord.

They sang: "Give thanks to the Lord, for He is good. His mercy endures forever."

Then all the people gave a mighty shout and praised God.

When the enemies of Judah heard that the Temple was being rebuilt, they came to Jerusalem and caused trouble, interfering with the work of rebuilding.

The work stopped for a long time.

Then the prophets Haggai and Zechariah spoke the words of the Lord to the Jews, encouraging them and urging them to begin rebuilding once more.

Once again their enemies tried to stop them. But this time a new king ruled over the empire. He knew about the proclamation of Cyrus, and he made a new proclamation: that the Temple should be rebuilt, and that no one should interfere with the rebuilding.

When at last the Temple was finished, it was dedicated with great rejoicing and many offerings.

Ezra
Ezra 7-10

The exiles had been in Jerusalem for some time before Ezra the scribe went there from Babylon. He was a descendant of Aaron the High Priest, and he was skilled in knowledge of the law of Moses.

He carried gifts of gold and silver from the king of Persia to Jerusalem.

When Ezra arrived in Jerusalem he was shocked to find that the people had already departed from the ways of their God. They were living among the peoples of the land and their children were marrying from among these peoples.

Ezra wept and he said: "O my God, I am ashamed. Even after You spared us to return to our land, we are breaking Your commandments."

Then Ezra spoke to the people and made them agree to put aside their foreign wives.

Nehemiah
Nehemiah 1-13

Nehemiah was a cupbearer to the king of Persia and lived in the royal palace in Shushan. His family had been exiled from Judah and he was interested in the rebuilding of Jerusalem.

When he learned that the Temple had been rebuilt, he rejoiced. But when he was told that the walls and gates of the city were still in ruin, he mourned and fasted and prayed to God that he might be able to help his people.

Nehemiah went before the king of Persia and asked permission to travel to Judah to help his people.

The king agreed to let him go and gave him letters to all the rulers along the way, so that he would have a safe journey.

Nehemiah arrived in Jerusalem and inspected the city, its ruined walls and gates. Then he spoke to the leaders and priests and told them why he had come and he assured them of God's help.

Then plans were made to do the work. Each family became responsible for a different part of the wall or for a gate.

While the work was being done, enemies of Judah came out to stop the building.

Nehemiah heard of this and made a plan: every day and every night the workmen took turns. Half of the men were armed and stood watch while the other half worked at the rebuilding. Even they kept their swords nearby as they worked.

In this way the great wall of Jerusalem was rebuilt in fifty-two days.

Then Nehemiah became governor and took a census of all the exiles who had returned.

And Ezra read the books of the law to the people, so that they would know and do all the commandments of the Lord.

A public ceremony was held for the reading of the law. All day Ezra read; then Nehemiah, Ezra, and the Levites and all the people praised God. They bowed their heads in worship and the word of the Lord went forth in Jerusalem.

Malachi
Malachi 2-4

About fifty years after Ezra and Nehemiah had read the laws of Moses to the people of Jerusalem, the prophet Malachi spoke to the people about their immorality and indifference.

He asked: "Have you forgotten God so soon, that you have turned away from Him?"

Malachi urged the people to keep God's commandments. "Observing rituals is not enough," he preached. "You must have inner commitment as well."

From time to time, there had been hopes of a Messiah, a leader sent by God who would rule the Jews and release them from all oppression.

But none had appeared.

Malachi's message included the promise of a Messianic Age:

"Have we not all one Father? Has not one God created us? God will send His messenger to prepare the way. Then the Lord you seek will come.

"There will be a day of the Lord when Israel will be purified and the wicked will be destroyed. Then the hearts of the parents will be turned to the children and the hearts of the children to the parents."

The Book of Jonah

The story of the prophet Jonah who was sent by God to save the people of Nineveh.

Jonah Flees from God
Jonah 1

The word of the Lord came to Jonah, saying: "Go and preach in the city of Nineveh in

Assyria, for the wickedness of its people is great."

Jonah did not want to go to Nineveh. The people there were not believers in God, and Jonah thought God should not be concerned about them. He thought it was not his responsibility to save them. In order to flee from the Lord, he went down to Joppa where he boarded a ship for Tarshish.

The ship set sail and immediately a great wind began to blow over the sea. There was such a mighty storm that the ship was in danger of breaking apart.

The seamen became afraid and each one called on his own god to save the ship. They threw overboard the goods they were carrying in order to make the ship lighter. Even this did not help. The waves rose higher and dashed against the side of the ship.

"Someone on board has done evil and caused this to happen," said the sailors. "We must find out who it is."

They cast lots and the lot fell to Jonah. They told him and asked: "Who are you, and where are you from, that you have caused this storm?"

Jonah answered: "I am a Hebrew and I am fleeing from the God who made heaven and earth. I can no longer hide from Him. It is because of me that this great storm has happened. You must throw me overboard; then the sea will become calm once again."

The men rowed harder to save the ship, but the storm became worse.

Then they called upon the Lord, saying: "Do not let us perish because of this man. And do not hold us responsible for his life because of what we are about to do. You, O Lord, have done this thing."

So saying, they tossed Jonah into the sea. At once the sea became calm, and the men had great fear of the Lord. They offered sacrifices and made vows to Him.

Jonah at Nineveh

Jonah 2-3

The Lord sent a great fish to swallow Jonah. He was inside the fish for three days and three nights, and he prayed to the Lord:

"Out of my trouble I called the Lord
And He answered me.
He cast me into the heart of the sea
And the waves passed over me.
I will sacrifice with the voice
    of thanksgiving,
What I have vowed, I will do."

Then the Lord spoke to the fish and it vomited Jonah out onto dry land.

The word of the Lord came to Jonah a second time, saying: "Go to Nineveh, and preach the message that I will tell you."

This time Jonah went to Nineveh as the Lord commanded. And he told the people that because of their wickedness, Nineveh would be destroyed in forty days.

When the king of Nineveh heard this, he proclaimed a fast, saying: "Let no one eat or drink or taste any food. Neither man nor beast shall eat. Let everyone turn from evil ways and seek God. Perhaps then God will turn His anger away from us, and we will be saved."

All the people of Nineveh believed in God and listened to their king. They fasted and mourned and they turned away from their evil ways, saying: "Who knows? God may turn away His anger if we turn to righteousness."

When God saw how they turned away from evil and repented their wrongdoings, He did not destroy the city.

Jonah's Anger

Jonah 4

Jonah was displeased with the Lord and angry that Nineveh had been saved. He spoke to the Lord, saying: "This was what I hoped to prevent when I ran away to Tarshish. I knew You to be a gracious God, slow to anger, showing great kindness and love and not wanting to do evil.

"Now, Lord, I ask You to take my life. I am not worthy to live."

Jonah left Nineveh and built himself a booth for shelter. From there he could watch to see what would become of the city.

God caused a plant to grow up over Jonah's shelter, to shade him from the sun. But early the next morning, God caused the plant to be eaten by a worm. The plant withered and died. Then the sun and the wind beat down on Jonah and he became uncomfortable.

Again he said: "It is better for me to die than to live."

God asked Jonah: "Is it right for you to be so angry because of the plant?"

Jonah answered: "Yes, I am right to be angry, angry enough to die."

And the Lord said: "You are angry about the plant and you have pity for it. It gave you no trouble; you neither planted it nor helped it grow. It came up in a night and perished in a night.

"Now, is it wrong for me to have pity on Nineveh, a great city with thousands of people who could not tell right from wrong? Should I not have pity for them?"

The Book of Psalms

The psalms are songs associated with King David, although he did not write them all. Many refer to events that happened long after his death. The psalms were written by different people at different times and have different themes.

Most of the psalms praise and give thanks to God for the wonders of nature and for being a source of help to man.

They are used as a regular part of church and synagogue worship. Altogether there are one hundred and fifty psalms.

Psalm 19

a song of praise

> The heavens declare the glory of God
> And the firmament shows His
> handiwork . . .
> The law of the Lord is perfect,
> restoring the soul;
> The testimony of the Lord is sure,
> making wise the simple;
> The precepts of the Lord are right,
> rejoicing the heart;
> The commandments of the Lord are pure,
> enlightening the eyes;
> The fear of the Lord is clean,
> enduring forever;
> The ordinances of the Lord are true,
> and righteous altogether.
> They are to be desired more than gold,
> even much fine gold . . .

Let the words of my mouth
And the meditation of my heart
Be acceptable to the Lord,
Who is my rock and my redeemer.

Psalm 23

a song of trust

The Lord is my shepherd, I shall not want;
He makes me to lie down in green pastures;
He leads me beside still waters,
He restores my soul;
He leads me in paths of righteousness
For His name's sake;
Though I walk through the valley
    of the shadow of death,
I fear no evil,
For the Lord is with me.
His rod and His staff, they comfort me;
He prepares a table before me
    in the presence of my enemies;
He anoints my head with oil,
    my cup runs over;
Surely goodness and mercy shall follow me
    all the days of my life,
And I will dwell in the house of the Lord
    forever.

Psalm 24

a song of praise and righteousness

The earth is the Lord's, and the fullness
    thereof,
The world and all who dwell therein;
For He has founded it upon the seas
And established it upon the waters.
Who shall ascend the mountain of the Lord?
Who shall stand in His holy place?
He who has clean hands and a pure heart,
Who has not taken the name of the Lord in
    vain, nor sworn deceitfully;
He will receive blessing from the Lord
And righteousness from the God of his
    salvation;
Such is the generation of those who seek
    Him,
That seek the face of the God of Jacob.
Lift up your heads, O gates,
And be lifted up, everlasting doors!
So the King of glory shall come in.
Who is the King of glory?
The Lord, strong and mighty,
The Lord, mighty in battle.
The Lord of hosts, He is the King of
    glory.

Psalm 100

a song of joy and praise

Make a joyful noise unto the Lord, all
    the lands;
Serve the Lord with gladness;
Come before His presence with singing.
Know that the Lord, He is God;
It is He that has made us, and not we
    ourselves;
Enter into His gates with thanksgiving.
And into His courts with praise;
Give thanks to Him, and bless His name;
For the Lord is good, His mercy endures
    forever,
And His truth to all generations.

Psalm 118

a song of thanksgiving

Out of my distress I called on the Lord,
The Lord answered and set me free.
The Lord is for me, I will not fear;
What can man do to me?
It is better to seek refuge in the Lord
Than to trust in man;
It is better to seek refuge in the Lord
Than to trust in princes . . .
The Lord is my strength and my song,
He has become my salvation . . .
The Lord has caused me to suffer,
But has not given me over to death.
Open the gates of the righteous,
I will enter them and give thanks unto
    the Lord . . .
This is the day which the Lord has made,
Let us rejoice and be glad in it . . .
Give thanks unto the Lord, for He is good,
His mercy endures forever.

Psalm 137

a song of the exile

By the rivers of Babylon,
We sat down and wept
When we remembered Zion;
We hung up our harps
On the willows there:
For there our captors required us to sing,
    saying:
"Sing us a song of Zion."
How shall we sing the Lord's song

In a strange land?
If I forget you, O Jerusalem,
Let my right hand wither;
Let my tongue cleave to the roof of my
    mouth
If I forget Zion,
If I do not place Jerusalem
Above my greatest joy. . .

Psalm 126

*a song of thanksgiving for the return to
Jerusalem*

When the Lord restored Zion,
We were like dreamers;
Our mouth was filled with laughter,
And our tongue with singing;
Then they said among the nations:
"The Lord has done great things for them.
Yes, The Lord has done great things for
    them."
And we are glad.
Restore our fortunes, O Lord,
As waters return to the desert;
May those who sow in tears, reap in joy;
He that goes forth weeping
Shall come home with shouts of joy.

The Book of Proverbs

*A book of sayings and practical
wisdom, of instructions for everyday
life. It speaks of knowledge and
righteousness, duty and responsibility,
reward and punishment.*

*King Solomon, known for his wisdom,
wrote many of the proverbs. Others
were written by wise men of later times.*

Selections from the Book of Proverbs:

The memory of the righteous is a blessing,
    but the name of the wicked will rot.
The mouth of the righteous is a fountain of
    life,
        but the mouth of the wicked conceals
        violence.

Hatred stirs up trouble,
    but love covers all offenses.
Wise men store up knowledge,
    but the babbling of a fool brings ruin.
He who heeds instruction is on the path to
    life,
    but he who rejects it goes astray.
The Lord is far from the wicked,
    but He hears the prayer of the righteous.
Pride goes before destruction,
    and a haughty spirit before a fall.
He who is slow to anger is better than the
    mighty,
    and he who rules his spirit than he who
    takes a city.
To do righteousness and justice
    is more acceptable to the Lord than
    sacrifice.
He who keeps his mouth and his tongue
    keeps himself out of trouble.
A good name is to be chosen rather than
    great riches,
    and righteousness is better than silver
    or gold.
A wise son makes a glad father,
    but a foolish son is a sorrow.
Train up a child in the way he should go,
    when he is old he will not depart from
    it.
He who spares the rod hates his son,
    but he who loves his son disciplines
    him.
A soft answer turns away wrath,
    but harsh words stir up anger.

A Woman of Valour
Proverbs 32

A woman of valour who can find?
She is far more precious than rubies;
The heart of her husband trusts in her . . .
She does him good and not harm
All the days of her life . . .
She rises while it is still night
And provides food for her household . . .
She opens her hand to the poor
And reaches out to the needy . . .
Strength and dignity are her clothing;
She opens her mouth with wisdom;
She teaches the ways of kindness;
She looks after the ways of her household,
And is not idle.
Her children rise up and call her blessed,
And her husband praises her, saying:

"Many women have done well,
But you surpass them all."
Charm is deceitful and beauty is vain,
But a woman who reveres the Lord is to be
    praised.

The Book of Job

A poetic drama dealing with the testing of faith in the face of great suffering.

A Righteous Man
Job 1

There was a man in the land of Uz whose name was Job. He was a righteous man who feared God and turned away from evil.

Job had seven sons and three daughters, and many flocks and herds. He also had many servants. He was the richest man in his part of the country.

God and Satan
Job 1

One day the sons of God came before the Lord and Satan came with them.

The Lord asked Satan: "Where have you been?"

Satan answered: "I have been travelling around the earth."

The Lord asked: "Have you seen Job? There is no one like him in all the earth. He is a righteous man who fears God and turns away from evil."

Satan answered: "Why should Job not praise God? You have looked after him and protected him and his household. You have blessed him in every way, with family and with riches. But, if all this is taken from him, he will surely turn away from You and curse You."

The Lord said to Satan: "Whatever Job has shall be in your power. Only do not touch Job himself."

Then Satan left the presence of the Lord.

Job's Misfortunes
Job 1-2

One day a messenger came to Job saying: "While your oxen were plowing and your don-

keys were grazing, a band of Bedouins attacked and seized them. All the men in the fields were killed. I alone escaped to tell you what happened."

While he was speaking, another messenger arrived, saying: "Lightning has struck and completely destroyed your sheep and the shepherds who were tending them. I am the only one who escaped."

While this man was speaking, a third man arrived and said: "The Chaldeans, in three groups, attacked your camels and drove them away. All the camel-keepers were slain except for me. I am the only one left, and I escaped to tell you what happened."

While this messenger was speaking, still another came running to Job, and said: "Your sons and daughters were gathered together in your eldest son's house, when a great wind struck the house and destroyed it. Everyone inside was killed. Of all your children and their servants I am the only one left."

Then Job threw himself on the ground in mourning and worshipped the Lord, saying: "The Lord has given, and the Lord has taken away. Blessed be the name of the Lord."

In all this, Job did not sin or blame God.

Satan Questions God
Job 2

Again the sons of God came before the Lord, and Satan came with them.

The Lord asked Satan: "Have you seen Job in your travels? There is no one like him in all the earth. He is a righteous man who fears God and turns away from evil. With all that you have made happen to him without cause, his faith is still strong."

Then Satan said: "A man will give all that he has for his life. Touch his bone and his flesh; inflict him with disease. Then he will curse You."

The Lord said: "He is in your power, only do not let him die."

Satan left the presence of God. And he inflicted Job with leprosy so terrible that, from the soles of his feet to the top of his head, he could not relieve the discomfort.

Job's wife spoke to him, saying: "Do you still have faith in God? Curse Him and ask Him to let you die!"

But Job answered: "You speak like a senseless woman. Shall we receive only good from God, and not evil?''

Still Job did not speak evil of God or blame Him.

Job's Friends

Job 2-3

Three of Job's friends heard of all his misfortunes. They came to comfort him and offer their sympathy.

When they saw Job, they hardly knew him. They wept for him and mourned. They stayed with him for a week without saying a word, and they saw that Job's suffering was very great.

Then Job began to speak, bewildered over his undeserved suffering. He cursed the day that he was born, and he asked:

"Why does God give life to him who
   is in misery,
And to those who are in great distress,
Who wish for death, and wish in vain?
Groans pour forth from me,
I have no peace; trouble keeps coming.''

Then the first of Job's friends tried to comfort him and bring him hope.

He praised Job for all the good he had done in the past, for his honesty and his wisdom.

Then, believing that God punishes only the guilty, he asked Job: "Was an innocent man ever destroyed?

"Seek God. Do not despise Him. God wounds and He will bind up. Surely He will deliver you from trouble.''

Job answered his friend saying: "Surely my suffering is greater than my wrongdoing.''

Then Job called on God, asking why such misfortune had come to him.

Job's second friend spoke to him, saying: "Surely God acts with justice. If you will seek God, if you are pure and upright, He will answer and reward you. Where there is punishment, there must be wrongdoing. God does not punish a blameless man. With God there is justice.''

Job answered: "God is not a man that I can answer Him. God is greater than man can ever imagine. He is wise and mighty. And He destroys both the innocent and the wicked. I believe I am innocent.

"I only appeal to God for mercy, to let me alone, so I may find a little comfort before I die. I only ask that He tell me of any wrongdoing and pardon me.''

Then the third of Job's friends spoke to him. He accused Job of evil, of secret wrongdoing, and urged him to examine his life carefully, saying: "You say your life is pure and good, and you have not sinned. You must turn your mind to God and completely banish sin from your life. Then you will have hope.''

Job answered with bitterness: "No doubt you three know everything. Have pity on me. Do not persecute me.

"I appeal directly to God; it is from God that I wish to understand. From God I want to learn the truth. Though He causes me to suffer, I will trust Him. And I say before Him that I have done no wrong.''

Then he spoke to God: "Why, O Lord, am I persecuted? And why am I tried? If I have done wrong, I know it not. Show me Your ways, O Lord, that I might understand.

"Often the wicked seem to go unpunished. Perhaps my suffering is not related either to righteousness or wrongdoing. I call upon Your justice and mercy, though I cannot understand Your ways.''

Then Job spoke to his friends again, saying: "Man's wisdom is to revere God and live a righteous life. Only God has true wisdom and understanding. Even if He causes my death, I will continue to trust in Him.''

Elihu's Advice

Job 32-37

Now Elihu, a younger man who had been listening to Job and his friends, spoke up. He was angry with Job's friends because they had given no answers and no comfort. They had only accused him of wrongdoing. And Elihu was angry with Job because he had tried to justify his life and actions before God.

Elihu said to them: "God is greater than man and reveals Himself to man through dreams and through suffering. Therefore suffering has meaning and value for man. Stop and consider the wondrous works of God. He is perfect in knowledge and He knows all. He does no unjust thing.

"Tell God that since you have suffered, you will not offend Him. Then understanding will come. The case is before the Lord.''

140

The Lord Speaks

Job 38-42

Then the Lord spoke to Job out of a whirlwind. He spoke to the littleness of man in the presence of the great mystery of creation, saying: "Where were you when I laid the foundations of the earth? Who shut in the seas and formed the clouds? Who caused the dawn to know its place? And who stored up the snow and hail and rain and dew? Can you lift up your voice to call forth floods and lightning?"

God said: "Look away from your own suffering and look to the wonders around you. Renew your faith in the wisdom, justice and goodness of the Lord even though you cannot entirely understand them."

Job listened intently, and he answered: "How small I am. I questioned, and I will go no further. I know that God can do all things; that nothing with God is impossible. I have asked only what I did not understand, things too awesome for me.

"Hear me: If I have doubted You, O Lord, I repent, for I am only dust and ashes."

Then, although his questions were still not answered, Job found comfort in his faith, and in his belief in a God of such greatness that no man can fully understand His ways. At last Job was at peace with his faith, a faith that could remain strong even in the midst of pain and suffering.

The Lord healed Job and gave him special powers to pray for his friends. People came to Job: his family and his friends and all who had known him.

The Lord blessed Job's later days until he had twice as much riches as before. He had seven sons and three daughters and many grandchildren and great-grandchildren.

And Job died a very old man, having lived a full life and having believed in the Lord.

The Book of Ecclesiastes

Ecclesiastes is a preacher, Koheleth, addressing his congregation. He expresses both hope and hopelessness. He speaks of the beauty of life and yet of life's injustice.

According to tradition, King Solomon was thought to have written this book. However, scholars believe it was written at a later time.

Ecclesiastes questions the meaning of life, saying:

"Vanity of vanities, all is vanity.
What does man gain by all the work
at which he toils under the sun?
A generation goes, a generation comes,
but the earth remains forever;
The sun rises and the sun goes down,
and hurries to where it rises . . .
What has been is what will be,
what has been done is what will be done,
and there is nothing new under the sun."

Koheleth says he has tried to seek the meaning of life. He has searched for pleasure, for wealth and for wisdom.

"I have seen everything," he says, "and it is all like striving after the wind, for nothing seems to have lasting value."

Finally he comes to the conclusion that the enjoyment and acceptance of life is God's gift to man, that man's purpose is to have reverence for God and to accept His law. He says:

"For everything there is a season and a time for everything under heaven:
a time to be born, and a time to die;
a time to plant, and a time to pull up
what is planted;
a time to kill, and a time to heal;
a time to tear down, and a time to build up;
a time to weep, and a time to laugh;
a time to mourn, and a time to dance;
a time to embrace, and a time to refrain from embracing;
a time to seek, and a time to lose;
a time to keep silent, and a time to speak;
a time to love, and a time for peace . . ."

"Everything is in the hand of God," says Koheleth. "Enjoy life while you have it, for life is good and has many rewards.

"Often things do not go well and much in life seems futile. Men may question, become disappointed or even suffer, but there is always hope. If you do your duty, God will not fail you.

"The end of the matter is this: fear God and keep His commandments. This is the whole duty of man."

The Song of Songs

(Also called the "Song of Solomon")

According to tradition, King Solomon was its author. Its origin was probably in folk love songs adapted for the wedding of King Solomon and interpreted as a symbolic expression of God's love for His people. The Song of Songs is a collection of poetry with lines of beauty and tenderness. Country scenes, springtime and expressions of love:

"The winter is past,
 the rain is over and gone;
Flowers appear on the earth,
 the time of singing has come,
And the voice of the turtledove
 is heard in the land.

The fig tree puts forth figs,
 and the vines are in blossom,
  giving forth fragrance,
Arise, my love, my fair one,
 and come away . . ."

The story is told of a beautiful young maiden betrothed to a shepherd whom she loves. She is taken away to the palace of a king. He tempts her with his love and riches, but she remains faithful to her shepherd.

The young girl continually vows her love, saying: "My beloved is mine and I am his."

Finally, impressed by her faithfulness, the king sends her back to the one she loves.

In the symbolic interpretation of the Song of Solomon, the shepherd represents God. The king is the symbol of temptation trying to lure God's people (the beautiful maiden) away from their faithfulness.

Just as, in the story, the young girl remains faithful and true no matter what temptations are put before her, God's people are encouraged to remain faithful to Him no matter what happens.

NEW TESTAMENT

Time and Place

From the time of the return of the Jewish people from exile in Babylon, although they established a separate community and rebuilt the Temple of Jerusalem, Israel was not free.

First under Persian rule, then conquered by Alexander the Great, and later occupied by the great empires of Egypt (under the Ptolemies) and of Syria (under the Seleucids), the Jews became fairly prosperous and were allowed to worship according to their Law. But they yearned for the day when Israel would be free.

In response to the Syrian king's effort to suppress their religion, the Jews rebelled and, under the Maccabean and Hasmanean kings, were independent for almost a century.

Then the little nation was conquered by Rome, which made King Herod the ruler over Judea. He claimed to be a Jew, but his cruelty and greed made life hard for the God-fearing people of Israel.

The Gospel of Jesus

The story of Jesus told by four evangelists: Matthew, Mark, Luke and John, each in his own way. The order of events, the specific stories and the emphasis of teaching vary somewhat among the four, but together they form the basic "Gospel," a word meaning "good news."

Zacharias and Elizabeth
Luke 1

In the days of Herod, king of Judea, there was a priest named Zacharias who lived in Jerusalem. He and his wife Elizabeth were righteous people keeping the commandments of the Lord. They were growing old and they had no children.

One day while Zacharias was performing his duties in the Temple, an angel of the Lord spoke to him, saying: "Do not be afraid. Your prayers for a child will be answered. You and your wife will have a son and you shall call him John.

"He will be filled with the Holy Spirit and he will become great in the sight of the Lord. He will drink no wine nor strong drink. Because of him, many of the children of Israel will turn again to the Lord their God."

Zacharias asked the angel: "How will this be? I am an old man and my wife is beyond the time of having children."

The angel answered: "I am Gabriel and I was sent from God to speak to you. Now, from this time until these things happen, you will be unable to speak. You will be silent because you did not believe my words."

The people wondered why Zacharias was in the Temple for such a long time. When he came out, he could not speak a word; he could only make signs.

Zacharias went home, and soon Elizabeth knew that she was going to have a child.

The Announcement of the Coming of Jesus

Luke 1

Six months after he had visited Zacharias, the angel Gabriel was sent to Nazareth, a town of Galilee. God sent him to a young girl named Mary, a cousin of Elizabeth and the wife of Zacharias. Mary was betrothed to a man named Joseph, a carpenter, who was a direct descendant of King David and the royal house

of Israel.

The angel appeared to Mary, saying: "Hail, Mary! the Lord is with you and you are blessed among women."

Mary was troubled at this greeting; but Gabriel said: "Do not be afraid, for the Lord is with you. You will bear a son, and his name shall be Jesus. He will be great and will be called 'Son of the Most High.' He will reign over the house of Jacob forever, and his kingdom will never end."

Mary asked, in wonder: "How can this be, for I have no husband?"

The angel answered: "The Holy Spirit will come to you and the power of the Most High also. Therefore the child will be holy, and shall be called the Son of God.

"Now your cousin Elizabeth in her old age will also have a son. For with God nothing is impossible."

Mary replied: "Let it happen according to your word, for I am the handmaid of the Lord."

The angel Gabriel left Mary. And Mary hurried to the hill country, to the house of Zacharias and Elizabeth.

When Elizabeth heard Mary's greeting from the doorway she was filled with the Holy Spirit and she called out: "Blessed are you among women, and blessed is the son you shall have. Why should you, the mother of my Lord, come to visit me?"

Mary, filled with the spirit of God, spoke, saying:

> "My soul praises the Lord
> And my spirit rejoices in God;
> He that is mighty has done great things
>   for me, and holy is His name.
> His mercy is upon those who fear Him.
> He has shown strength with His arm;
> He has put down the mighty and raised
>   up those of low degree;
> He has helped His servant Israel
> As He spoke to our fathers,
>   to Abraham and his descendants forever."

Mary stayed with Elizabeth for a while and then returned home.

The Birth of John the Baptist

Luke 1

When Elizabeth's baby was born, all her family and friends rejoiced with her. On the

eighth day, they came to name the baby. They would have called him Zacharias for his father, but Elizabeth spoke up, saying: "His name shall be John."

Everyone said: "But this is not a name of your family."

Then they went to Zacharias to ask him, even though he could not speak. Zacharias asked for a tablet, and he wrote on it: "His name is John."

As Zacharias wrote, his tongue was loosened and he spoke, blessing the name of the Lord.

All who heard of these things marvelled and knew that the Lord was with this child.

Zacharias was filled with the Holy Spirit and prophesied, saying:

"Blessed be the Lord, God of Israel;
He has visited and redeemed His
    people;
He has raised up a horn of salvation
    for us in the house of David,
As He spoke through the prophets
    of old:
That we should be saved from our
    enemies
To remember His holy covenant,
The promise that He made to our father
    Abraham;
That we might serve Him without fear
In holiness and righteousness all of
our lives.
This child will be the prophet of the
    Most High;
He will go before the Lord to prepare
    the way,
To give knowledge of salvation to the
    people
In forgiveness of their sins,
Through the tender mercy of God;
To give light to those who are in
    darkness and in the shadow of death,
To guide us in the way of peace."

The child John grew and became strong in spirit.

The Birth of Jesus
Matthew 1, Luke 2

Joseph, the carpenter who was betrothed to Mary, was worried because Mary was to have a child, and they were not yet married.

But an angel appeared to Joseph in a dream, saying: "Do not be afraid to marry Mary. The baby she will have is of the Holy Spirit. She will have a son and his name shall be Jesus, which means 'God is salvation.' This will happen to make the words of the Lord come true, the words spoken by the prophets promising that a saviour would appear."

Joseph awakened from his dream and did as

the angel had commanded. He married Mary and waited for her son to be born.

At this time the Roman Emperor ordered that a census be taken of all the people in the Empire. So Joseph took his wife and went from Nazareth in Galilee to the city of David, called Bethlehem, in Judah. He was of the house of David and was to be counted there.

It was a long journey to the little town of Bethlehem and Mary rode on a donkey. There were so many people in the town already that there was no room for them at the inn. A place was found for them in the stable.

While they were there, the baby was born. Mary wrapped her son carefully and placed him on straw in a manger.

That night in the fields near Bethlehem a group of shepherds were looking after their sheep. Suddenly an angel of the Lord appeared to them and a great light shone all around them. They were filled with fear.

The angel spoke to them, saying: "Do not be afraid. I have good news of a great joy for all the people. This day in the city of David, a saviour has been born. He is Christ the Lord.

"This will be a sign to you: you will find a baby lying in a manger, wrapped in swaddling clothes."

Then suddenly there appeared to the shepherds a great number of heavenly angels singing: "Glory to God in the highest, and peace on earth to all with whom the Lord is pleased.

The angels disappeared. The shepherds hurried to Bethlehem to see the great miracle that had taken place.

In the stable they found Mary and Joseph, and they saw the baby lying in a manger. They told everyone what the angel had said to them

about the child. All the people who heard marvelled at these things. Then the shepherds praised God and glorified His name.

Jesus Presented in the Temple
Luke 2

When the baby was eight days old he was given the name of Jesus. And when the time came for their purification according to the law of Moses, Mary and Joseph took the baby to Jerusalem, to present him to the Lord and to make a thanksgiving offering in the Temple. Joseph took two pigeons as his sacrifice.

There was a righteous man in Jerusalem named Simeon who longed for the coming of the saviour that God had promised. The Holy Spirit revealed to him that he would surely see the Lord's Christ before he died.

The day that Mary and Joseph brought the baby Jesus to the Temple, Simeon was there. He lifted Jesus in his arms and blessed God, saying: "Now I can die in peace, for my eyes have seen Your salvation, which You have prepared in the presence of all peoples."

Then Simeon asked God's blessing on Mary and Joseph and said to Mary: "This child will cause the fall and rising again of many people in Israel. Many shall speak against him. Through him a sword will pierce your soul

also, and through him, the thoughts of many will be made known."

The Visit of the Wise Men
Matthew 2

Wise men came to Jerusalem from the east, asking: "Where is the child who has been born to be king of the Jews? We saw his star in the east, and we have come to worship him."

When Herod, the king, heard this, he was troubled. He sent for all his priests and scribes. And he asked them where the Christ could be found.

They answered, saying: "In Bethlehem, for so it has been written by the prophet Micah:

"Out of Bethlehem in Judah shall come a governor to rule the people Israel."

Herod called the wise men to him. Secretly he sent them to Bethlehem to search for the child, ordering them to report back to him.

"When you have found him," said Herod, "come and tell me so I too may go to worship him."

The learned men left the king and began their journey. The star which they had seen in the east went before them. They followed the star until it stood over the stable where the baby was lying.

When they went into the stable and saw the child with his mother Mary, they bowed down and worshipped him. Then they offered him gifts that they had brought: gold and frankincense and myrrh.

The wise men had been warned by God in a dream not to return to Herod. So they left the baby Jesus to return to their own country by a different way.

The Flight to Egypt
Matthew 2

The wise men left the stable and started for home. Then an angel of the Lord appeared to Joseph in a dream, saying: "Take the child and his mother and go to Egypt, for King Herod has heard about the birth of the child. He will send messengers to search for him and kill him."

So Joseph, Mary and Jesus journeyed to Egypt and stayed there until after the death of King Herod.

This was done to fulfil the words of the Lord spoken by the prophet Hosea: "Out of Egypt I have called My son."

When the wise men did not report the whereabouts of the baby to the king, he became

very angry. He ordered his men to go to Bethlehem and kill all male children less than two years old.

When King Herod died, an angel again appeared to Joseph. This time the angel directed Joseph to take the child and his mother back to Israel.

So they returned to Israel and settled in Nazareth in the district of Galilee, for the prophet Isaiah had said: "He shall be called a Nazarene."

The Twelve-Year-Old Jesus

Luke 2

Jesus grew up in Nazareth and went to school there. He helped Joseph in his carpenter's shop. He grew strong in spirit and wisdom, and the Lord blessed him.

According to custom, every year at the Passover, Joseph and Mary took the child Jesus to the Temple in Jerusalem. Many others also made the journey, and after the feast which lasted seven days, they all returned home.

When Jesus was twelve years old, he was taken to Jerusalem as usual. But this time, when Mary and Joseph started for home with a large group of people, Jesus stayed behind in Jerusalem. After a day's journey, Mary saw that Jesus was not with the group, so she and Joseph hurried back to Jerusalem to find him.

Three days later they found Jesus in the Temple, sitting with the teachers. He was asking questions and listening intently. Everyone there was amazed at the understanding of the boy, at the questions he asked and the comments he made.

Mary asked: "Why have you done this? Your father and I have been worried about you."

Jesus answered: "Why have you looked for me? You should have known that I would be in my Father's house."

They did not understand his answer, but took him back to Nazareth with them.

Jesus was an obedient son. He continued to grow in strength and in wisdom and to be blessed by the Lord.

The Baptism of Jesus
Matthew 3, Mark 1, Luke 3, John 1

John, the son of Zacharias and Elizabeth, was six months older than his cousin Jesus. Jesus lived in the city of Nazareth; John grew up in the wilderness.

John wore a coat of camel's hair and a leather belt around his waist. He ate the foods of the wilderness, wild honey and locusts.

The word of God came to John in the wilderness. It was during the reign of the Roman Emperor Tiberius Caesar; Pontius Pilate was governor of Judea and Herod An-

tipas ruled Galilee.

John heard the word of God and went from the wilderness into the countryside around the river Jordan. There he preached repentance for the forgiveness of sins.

This fulfilled the prophesy of Isaiah: "It shall be the voice of one crying in the wilderness to prepare the way, saying that the crooked shall be made straight and the rough made smooth, and that all men shall see the salvation of God."

Many people came to John and heard his preaching. They confessed their sins and were baptized by him. They asked his advice and he spoke to them, telling them what they must do to live a righteous life.

"Let the man who has two coats share with the man who has none," said John. "Let the man who has food also share."

To the tax collectors he said: "Collect no more than is legal and just to collect."

To the soldiers: "Do not rob any man by violence and never accuse a man falsely."

People who came to John wondered if he was the Messiah. To them he said: "I baptize with water, but one is coming who is mightier than I. I am not worthy even to stoop down and touch his sandals. He will baptize with the Holy Spirit."

One day Jesus, by then a young man, came from Galilee to the Jordan to be baptized by John.

John knew at once who Jesus was and he asked: "You have come to me to be baptized? I should be baptized by you."

Jesus answered: "But you must baptize me now, for we must do all things that are righteous."

John agreed, and he baptized Jesus in the river Jordan.

As Jesus came out of the water the heavens opened and the Holy Spirit descended upon him like a dove. A voice spoke to him, saying: "This is My beloved son, with whom I am greatly pleased."

The Temptation of Jesus
Matthew 4, Mark 1, Luke 4

After Jesus was baptized by John, the spirit of God led him into the wilderness to be tempted by the devil. Jesus fasted for forty days and forty nights. Afterward he was very hungry.

The devil said to him: "If you are hungry, and if you are the son of God, make this stone become bread."

Jesus answered: "It is written that men shall not live by bread alone, but by the words of God."

Then the devil took him to the holy city to the highest part of the Temple. He said: "If you are the son of God, throw yourself down from this place. If you are, it is said that angels will be in charge of you to protect you."

Jesus answered: "It is written that you should not tempt the Lord your God."

Then the devil took Jesus to the top of a very high mountain and showed him all the nations of the world, saying: "If you will worship me, all these nations will be yours. Then you will be rich and powerful."

Jesus answered: "No, for it is written that you shall worship the Lord your God and no other."

Then the devil left Jesus, and angels came to look after him.

Jesus' Ministry
Matthew 13, Mark 4-6, Luke 4, 8

Jesus was about thirty years old when he began his ministry.

In Nazareth he went into the synagogue and read from the Book of Isaiah: "The spirit of the Lord is upon me; He has anointed me to preach good tidings to the poor, to proclaim

freedom to the captives and the oppressed, to restore sight to the blind and to proclaim the year of the Lord."

Then he closed the book, and all who were there watched him. He said: "Today this prophecy is fulfilled and you have heard it."

All there were astonished and they asked: "Where did this man get his wisdom? How can he do all this? His mother is Mary. Is his father not Joseph, the carpenter? Where did he get such power?"

They were offended by him, and did not believe in him.

But Jesus said: "A prophet is often without honour in his own house and in his own country. He is not acceptable in his own land."

Jesus and the Fishermen

Matthew 4, Mark 1, Luke 5,8, John 1

Jesus left Nazareth and travelled to Capernaum on the Sea of Galilee. There, too, he preached, saying: "Repent, for the kingdom of heaven is near."

As he was walking along the coast of the Sea of Galilee, Jesus saw two fishermen casting their nets into the water. They were brothers, Simon and Andrew.

Jesus got into Simon's boat and asked him to push it out from shore. Simon did so, and Jesus preached to the people from the boat. They stopped what they were doing and listened to him.

Then Jesus said to Simon: "Now we will go out into deep water and let down the nets to bring in some fish."

Simon replied: "We have sat in our boats all night with the nets out and we have caught nothing. But if you say to do it, we will."

When they had rowed out to deep water, they let down the nets. Immediately a great number of fish swam into them. There were so many that the nets could not hold them all.

Simon and Andrew called their partners James and John, who were also brothers, to come out and help them. Together, they filled both boats so full of fish that they nearly sank.

All four men were amazed at the number of fish they had caught.

Then Jesus said to them: "Follow me, and I will make you fishers of men."

When they reached shore with their great catch, all four men left their nets and their boats to go with Jesus. These were the first of his many disciples: Simon who was also called Peter and his brother Andrew, and the brothers James and John.

The Miracle of Changing Water into Wine
John 2

Jesus and his four disciples travelled throughout the district of Galilee. He attended a wedding feast at Cana in Galilee. His mother, too, had been invited to the wedding.

After a while, all the wine had been used up. Mary came to tell him, and he said: "Why have you told me? It is not yet time for me to act."

But his mother said to the servants: "Listen to my son. Do whatever he asks of you."

There were six large water jugs standing at the doorway to the house. They were used by all who entered to purify themselves.

158

Jesus told the servants to fill all of the jars with clean water. They did so. Then he said: "Now, dip some out and take it to the master of ceremonies." They did as Jesus asked.

When the master of ceremonies drank from the jug, he was astonished. He had been told there was no more wine, yet this was wine. And it was excellent.

Then the man called the bridegroom and said: "Everyone serves the best wine first. Then, when the guests have been drinking for a while,

the poor wine. But you have kept the best for last."

When the disciples saw this sign by Jesus, they believed in him.

Preaching in the Synagogue
Matthew 8, Mark 1, Luke 4

In Capernaum, Jesus went into the synagogue on the sabbath. Simon, Andrew, James and John were with him. There Jesus taught, and the people listened.

Everyone was surprised at the preaching of Jesus, for he spoke with authority.

A man possessed by an unclean spirit called to Jesus: "Why are you here? What have you to do with us? Have you come to destroy us, Jesus of Nazareth?"

Jesus spoke: "Be silent and come out!"

The unclean spirit caused the man to shake and cry out, and then it came out of him.

All the people were amazed, and they asked: "What happened? Is this a new teaching? This man even has authority over unclean spirits; they obey him." They marvelled at what Jesus had done.

When Jesus and his followers left the synagogue, they went to the house of Simon and Andrew. There Simon's mother-in-law was sick with fever.

Jesus went to the sick woman, took her by the hand and lifted her up. Immediately the fever left her. She got up and was able to serve them.

After that, the fame of Jesus spread throughout the whole district of Galilee.

That night after sundown, many people came to Jesus. Those that were sick with disease were brought to him and those that were possessed by evil spirits were also brought. A great crowd gathered.

Jesus healed many who were sick, and cast out many evil spirits.

In the morning Jesus rose before daylight and went out alone to pray. Simon and the others followed him, saying that many people were looking for him and seeking his help.

Jesus said: "We will go on to other towns to preach, for that is my purpose."

So Jesus went throughout Galilee, preaching in the synagogues and healing and casting out evil spirits.

Jesus and the Leper

Matthew 8, Mark 1, Luke 5

A leper came to Jesus, kneeling before him. And he said: "If you will, you can make me clean."

Jesus stretched out his hand and touched the man, saying: "I will; be clean."

Immediately the man was cured: his skin became smooth; the leprosy was gone.

Then Jesus sent the man away, saying: "Tell no one what has happened. But go to the priest and make a thanksgiving offering as commanded by the laws of Moses."

But the man went out and told everyone about the healing. The news spread to such an extent that Jesus could not even enter towns or cities, because people streamed forth from every direction to meet him.

Healing the Paralytic

Matthew 9, Mark 2, Luke 5

Jesus went back to Capernaum. So many people gathered to greet him that they could not even get near the door of the place where he was preaching.

A man who was paralyzed was being brought to Jesus, carried on a stretcher by four men. When they saw that they could not get near the house, the four men put down the stretcher and climbed up on the roof and made an opening in it. Then they let the stretcher down inside, through the opening.

When Jesus saw their great faith, he said to the man on the stretcher: "Your sins are forgiven."

The scribes and teachers of the law who had gathered to listen to Jesus preach heard this.

And they thought: "Only God can forgive sins. Who is this man? He speaks blasphemy!"

Jesus, knowing that they questioned him, asked: "Why do you question? Which is easier to say: 'Your sins are forgiven' or 'Rise up and walk?' "

Then he turned to the man who was paralyzed, saying: "So you will know that the Son of Man can forgive sins, I say to you: rise up and go home."

Immediately the man got up and walked out, carrying the stretcher with him.

Everyone who saw this was astonished for they had never seen anything like it.

In the Fields on the Sabbath
Matthew 12, Mark 2, Luke 6

One sabbath, Jesus and his disciples were walking through a field. The disciples were hungry and began to pick ears of grain, rubbing them in their hands to loosen the grain.

When the Pharisees saw this, they spoke to Jesus about it. The Pharisees believed in the strict observance of the sabbath laws, so they said: "This is the sabbath. Why are you doing what is forbidden on this day?"

Jesus answered: "Do you know what David did when he and his followers were hungry? They went into the Temple and ate some of the bread which only the priests are supposed to eat."

Then he said: "The sabbath was made for man, not man for the sabbath. The Son of Man is lord of the sabbath."

The Man with the Withered Hand
Matthew 12, Mark 3, Luke 6

On another sabbath, Jesus entered the syna-

gogue to teach. A man with a withered right hand was there.

The scribes and the Pharisees, who were teachers of the Jewish religion, watched to see if Jesus would heal on the sabbath, so they might accuse him. Jesus knew what they were thinking, and he called the man to him.

He asked those who were watching: "If you have one sheep and it falls into a deep pit on the sabbath, would you leave it there? Or would you reach in and lift it out? How much more valuable is a man than a sheep? Is it better on the sabbath to save life or destroy it?"

Then he said to the man: "Hold out your hand." He did, and it was healed and well, like the other.

The Pharisees left the synagogue to plan what they might do about Jesus.

Healing the Invalid on the Sabbath
John 5

In Jerusalem near the sheep market was a pool of water which had special powers. At certain times the water moved and was stirred up.

Around the pool were many sick people, people who were lame and paralyzed and blind. One man who had been an invalid for thirty-eight years was lying far from the water.

Jesus saw the man and asked: "Do you want to be healed?"

The man answered: "Yes, but there is no one to help me down into the water."

Jesus said: "Rise now, pick up your mat and walk." At once the man was healed. He picked up his mat and walked away.

This happened on a sabbath. When the Pharisees saw the man carrying his mat, they said: "Today is the sabbath. It is unlawful for you to be carrying on the sabbath."

The man answered: "The one who healed me told me to lift up my mat and walk."

They asked him: "Who was the man?" But he did not know.

Later he saw Jesus in the Temple, and Jesus spoke to him, saying: "Now you are well. If you sin no more, nothing else will happen to you."

Then the man knew who had healed him, and he told the Pharisees.

Again they accused Jesus of breaking the laws of the sabbath.

Jesus answered them: "My Father is working, and I am working too. A son can do nothing alone, only what he sees his father doing. As the Father brings the dead to life, so can the son give life."

Then they determined to destroy Jesus. He not only violated the sabbath, but he had called God his Father and had made himself equal to God.

Choosing the Twelve Apostles
Matthew 10, Mark 3, Luke 6, John 1

Jesus journeyed throughout the district of Galilee with the four fishermen from Capernaum who had been his first followers. Soon after that, he met a man from Bethsaida whose name was Philip. He joined the others, and together they became disciples of Jesus.

They travelled through cities and villages. Everywhere they went, Jesus taught in the synagogues, preaching to the people and healing them. And everywhere, crowds followed him and he gathered many other disciples.

One evening Jesus went into the hills to pray. All night he prayed to God. In the morning he called his disciples to him and from among them all, he chose twelve whom he named apostles.

The twelve apostles were: Simon Peter and his brother Andrew, and James and John who were the sons of Zebedee the fisherman. Then there were Philip and Bartholomew, Thomas and Matthew the tax collector, James the son of Alphaeus, Thaddeus, Simon the Zealot, and Judas Iscariot.

Jesus gave them power to heal all kinds of disease and sickness and to cast out evil and unclean spirits.

The Sermon on the Mount
Matthew 5-7, Luke 6,11

Jesus continued to travel, teaching and preaching and healing. His fame spread far and wide. Great crowds came to him from everywhere: from Galilee, Jerusalem and Judea. Even from Decapolis, beyond the river Jordan, people came to follow him.

Leaving the large number of people that had gathered around him, Jesus went alone into the mountains. There his disciples came to him, and he spoke to them, teaching them many things:

162

The Beatitudes
Matthew 5

"Blessed are the poor in spirit, for
theirs is the kingdom of heaven.
Blessed are those who mourn, for they
shall be comforted.
Blessed are the meek, for they shall
inherit the earth.
Blessed are they who hunger and thirst
for righteousness, for they shall be
satisfied.

Blessed are the merciful, for they shall
receive mercy.
Blessed are the pure in heart, for they
shall see God.
Blessed are the peacemakers, for they
shall be called God's children.
Blessed are those who are persecuted
for the sake of righteousness, for
theirs is the kingdom of heaven.
Blessed are you when men despise you,
curse you, persecute you and speak
evil against you falsely because of me.
Rejoice and be glad, for your reward
is great in heaven,
for so were the prophets persecuted
before you."

To the Disciples
Matthew 5, Luke 11

"You are the salt of the earth. If salt loses its taste, how can its saltiness be restored? It is then not good for anything, except to be thrown away and stepped on.

"You are the light of the world. A city on a hill cannot be hidden. Men do not light lamps to put them under a bushel, but to put on a stand to give light. Let your light so shine before men, so that seeing your good works, they will glorify your Father in heaven."

The Law and the Prophets

Matthew 5

"Do not think I have come to destroy the law and the prophets of old. Instead I have come to fulfil them.

"Truly not one bit shall be removed from the law until it all is accomplished. Whoever breaks any of the commandments, even the least of them, shall be the lowest in all the kingdom of heaven. But whoever does and teaches all the commandments shall be great.

"Unless your righteousness is greater than that of the Pharisees and the scribes, you will never enter the kingdom of heaven.

"You have heard it said that you shall not kill, that whoever kills is in danger of punishment. But I say that anyone who is angry with his brother is in danger of punishment, and whoever insults his brother shall be in danger of hell fire.

"If you go to make an offering at the altar, and remember that anyone holds something against you, leave your offering and go first to make peace with that person. Then make your offering.

"Make friends with those who accuse you, who take you to court; for if you are judged against and put into prison, you will not get out until the last penny has been paid.

"You have heard it said that you shall not commit adultery. But I say that one who even looks at another with lust has already done so in his heart. If your eye causes you to sin, it is better to pluck it out and lose an eye than have your whole body thrown into hell.

"It was also said that you shall not swear falsely, but shall do what you have sworn to do. But I say do not swear at all, either by heaven or earth. Say simply 'Yes' or 'No'; anything more is evil.

"You have heard 'An eye for an eye and a tooth for a tooth.' But I say if someone strikes you on the cheek, then turn the other cheek; do not resist an injury.

"Give to one who begs from you, and do not refuse one who comes to borrow.

"It has been said 'Love your neighbour and hate your enemy.' But I say love your enemies, bless those who persecute you, do good to those who hate you. For our Father in heaven makes the sun shine on both the good and the evil, and He sends rain on both the just and unjust.

You must be perfect, even as your heavenly Father is perfect."

Charity

Matthew 6

"Be careful not to do your good deeds openly in order for them to be seen by all. Then you will receive no praise from your Father in heaven.

"When you give charity, do it quietly. Do not shout it publicly as with trumpets to be praised by other men. When you give charity, do not let your left hand know what your right hand is doing. Let your charity be in secret. Your Father sees what is done in secret and will reward you."

Prayer

Matthew 6

"When you pray, do not be like the hypocrites who stand and pray where they can be seen, in the synagogues and on street corners. When you pray, go to your room and pray to your Father alone in secret. Your Father sees in secret and will reward you.

"In praying, do not use fancy words and empty sayings. Your Father knows what you need even before you ask it. Pray in the following way, saying:

Our Father who is in heaven,
Holy be Your name.
May Your Kingdom come, Your will be done
On earth as it is in heaven.
Give us this day our daily bread;
Forgive us our sins
As we forgive those who sin against us;
And lead us not into temptation,
But deliver us from evil."

Then he added: "If you forgive men their wrongdoings, your heavenly Father will forgive you. If you do not forgive men, neither will your heavenly Father forgive you."

True Treasures

Matthew 6-7

"Do not collect treasures on earth, treasures that moths and rust can damage or that thieves can steal, but store up treasures in heaven where neither moths nor rust do damage or thieves steal. Where your treasures are, your heart will be also.

"The eye is the lamp of the body. If your eye is good, your body will be full of light; but if your eye is not good, your body will be filled with darkness. And the darkness will be great indeed.

"You cannot serve two masters. Either you will hate one and love the other, or love the one and hate the other. You cannot serve both God and worldly things.

"Do not worry about life: what to eat or drink or what clothes to put on. Life is more than food; the body is more than clothing. Look at the birds: they neither plant nor harvest nor store up food. They are fed by your heavenly Father. Are you not of greater value than the birds?

"Consider the lilies of the field and how they grow: they neither spin nor sew. Yet not even Solomon was more handsome in all his glory. If God clothes the lilies so beautifully, how much more so will you be clothed?

"So do not worry about what to eat or what to drink or what to wear. Your heavenly Father knows you need them all. First seek the kingdom of God and righteousness, then these other things shall be yours also.

"Do not worry about tomorrow; tomorrow will take care of itself. Let each day's troubles be enough for that day.

"Do not judge others, so you will not be judged. As you measure others, so they will measure you.

"Why do you see a tiny speck in another's eye, but do not notice the larger one in your own? First take the larger one out of your own eye, then you can see better to take the speck out of his.

"Ask and you will receive; seek and you will find. Knock and doors will be opened for you. Is there any among you who, if your son asks for bread, would give him a stone? Or if he asks for a fish, would give him a serpent? If you, who are evil, know how to do good for your children, how much more will your heavenly Father give good things to you who ask?

"Do to others whatever you wish to be done to you; this is the law and the teaching of the prophets.

"Enter the narrow gate. The gate to destruction is wide and easy to pass through; there are many who go that way. The way that leads to life is hard; that gate is narrow and those who find it are few."

False Prophets
Matthew 7

"Beware of false prophets, of those who are wolves but come in sheep's clothing. You will

know them by their fruits. Can you get grapes from thorns? Or figs from thistles? Good trees bear good fruit, but a bad tree bears bad fruit. All trees that do not bear good fruit will be cut down and burned. So by their fruits you will know them.

"Not everyone who calls me 'Lord' shall enter the kingdom of heaven, only those who do the will of my Father who is in heaven. Many will ask me: 'Lord, did we not prophesy in your name and do great deeds in your name?' I will answer that I never knew them, and I will send away those that do evil.

"Everyone who hears these words I have spoken and does them will be like the wise man who builds his house on a rock. When it rains, when floods come and winds blow, the house will remain steady because it has been built on a rock.

"Those that hear my words and do not act according to them will be like the foolish man who builds his house on sand. When it rains, and the floods come and the winds blow, that house will fall because it has been built on sand."

When Jesus finished saying all these things, the disciples were astonished at his words and at his preaching. He taught them as one who had authority and not as a scribe giving interpretation of the law.

The Roman's Servant

Matthew 8, Luke 7

When Jesus came down from the mountain, great crowds followed him. As he entered the town of Capernaum, a centurion, a Roman officer, came to meet him.

The Roman spoke to Jesus, saying: "I have a servant who is paralyzed and suffering greatly."

Jesus said: "I will come to him."

Now the elders of the Jews were pleased. They said to Jesus: "He is worthy to have you do this for him. He has been good to our people, and has even built a synagogue for us."

As Jesus came near the house of the Roman, the man said to him: "Lord, I am not worthy to have you enter my house. But if you will only say the word, my servant will be healed.

"I am a man of authority with soldiers under me. If I tell my men to go, they go. If I say come, they come."

Jesus marvelled when he heard this and he said to all those who were with him: "Surely, I have never found such faith before, not even among the Jews."

To the Roman Jesus said: "Go, and it will be done for you as you have believed."

When the centurion returned home, he found his servant healed.

The Widow's Son

Luke 7

Jesus travelled to the city of Nain with his disciples and a great crowd followed him.

As he neared the gates of the city, a funeral procession was coming toward him. The man who had died was the only son of a widowed mother.

When Jesus saw the mother, he felt sympathy for her and spoke to her, saying: "Do not weep."

Then he touched the coffin. Those who carried it stood still, and Jesus said: "Arise, young man."

The dead man sat up in his coffin and began to speak.

Jesus had given him back to his mother.

Everyone who was there was overcome with fear. They glorified God and they said: "A great prophet has come among us. Surely God has visited His people."

This story, too, spread throughout the countryside, until all the people had heard of Jesus. Wherever he went people came to him for help, and he healed the sick and taught those who gathered around him.

The Greatest Prophet

Matthew 11, Luke 7

John the Baptist, who was Jesus' cousin, heard about the ministry of Jesus, about his healing and his preaching. He sent two of his disciples to Jesus to ask: "Are you the one who is to come, or shall we look for another?"

While John's messengers were with Jesus, they saw him cure many diseases and cast out evil spirits.

Then Jesus said: "Tell John what you have seen and heard: that the blind can now see, the lame can walk, the lepers are cleansed, the deaf can hear and the dead have been restored to life. Blessed is he who is not offended by me."

wanted John put to death. But the king hesitated to have John killed. He knew that John was a righteous man and that many people believed him to be a prophet.

Instead of ordering John's death, the king had him thrown into prison where he was kept for a long time.

It happened that on Herod's birthday, his wife's daughter Salome danced before the

When the messengers left, Jesus spoke to the people about John, saying: "When you went into the wilderness, what did you go out to see? Grasses blowing in the wind? A man dressed in fine clothing? Those who wear fine clothes are in the courts of kings.

"Did you go to see a prophet? Yes, and more than a prophet. This prophet, this man of the wilderness, is the one who was written about by the prophet Malachi, who said: 'Behold, I will send My messenger to prepare the way!'

"So I say: among all men, there is not a greater prophet than John the Baptist."

The Death of John the Baptist
Matthew 14, Mark 6

John the Baptist had many followers. He had been preaching about the sins committed by the people. He had been baptizing people and urging them to repent and ask forgiveness for their sins.

He had even spoken out against the wrongdoing of King Herod Antipas and his wife Herodias, for Herod had taken his brother's wife to be *his* wife. As a result, Herod's wife crowd that had gathered to celebrate. Herod was so pleased that he said to her: "Ask whatever you wish and it shall be yours, even to half my kingdom."

Salome asked her mother: "What shall I ask?"

The mother answered: "Ask for the head of John the Baptist."

So Salome went to the king and asked for the head of John the Baptist on a platter.

Now the king had promised her anything, and he could not break his word before all the people. Even though he was sorry to do it, he gave orders for John to be beheaded immediately and for his head to be given to the girl on a platter.

It was done, and Salome took the platter to her mother.

John's disciples came for his body and buried it. Then they went to tell Jesus.

When Jesus heard this, he went out to a deserted place by boat.

A Sinful Woman
Luke 7

One of the Pharisees asked Jesus to eat with him. They went into the house and sat down to eat.

A woman of the city who was known for her sinful life came to the house when she heard that Jesus was there. She brought a flask of ointment with her, and knelt at the feet of Jesus. Weeping, she wet his feet with her tears. Then she wiped them with her hair and anointed them with the ointment she had brought.

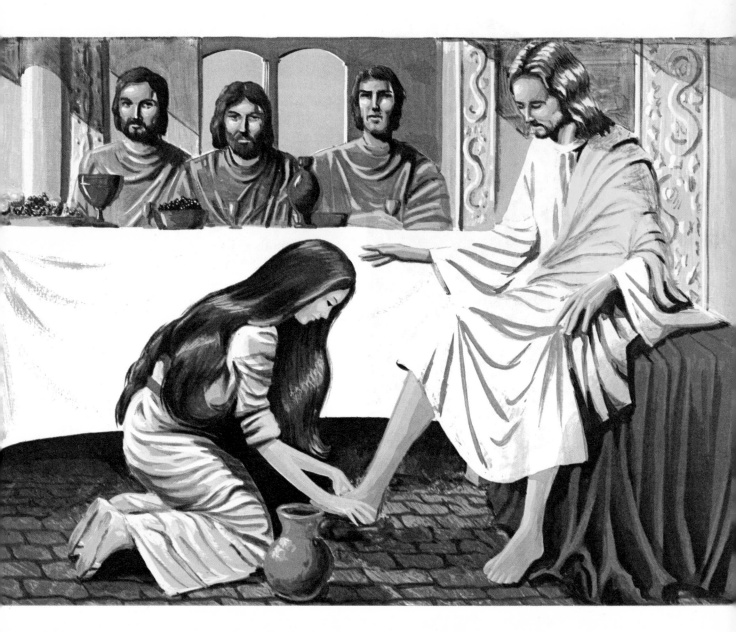

The Pharisee saw this and thought: "If Jesus were a true prophet, he would know this woman is a sinner and unfit to touch him."

Jesus, knowing the other's thoughts, said: "I have something to tell you: two people owed a man money. One owed him five hundred denarii and the other owed fifty. Neither of them could pay and he forgave them both. Which one would love him more?"

The Pharisee answered: "The one who owed him more would love him more, I suppose."

Jesus said: "Your judgement is right. Do you see this woman and what she has done? I came into your house and you gave me no water to wash my feet. But she washed my feet with her tears, and wiped them. You gave me no kiss, but she kissed my feet. You did not anoint me with oil, but she anointed my feet with ointment.

"Now, her sins which are many shall be forgiven, for she has shown much love. One who is forgiven little, loves little."

He said to the woman: "Your sins are forgiven. Go in peace: your faith is great and has saved you."

All who were there and saw and heard Jesus asked themselves: "Who is this that forgives sins?"

A House Divided
Matthew 12, Mark 3, Luke 11

On another occasion a man possessed with a devil and who was blind and dumb was brought before Jesus. Jesus healed him. The devil was cast out and the man could see and speak.

All the people were amazed, saying: "This must be the son of David."

But the Pharisees said: "Devils can only be cast out through Beelzebub, the prince of devils."

Then Jesus spoke, saying: "A kingdom divided against itself will fall. A house divided against itself cannot stand. If the devil casts out the devil, he is divided against himself. Then how could his kingdom stand?

"If I cast out devils through the prince of devils, how do your people cast them out? But if I cast out devils through the spirit of God, then the kingdom of God will come.

"How can one enter the house of a powerful man to steal his goods, unless he first ties up the strong man? Then he can steal from him. He that is not with me, is against me.

"Now I say this: all sins and blasphemy shall be forgiven except blasphemy against the Holy Spirit. That blasphemy will never be forgiven. Anyone who speaks against the Son of Man will be forgiven, but anyone who speaks against the Holy Spirit shall not be forgiven, either now or in the time to come.

"Good men bring forth good, and evil men bring forth evil. On the day of judgment, every man must give account for every careless word he has spoken. By their words will they be judged."

Then some of the scribes and Pharisees who had heard him asked for a sign from Jesus.

Jesus answered: "An evil generation seeks a sign. No sign shall be given except the sign of Jonah. Just as Jonah was inside the fish for three days and three nights, so the Son of Man will be three days and three nights in the heart of the earth."

Teaching by Parables

Matthew 13, Mark 4, Luke 8

Jesus travelled through every city and village, preaching and speaking of the kingdom of God. The twelve apostles went with him.

Several women travelled with him also: women who had been healed of illness or of evil spirits. These were Mary Magdalene who had been possessed by seven devils, Joanna the wife of Chuza, Susannah and others.

Great crowds gathered around Jesus wherever he went.

At the seaside he got into a boat and spoke to the people from there. He spoke to them in parables, stories about people that teach lessons about God.

The disciples asked: "Why do you speak to the people in parables?"

Jesus answered: "You have the power to know the secrets of the kingdom of God, but they have it not. Seeing, they do not see and hearing, they do not hear. Even hearing, they may not understand."

The Sower

Matthew 13, Mark 4, Luke 8

"A sower went out to sow his seed. Some seeds fell along the way and were eaten up by birds. Some fell on rocky ground where there was not much soil to grow in; these had no roots so they withered away. Some fell among thorns and the thorns grew and choked them out. Some went into good earth and grew and ripened, bringing forth fine grain.

"The meaning of the parable is this: the seed is the word of God. Those seeds that fall by the way are those words which are heard but are not believed and are lost.

"Those that fall on rocky soil are heard with joy, but have no roots. They are believed for a short time and easily wither away in times of temptation.

"The seeds among the thorns are those words which are heard and then are choked out by the riches and pleasures of life before faith in them ripens.

"But the seeds planted in good earth are the words of God that are heard and believed and looked after, growing and ripening to bring forth fruit."

Weeds

Matthew 13

"The kingdom of heaven is like a man who has sown good seeds. While he was sleeping, his enemy came and sowed weeds along with the wheat. And the two grew in the field together.

"The man's servants asked him if they should pull up the weeds that his enemy had planted. He answered: 'No, for you may pull up the wheat while pulling out the weeds. Let them grow together until they ripen. Then we will gather the weeds and burn them. After that, we will harvest the wheat.'"

Jesus explained to his disciples: "The one who sows good seeds is the Son of Man. His field is the world. The good seeds are those of the kingdom of God. The enemy who planted the weeds is the devil and the weeds are the sons of the devil.

"The time of harvest is the end of days and those who reap are the angels. Just as the weeds are gathered and burned, so the angels will gather up all who do evil and throw them into the fire. Then those who are righteous will shine like the sun in the kingdom of heaven."

The Mustard Seed

Matthew 13, Luke 13

"The kingdom of heaven is like a mustard seed which a man plants in his field. It is the smallest of seeds but it grows into a large plant. It becomes a tree and birds come to build their nests in its branches."

The Fishnet

Matthew 13

"The kingdom of heaven is like a net thrown into the sea to gather all kinds of fish. When it is full, it is pulled in. Then men sort out the good fish and keep them and throw away the bad. So it will be at the end of days.

"The angels will separate the evil from the righteous, throwing the evil ones into a furnace."

Jesus and the Apostles

Matthew 10, Mark 6, Luke 9

Jesus continued to travel, to heal and to perform miracles. He calmed a storm, cast out evil spirits and devils, healed the sick and even restored the dead to life.

Herod, who ruled Galilee, heard about Jesus: his teaching and preaching, his healing and the miracles he performed. Herod was puzzled and did not know who Jesus was. He thought he might be John the Baptist come to life again.

When Jesus heard about Herod's questioning, he went with his disciples to a lonely place. He called the twelve apostles to him and gave them power to heal and to cast out evil spirits. Then he sent them out two by two to carry the message: "The kingdom of God is at hand."

He said to them: "Take nothing with you except your walking staff. Take no food nor money nor extra clothing. Wear sandals on your feet.

"If you are received well in a place, stay and bless that place. If you are not treated well or the people do not listen to you, then leave that place. When you leave, shake off the dust from your feet as a testimony against the place and its people."

The apostles left Jesus and travelled two by two through many villages and towns, preaching the gospel and healing.

Then they returned to Jesus to tell him all that they had done and taught, and Jesus said: "Come away with me by boat and rest awhile."

Feeding the Multitude

Matthew 14, Mark 6, Luke 9, John 5

Many people saw Jesus and the apostles together and followed them until a great crowd had gathered. Then Jesus stopped along the way. He healed their sick and spoke of many things.

When it was evening, the apostles said to Jesus: "It is getting late. Let the people go into nearby villages for food and a place to stay."

Jesus answered: "They need not leave. Give them something to eat."

The disciples were surprised and they said: "We do not have enough money to buy food for so many." There were about five thousand people there, not counting women and children.

"How many loaves of bread have you?" asked Jesus.

They came back and said: "We have only five loaves and two fish, not enough for all these people."

Then Jesus commanded all the people to sit down on the grass. He raised his eyes to heaven, holding the five loaves and the two fish.

He blessed the loaves, broke them and handed them to the disciples to give to the people. He also divided the two fish.

He divided the loaves and the fish until everyone who was there had enough bread and enough fish to eat.

After they all had eaten, Jesus sent his disciples around to pick up left-over pieces, and there were twelve baskets full.

When the people saw what had been done,

they said: "This man is surely a prophet sent by God."

Then Jesus sent the multitudes away and told his disciples to go on ahead in a boat to Capernaum. And he went alone into the hills to pray.

Walking on the Water
Matthew 14, Mark 6, John 6

Jesus was alone praying in the hills and his disciples were in a boat going toward Capernaum when suddenly a storm began. It grew dark, strong winds blew and great waves arose on the sea.

When the disciples had been rowing hard for three or four miles, they saw Jesus coming toward them. He was walking on the water.

The men were frightened, but Jesus said: "Do not be afraid."

Peter called: "If it is really you, call me to come to you on the water."

Jesus said: "Come."

So Peter got out of the boat and started toward Jesus. When he saw the wind and the waves, he became frightened and started to sink, crying out: "Save me, Lord."

Jesus reached out to Peter and caught him, saying: "Why did you doubt? You have such little faith."

Then the two men got into the boat. At once the wind stopped, the sea became calm, and the boat landed at Gennesaret.

When the people there saw Jesus they marvelled at what had happened and they spread the word. The sick and the diseased were brought to Jesus so he could heal them. Many were made well simply by touching the fringe of the garment Jesus was wearing.

Then the disciples worshipped Jesus, saying: "You are surely the son of God."

Eating with Unwashed Hands
Matthew 15, Mark 7

The Pharisees and scribes came to Jesus from Jerusalem, and asked him: "Why do your disciples not act according to tradition? They no longer wash their hands before eating."

Jesus answered, calling them hypocrites: "Isaiah prophesied about you when he said: 'This people worship with their lips, but their heart is far away from Me; they teach the commandments of men as law!'

"You have put aside God's commandments. You are paying more attention to unimportant things, like washing."

Then Jesus spoke to all the people who had gathered, for wherever Jesus went, a crowd followed him.

He said: "Listen, and understand. It is not what goes into a man's mouth that can do him harm, but what comes out of his mouth."

The disciples told Jesus that the Pharisees had been offended by what he had said.

Jesus answered: "Leave them alone. They are like the blind leading the blind. And when the blind lead the blind, they will surely fall into a pit."

Then Peter said: "Explain the parable to us."

And Jesus replied: "Do you still not understand? Whatever goes into the mouth goes into the stomach and then passes out of the body. But what comes out of the mouth comes from the heart.

"Out of the heart come evil thoughts and wrongdoing of all kinds. These are the things which truly defile man. To eat with unwashed hands does not defile."

Jesus the Christ
Matthew 16, Mark 8, Luke 9

Jesus continued to travel. He went through the district of Tyre and Sidon, then through Decapolis back to the Sea of Galilee. From there he went by ship to Dalmanutha, and on

to Bethsaida. In all these places crowds gathered, and Jesus preached and healed wherever he went.

When he came to the district of Caesarea Philippi, he spoke with his disciples, asking: "What do men say about me? Who do they say I am?"

They answered: "Some think you are John the Baptist, others think Elijah and still others think you are one of the prophets."

Then he asked: "Who do you say I am?"

Simon Peter answered: "You are the son of the living God. You are the Christ."

Jesus said: "May you be blessed, Simon, for this has been revealed to you, not by flesh and blood, but by my Father who is in heaven.

"And you are Peter, the rock. On this rock I will build my church. Even the powers of death will not prevent it.

"I will give you the keys of the kingdom of heaven, and whatever you do on earth shall be done in heaven."

Then Jesus told them to tell no one that he was the Christ.

Predicting the Crucifixion

Matthew 16, Mark 8, Luke 9

Jesus began to tell his disciples what the future would bring. He told them he would go to Jerusalem and be rejected, and that he would suffer greatly from the priests and scribes and elders. He said that he would be killed and be raised again on the third day.

Then Peter said: "This shall never happen. God forbid that it should happen to you."

Jesus answered Peter, saying: "Get behind me, Satan. You are not a help to me, but a hindrance. You are only on the side of men, not of God."

Then Jesus spoke to them all. He said: "If any of you would follow me, you must deny yourself. Take up your cross and follow me. Whoever wishes to save his life will lose it, and whoever loses his life for my sake, will find it.

"What good will it do a man if he gains the whole world and loses his soul? What shall a man give in return for his life? The Son of Man with his angels will come in the glory of his Father. Then he will repay each man for what he has done.

"You will surely see the kingdom of God before you die."

The Transfiguration

Matthew 17, Mark 9, Luke 9

A few days later, Jesus took Peter, James and John up into a high mountain to pray. There he was transfigured before them: his face shone like the brightness of the sun and his clothing became intensely white, as white as light.

There, too, Moses and Elijah appeared, talking with Jesus.

Peter said: "Lord, it is good that we are here. Let us build three tabernacles: one for you, one for Moses and one for Elijah."

While Peter was speaking, a bright cloud came over them and a voice came out of the cloud saying: "This is My beloved son, listen to him."

Hearing the voice, the disciples bowed down and were afraid. Jesus came near and touched them, saying: "Rise up and do not be afraid."

They lifted up their eyes and saw only Jesus before them.

As they came down the mountain together, Jesus commanded them to tell no one of the vision until the Son of Man would be raised from the dead.

The disciples asked: "Do not the scribes say that Elijah must come first?"

Jesus answered: "Yes, Elijah must come first to restore all things. But I say to you that Elijah has already come and they did not know him. He suffered and the Son of Man will also suffer because of them."

Then the disciples knew that Jesus was speaking of John the Baptist.

The Boy with Epilepsy

Matthew 17, Mark 9, Luke 9

Jesus, Peter, James and John came down from the mountain together and saw that a crowd had gathered.

A man came to Jesus and knelt before him, saying: "Lord, my son is an epileptic. Have mercy on him and heal him."

Jesus shook his head saying: "O generation without faith, how long must I be patient with you?"

Then he said to the man: "Bring your son here."

The boy was brought to him, and the spirit seized the boy, causing him to fall down and become rigid. The boy's father asked for pity, saying: "Help him if you can."

Jesus replied: "If you can! Everything is possible to one who believes."

The father cried out: "I believe! Help my unbelief!"

Then Jesus called out the evil spirit. The boy was healed and returned to his father.

The disciples came to Jesus privately and asked: "Why is it that we could not cast out the spirit?"

Jesus answered: "Because you have such little faith. If you would have faith as tiny as a mustard seed, you could move a mountain. Then nothing would be impossible for you. Such faith comes through prayer."

Jesus and his disciples travelled on through Galilee and Jesus taught them, saying: "Remember my words: the Son of Man will be delivered into the hands of men. They will kill him and he will be raised up on the third day."

The disciples did not fully understand the words, but they listened and did not ask the meaning.

True Greatness

Matthew 18, Mark 9, Luke 9

The disciples discussed among themselves who was the greatest in the kingdom of heaven. They asked Jesus and he answered: "If anyone would be first, he must be last and the servant of all."

Then he called a child to him, and he said: "Whoever receives a child in my name, receives me. Whoever receives me, receives Him who sent me. He who is least among you is the one who is the greatest.

"Whoever causes one child who believes in me to sin, it would be better if he had a millstone around his neck and were thrown into the sea to drown. It is necessary for temptation to come, but woe to the one who brings temptation.

"See that you do not wrong even one child; not one shall perish. If your hand causes you to sin, or your foot or your eye, cut it off and throw it away. It is better to enter the kingdom of God maimed than to go to hell whole."

Then John said: "On the way we saw a man casting out spirits, using your name. We forbade him to do this for he was not one of your followers."

Jesus said: "Do not forbid such a man. One who does a righteous act in my name will not be able to speak evil of me. Therefore, he who is not against us is for us.

"If your brother sins against you, go and tell him. It shall be between you and him alone. If he listens, you have gained. If he does not, take others with you as witnesses. If he still does not listen, tell it to the church. If he does not listen to the church, let him be as a pagan to you. Whatever you bind on earth shall be bound in heaven and whatever you loose on earth shall be so in heaven.

"If two of you on earth agree about anything, it shall be done by my Father in heaven. Where two or three are gathered together in my name, I will be there in the midst of them."

The Unmerciful Servant

Matthew 18

Peter came to Jesus and asked: "How often shall my brother sin against me, and I forgive him? Seven times?"

Jesus answered: "Not seven times, but seventy times seven.

"The kingdom of heaven may be compared to a king who wished to settle an account with one of his servants. The servant owed the king ten thousand pieces of money. Since he could not pay, the master ordered him and all that he had to be sold, including his wife and children.

"The servant fell on his knees and begged his master to have mercy on him and patience until the debt could be paid. The master had pity on the servant and agreed to free him and release him from the debt.

"Now that same servant met another servant who owed him a hundred coins. He seized the man by the throat and threatened him. The man begged for mercy and patience, saying he would surely repay the debt. But the servant had no pity and had the other thrown into prison.

"When the master heard what had happened, he called the servant to him and said: 'I forgave you your debt because you asked me. I had mercy on you. Should not you have mercy on another?'

"In his anger, the master had his servant thrown into prison to stay until the debt could be paid.

"So also," said Jesus, "will my heavenly Father do to anyone who does not forgive his brother from his heart."

Seventy More Disciples

Matthew 10, Luke 10

Jesus left Galilee and went into Judea, beyond the Jordan river. Great crowds continued to follow him everywhere, and he healed them and taught them along the way.

Then he appointed seventy other disciples to join the twelve. He sent them ahead of him, two by two, into villages and towns.

He said to them: "The harvest is plentiful but the workers are few. Pray to the Lord to send forth workers.

"You go out as lambs among wolves; carry no purse nor bag nor extra clothing. When you enter a house say: 'Peace unto this house.' Stay there, eat and drink what is offered, for a worker deserves payment.

"When you are well received, tell the people that the kingdom of God is near. If you are not well received, leave that place and shake its dust from your feet. You can be sure that the kingdom of God is near and that place shall have its reward.

"Beware of men: they will question you and bring you before councils to testify.

"Whoever receives you, receives me; whoever rejects you, rejects me. Whoever rejects me, rejects Him who sent me."

The Good Samaritan
Luke 10

A lawyer stood up and called out, to test Jesus: "Teacher, what should I do to have eternal life?"

Jesus answered: "What is written in the law?"

The lawyer said: "You shall love the Lord your God with all your heart and all your soul and all your might. And you shall love your neighbour as yourself."

Jesus said to him: "Your answer is right. Do these things and you will live."

But the lawyer asked: "Who is my neighbour?"

Jesus replied: "A man was going from Jerusalem to Jericho. Robbers took his clothes, beat him and left him for dead. A priest came down the road and saw him and passed him by. Then a Levite also came along and saw him lying there and did not stop.

"But a Samaritan came down the road and saw the man. He had compassion and went over to the man to help him. He put bandages on his wounds, placed him on his own animal and took him to an inn and looked after him.

"When it was time for him to leave, the Samaritan gave the innkeeper some money to take care of the man, adding: 'If you spend more, I will repay you when I return.'

"Now I ask you," said Jesus, "which was truly a neighbour to the man who was robbed?"

The lawyer answered: "The one who showed mercy and helped him."

Then Jesus said: "Go and do likewise."

The Rich Young Man
Matthew 19, Mark 10

A young man came to Jesus and asked: "What good deed shall I do to have eternal life?"

Jesus answered: "No one is good but God. You know the commandments; keep them."

The young man said, "I keep the commandments; what more must I do?"

Jesus answered: "If you wish to be perfect, sell all that you have and give it to the poor. Then come and follow me. Your treasure will be in heaven."

The young man heard this and went away sadly, for he had many possessions.

Then Jesus spoke to his disciples, saying: "It will be hard for a rich man to enter the kingdom of God. Indeed, it is easier for a camel to go through the eye of a needle than for a rich man to enter heaven."

The disciples asked: "Then who can enter heaven and be saved?"

Jesus answered: "With God, all things are possible. In the new world, when the Son of Man will sit on his throne, you who have followed me will also sit on thrones. You will sit on twelve thrones to judge the twelve tribes of Israel.

"Everyone who has given up his possessions or his family, whether houses or lands or father or mother or brothers or sisters or wife or children, all who have given these up for my sake and for the gospel shall have everlasting life. And many of the first shall be last and the last shall be first."

The Blessing of the Children
Matthew 19, Mark 10, Luke 18

People continued to come to Jesus to be healed and blessed and to ask him questions.

They brought their children to him so he

might touch them and pray. The disciples scolded the people for bringing even infants to Jesus.

But Jesus said: "Let the children come to me; do not stop them. For the kingdom of God belongs to such as they. Truly whoever does not receive the kingdom of God like a child shall not enter into it."

Then Jesus took the children and placed his hands upon them and blessed them.

Workers in the Vineyard
Matthew 20

Jesus continued speaking to his disciples, saying: "The kingdom of heaven is like the man who went out early in the morning to find workers for his vineyard. He set a price, and they agreed, that their wages would be one denarius a day. Then they went to work.

"Later in the day, the man saw others and hired them, too, saying: 'Work for me and I will give you whatever is just.'

"Every three hours he hired more men until at the eleventh hour he hired the last group.

"When evening came, all the workers were paid, beginning with the last up to the first.

"Every worker was paid the same: one denarius. Those who were hired first and worked longest expected more. They complained when the others were paid the same amount.

"The owner answered: 'I am doing no wrong. You agreed to work for one denarius, so take what belongs to you. I decided to give to the last the same as to the first. Do you think I should not be so generous?'

"The last shall be first and the first last."

The Lost Sheep and the Lost Coin
Luke 15

The Pharisees and scribes continued to accuse Jesus. They said: "This man receives sinners and eats with them."

Jesus told them a parable: "If a man has a hundred sheep and one goes astray, does he not leave the many to go after the one that has strayed? When he finds it, does he not rejoice more over finding the one that was lost than over the other ninety-nine?

"So it is that there is more joy in heaven over one sinner who repents than over ninety-nine who do not need to repent."

Then he said: "Likewise, if a woman has ten silver coins and loses one, she lights a lamp to look for the lost coin. She sweeps and searches for it until she finds it. Then she rejoices over finding the coin that was lost.

"So there is joy among the angels of God over one sinner who was lost and repents."

The Prodigal Son, the Forgiving Father
Luke 15

"There was a man who had two sons. The younger son asked his father for the share of property that would be his. So the father divided his wealth between the two sons.

"Soon afterwards the younger son took all that was his and journeyed to a distant country. There he spent all his money quickly and unwisely. A famine came to that land and the son had nothing to eat. He hired himself out to feed pigs and would have been happy to eat even the food of the pigs when he decided to go home again to work for his father. He thought that even his father's servants were better off than he.

" 'I am not worthy to be my father's son!' he thought, 'So I will ask him to treat me as a servant.'

"The son set out for home. His father saw him at a distance and ran to meet him and embrace him. But the son said: 'Father, I have sinned against you and against heaven; I am no longer worthy to be called your son.'

"The father ordered his servants to bring a fine robe, a ring and sandals and to kill the fattened calf so that they could celebrate his son's return. He had thought the son dead or lost, and now he was found.

"All was done as the father ordered. When the elder son returned from working in the fields, he heard music and laughter. He asked a servant what it meant. The servant told him all that had happened: that his brother had come home and his father had killed the fattened calf because the brother had returned home safely.

"The elder brother became angry and refused to go inside. His father came out to him and the son said: 'Father, I have served you all these years and never disobeyed you. Yet you never killed the fattened calf or had a celebration for me. But when my brother comes home, even though he wasted his inheritance, you do all this for him.'

"The father answered his elder son, saying: 'You are always with me and all that I have is yours. It is proper to be glad and celebrate your brother's return, for he was lost and now he is found.' "

Lazarus and the Rich Man
Luke 16

Jesus told another parable: "There was a rich man who had fine clothes and feasted well every day. At his gate sat a poor man whose name was Lazarus. He was covered with sores, a beggar who wished only for scraps from the rich man's table.

"The beggar died and the angels took him to sit at the side of Abraham. The rich man also died and was buried. He was taken to hell and looked up toward heaven. He could see Lazarus in the bosom of Abraham and he cried out for mercy, saying that he was being tormented by the heat and flames.

"Abraham answered: 'Remember, in your lifetime you received good things and Lazarus suffered. Now he is comforted and you are suffering. There is a great space between us. No one can pass from here to there or from there to here.'

"Then the rich man asked Abraham to send a messenger to his brothers to warn them, so the same thing would not happen to them. But Abraham said: 'They have Moses and the prophets; let them live according to the laws and sayings. If they do not want to listen, even one who rises from the dead could not persuade them.' "

The Ten Lepers
Luke 17

On the way to Jerusalem Jesus and his disciples travelled through Samaria and Galilee. As they entered a certain village, ten lepers called out: "Jesus, Master, please have mercy."

Jesus saw them and told them to go to the priests. They went and were cleansed.

One of them, a Samaritan, when he was healed, came back to Jesus and praised God in a loud voice. Then he fell before Jesus, giving thanks.

Jesus said: "Were not ten cleansed? Where are the other nine? Has only one, a Samaritan and a foreigner, given praise to God?"

He said to the man: "Go your way in peace; your faith has made you well."

On Prayer
Luke 18

Jesus told this parable to some who were

proud of their own righteousness and looked down on others: "Two men, a Pharisee and a tax collector, went to the Temple to pray.

"The Pharisee spoke to God saying: 'I am glad I am not like other men: unjust, unkind and doing evil. I am righteous, I fast and give a tenth of all that I have to charity.'

"Now the tax collector stood far off, not even raising his eyes to heaven and he said: 'God, be merciful to me, for I am a sinner before You.'

"The second man went home more justified than the other. Whoever exalts himself above others shall be humbled, and whoever humbles himself shall be exalted."

Foretelling the Future
Luke 18

When Jesus and his disciples were on the road to Jerusalem, he called the twelve apostles to him to tell them what would happen:

"The Son of Man will be delivered into the hands of the priests and scribes. He will be con-demned to death by them and given over to the Gentiles. They will treat him shamefully by mocking him and spitting on him and they will kill him. On the third day he will rise.

"The Son of Man did not come to be looked after and cared for, but to minister to others and to give his life for many."

Sight Restored to a Blind Man
Luke 18

As Jesus neared Jericho, a blind man heard the crowds coming and called out, asking who was there. They said: "It is Jesus of Nazareth."

The blind man called: "Son of David, have mercy on me."

Jesus stopped and ordered that the man be brought to him. He asked: "What do you want me to do for you?"

The man answered: "Lord, let my sight be restored."

Jesus said: "You will see again; your faith has made you well."

The man's sight was restored and he glorified

God. All the people who were there praised God.

Zaccheus the Tax Collector
Luke 19

Jesus entered Jericho. There the chief tax collector, a rich man named Zaccheus, tried to see Jesus. Zaccheus was a small man and could not see Jesus because of the crowd, so he climbed a sycamore tree.

When Jesus came to that place he looked up and, seeing Zaccheus, called to him, saying: "Come down, I will stay at your house."

When the people saw this, they said: "He is going to the house of a sinner to be a guest."

Zaccheus said to Jesus: "Lord, I give half of what I have to the poor. If I have treated a man falsely, I repay him fourfold."

Jesus said to him: "Today salvation has come to your house for you are a son of Abraham. The Son of Man has come to find and to save the lost."

Mary and Martha
Luke 10

It happened in the village of Bethany near Jerusalem that a woman named Martha received Jesus in her house. Her sister Mary was also there and sat at the feet of Jesus to listen to his words.

Now Martha was busy with household duties and with serving Jesus. And she said to him: "Tell my sister to help me. She lets me do all that must be done."

Jesus answered: "Martha, Martha, you are careful and worry about many things, but only one thing is necessary. Mary has chosen to do that and it shall not be taken away from her."

Lazarus Raised from the Dead
John 11

Jesus was on a trip beyond the Jordan when he received word that Lazarus, the brother of Mary and Martha, was very ill.

To his disciples Jesus said: "Our friend Lazarus must be awakened from his sleep. Let us go back into Judea."

The disciples asked: "Are you going there again? They are seeking to kill you. But if you go, we will go with you."

Thomas said to the others: "We will go, so we may die with him."

When Jesus arrived at Bethany, Lazarus had already died and been buried for four days. Many Jews from Jerusalem had come to comfort Mary and Martha and were still there.

Martha met Jesus on the way and said: "My brother would not have died if you had been here. I know that whatever you ask of God will be granted to you."

Jesus spoke: "Your brother will rise again."

Martha was puzzled and said: "I know that he will rise on the last day."

Jesus spoke again, saying: "I am the resurrection and the life. Whoever believes in me shall live even though he is dead. Whoever lives and believes in me shall never die. Do you believe this?"

Martha answered: "Yes, Lord, I believe that you are the son of God, the Christ who was promised to come into the world."

Then Martha hurried to her sister, saying quietly: "The Master has come."

Mary went quickly to meet Jesus on the road. When the Jews saw her go out they followed her, thinking that she was going to her brother's grave to weep.

When Jesus saw Mary weeping, he wept also.

All who were there saw how Jesus had loved Lazarus. But some said: "This man, who has cured lepers and opened the eyes of the blind, could he not have kept Lazarus from dying?"

Then Jesus went to the cave where Lazarus was buried, and there was a stone closing it. He said: "Take away this stone."

They said: "But he has been dead four days."

Jesus answered: "If you believe, you will see the glory of God."

The stone was taken away. Jesus raised his eyes to heaven and said: "Father, thank You for hearing me. I know You always hear, but I want the people to know that You have sent me."

Then with a loud voice, he called: "Lazarus, come out!"

The dead man came out. His hands and feet were bound with cloth and his face was wrapped. Jesus ordered the cloths taken off so that Lazarus could move easily.

Many of the people who had seen this believed in Jesus. But some went to the Pharisees to tell them what Jesus had done.

Meeting of the Priests and Pharisees
John 11

The chief priests and the Pharisees called a council, for they did not know what to do about Jesus.

They said: "This man performs many miracles. If he goes on like this, everyone will believe in him. Then the Romans will come and destroy us all."

Caiaphas, the high priest that year, spoke, saying: "It is better for one man to die for the people than for the whole nation to perish."

These words he spoke were a prophecy that Jesus would die for the nation; not only for the nation, but also to unite all the children of God that were scattered.

From that time on they continued to look for a way to put Jesus to death.

After this, Jesus could no longer walk openly in the streets and towns. Instead he went into Ephraim near the wilderness and stayed there with his disciples.

It was near the time of the Passover, when many people travelled to Jerusalem to purify themselves at the Temple and to make offerings. There was much guessing about whether Jesus would come to the Temple, for the priests and Pharisees had given orders that if anyone knew where Jesus was, he should tell them so they could arrest him.

Entry into Jerusalem
Matthew 21, Mark 11, Luke 19, John 12

Near Bethpage and Bethany on the way to

Jerusalem was a hill called the Mount of Olives. When Jesus reached this place, he sent two of his disciples into a nearby village, saying: "In the village you will find a colt tied up. It has never before carried a man. You must untie it and bring it to me. If anyone asks why, you must say: 'The Lord needs it.' "

The two disciples went to the village and found the colt just as Jesus had said. When they were asked why, they answered: "The Lord needs it."

They brought the colt to Jesus, placed some garments on its back and helped Jesus up onto it. As he rode along, many in the crowd placed clothes on the road in front of him. Others cut branches from nearby trees and put them on the road too.

At the foot of the Mount of Olives, all the followers of Jesus rejoiced and praised God with loud voices. They shouted: "Blessed is the one who comes in the name of the Lord. Peace in heaven. Glory to the highest."

And they said: "This is the prophet Jesus from Nazareth in Galilee."

When he came near Jerusalem, Jesus wept and said: "If only you knew what would bring peace, but it is hidden from you. The day will come when your enemies will surround you and hem you in. They will kill you and your children because you did not know when God visited you."

Driving out the Moneychangers

Matthew 21, Mark 11-12, Luke 20

Jesus entered Jerusalem and went directly to the Temple. He drove out all those who were doing business there, changing money and buying and selling. And he overturned the tables of the moneychangers, saying:

"It has been written: 'My house shall be a house of prayer for all people,' but you have made it a place for business and a den for thieves."

Every day Jesus taught in the Temple and the people listened. They brought their blind and lame and diseased to him and he healed them.

The priests and scribes and elders were displeased when they saw the children crying out, saying: "Glory to the son of David."

Jesus said: "Have you never read: 'Out of the mouths of babes comes perfect praise'?"

Then Jesus left them and went back to Bethany.

About Authority

Mark 11, Luke 20

One day, the priests and scribes and elders asked Jesus: "Who gave you authority to do all the things that you do?"

Jesus answered with a question, asking: "Was the baptism of John from heaven or from men?"

They discussed it among themselves, saying: "If we say from heaven, he will ask us why we did not believe John. If we answer from men, the people will stone us because they think John was a prophet."

They answered: "We do not know."

Then Jesus said: "Then I will not tell you where my authority comes from."

Parable of the Vineyard Workmen

Matthew 21, Mark 12, Luke 20

Jesus told the people a parable about authority:

"A man planted a vineyard and then left the country, renting his vineyard to tenants for a long time. At the harvest season, he sent a servant to the tenants to collect some fruit. The tenants beat the servant and sent him away. The man sent other servants, but the tenants beat them too and sent them away empty-handed.

"Then the man sent his son, for he thought the tenants would respect him. But when the tenants saw the son, they thought: 'This is the son who will inherit the land. If we kill him, we will have his inheritance.' So they killed the man's son."

Jesus asked: "When the owner of the vineyard comes, what will he do?"

The people answered: "He will come and kill the tenants and give the vineyard to others who will give him his share of the fruits."

Jesus said: "In the same way the kingdom of God will be taken away from you and will be given to those who will produce the fruits of it."

When the priests, Pharisees and scribes heard this, they knew that Jesus had spoken of them and had told the parable against them. They wanted to arrest him, but they were afraid because of all the people who believed in him.

Taxes to Caesar

Matthew 22, Mark 12, Luke 20

The Pharisees and scribes watched Jesus and sent spies to listen to him in order to trap him in what he said. Then they would deliver him into the power of the governor.

The spies questioned Jesus. They asked: "We know that you teach the truth and know the ways of God. Now tell us whether it is lawful to pay taxes to Caesar."

Jesus saw that they were trying to trap him. He said: "Hand me a coin. Whose name and whose picture is on the coin?"

They answered, saying: "Caesar's."

Then Jesus said: "Therefore, give to Caesar the things that are Caesar's and give to God the things that are God's."

They all marvelled at his words and went away.

The Questioning of Jesus

Matthew 22, Mark 12, Luke 20

The Sadducees, who did not believe in the idea of resurrection, came to Jesus and asked him a question: "Moses said that if a man dies

having no children, his brother must marry the widow so there will be children in that family. Now, there were seven brothers in one family. The first married and had no children. He died and the second married the widow and also had no children; then the third and fourth, down to the seventh. After them all, the woman died.

"In the resurrection, whose wife will she be, for she had seven husbands?"

Jesus answered: "You know neither the teaching of scripture nor the power of God. When the dead are raised, there is no marriage. All are like angels. In the book of Moses, what did God say to him about resurrection? He said: 'I am the God of Abraham, Isaac and Jacob.' So He is not a God of the dead but of the living."

When the crowd heard this, they marvelled at his teaching.

Then the Pharisees came to question Jesus to test him. A lawyer among them asked: "Which is the greatest commandment?"

Jesus answered: "The first great commandment is: 'You shall love the Lord your God with all your heart, with all your soul and with all your mind.' The second is: 'You shall love your neighbour as yourself.'

"All the laws and the teachings of all the prophets depend on these two commandments."

On False Religion

Matthew 23, Mark 12, Luke 20

Jesus spoke to his disciples and to all the crowds that had gathered: "Beware of the scribes. They know the laws of Moses, so do and practise all that they tell you to do. But do not do what they do, for they do not practise what they preach.

"They love places of honour, to be seen by the people, and to be called teacher and rabbi."

To the scribes and Pharisees he said: "You all have one teacher and one Father who is in heaven. And you have one master, the Christ. Woe to you, scribes and Pharisees. You are hypocrites! You close the kingdom of heaven against men. You are like tombs which have been whitewashed, appearing beautiful outside, but filled with uncleanness. You appear righteous, but you are filled with evil."

Then Jesus cried out: "O Jerusalem, Jerusalem: you kill prophets and turn away those who are sent to you. You will not see me again until you say: 'Blessed is the one who comes in the name of the Lord.'"

Predictions of the Future

Matthew 24, Mark 13, Luke 21

Jesus and his disciples left the Temple. As they were going out, Jesus spoke to them about the Temple.

He said: "The day will come when the stones of this building will come down, one upon the other. Then the Temple will be destroyed."

The disciples asked him when this would happen. And they asked what would be the signs of his coming and of the end of days. Jesus answered them, saying:

"Be careful. Many men will come and claim to be the Christ, and they will say that the end has come. They will deceive many people, but you must not be deceived and led astray by them.

"You will hear of wars, but do not be alarmed for these things must happen before the end. There will be suffering and famine and earthquakes; nations and kingdoms will rise up against one another. All these sorrows will come before the end comes.

"Understand these things: you will endure many hardships and be put to death. You will be hated and persecuted because of me.

"Many people will leave the way; they will hate one another, and love will grow cold. But those who endure it all, whose faith is strong, will be saved. False Christs and false prophets will arise, but remember: I have warned you of these things.

"This message must be preached throughout the world as a testimony to all the nations. Then the end will come."

The End of Days

Matthew 24, Mark 13, Luke 17, 21

Jesus spoke of the end of time, saying: "After the suffering and the troubles I have spoken about, the sun will be darkened, the moon will not shine and the stars will fall from the sky. Indeed, all the powers of the heavens will be shaken.

"Then the sign of the Son of Man will appear in the heavens and all the peoples of the earth will mourn. They will see the Son of Man coming on the clouds. He will come with great power and glory. And he will send his angels with a great sound of trumpets. They will gather together all the chosen ones from the ends of earth to the ends of heaven.

"Learn a lesson from the fig tree: when its branches become tender and its leaves begin to show, summer is near. So it will be with the end of days: when all these things happen as I have said, you will know the time is near.

"All these things must happen. Heaven and earth will pass away, but my words will not.

"No one, not even the angels in heaven, will know when the time will come. Only my Father knows. Watch and be prepared, for you will not know at what hour your Lord will come. Just as the man who was robbed: if he had known what time the thief would come, he would have watched and would not have been robbed.

"You must be ready, for you will not know when the Son of Man will come. Blessed is the man who does his duty and is ready when his master comes."

The Kingdom of Heaven

Matthew 25

Jesus continued speaking to his disciples, saying:

"The kingdom of heaven can be compared to ten bridesmaids who went out to meet the bridegroom. They took their lamps with them, but five were wise and five were foolish. The foolish ones took lamps, but no oil, with them. The wise took oil along with their lamps.

"The bridegroom was delayed and did not arrive until midnight. Then the ten bridesmaids went out hurriedly with their lamps. The foolish said: 'Give us some of your

oil.' The wise answered: 'Then there would not be enough for any of us; go and get some for yourselves.'

"So the bridegroom and those who were ready went to the wedding feast. When the others came, the door was shut.

"Therefore, I say: watch and be ready, for no one knows when the day or the hour will be.

"The kingdom of heaven will be like a man going on a journey who called his servants to trust them with his property: to one servant he gave five gold coins, called talents, to another he gave two gold coins, to the third he gave one. Each was given according to his ability.

"The man who received the five traded with them and made five more. The man who had two did the same thing and made two more. The man who received only one made a hole in the ground and buried it.

"After a time the master came to settle accounts with his servants. The man who had been given the five came to his master, bringing five more.

"The master said: 'Well done, good and faithful servant. You have been faithful over the little I gave you, now I will put you in charge of much. You have brought joy to your master.'

"The man who had been given two, brought the two and the two he had made. To him the master said the same thing: 'Well done, good and faithful servant. You have been faithful over a little, now I will put you over much. You have brought joy to your master.'

"The third man came forward with the one gold coin, saying: 'I know you are a hard man, reaping where you do not plant and harvesting where you do not work, so I hid your coin. Here, this is yours.'

"The master answered: 'You are a wicked and lazy man. You should have invested my money so I would have received it with interest. The coin shall be taken from you and given to the man who has ten.' "

Then Jesus said: "To everyone who has and uses what he has wisely, more will be given and he will have much. But from the man who has little and does not use it wisely, even what little he has shall be taken away. So the worthless servant shall be cast out into the darkness."

The Day of Judgement
Matthew 25, Luke 21

The disciples continued to listen to the words of Jesus:

"When the Son of Man comes, all the angels will be with him and he will sit on a glorious throne. All the nations will come before him

and he will separate them as a shepherd separates the sheep from the goats. He will place the sheep at his right hand and the goats at his left.

"He will say to the sheep at his right: 'Come, you are the blessed of my Father, inherit the kingdom which was prepared for you from the beginning of the world. I was hungry and you fed me, I was thirsty and you gave me drink, I was naked and you gave me clothes, I was a stranger and you welcomed me. I was sick and you came to me, I was in prison and you visited me.'

"The righteous will answer, saying: 'When did we do these things?'

"And the King will say: 'Just as you did it for any of my people, it was as if you did it to me.'

"Then he will turn to those at his left and send them away, saying: 'You shall enter into eternal fire for I was hungry and you gave me no food, I was thirsty and you gave me no drink, I was naked and you gave me no clothes, I was a stranger and you did not take me in, I was sick and in prison and you did not come to me.'

"They, too, will answer, asking: 'Lord, when did we do these things?'

"Again the Son of Man, the King, will answer: 'As you did not do for even the least of my people, it was as if you did not do for me.'

"Then the wicked shall go into eternal punishment and the righteous into eternal life."

Every day Jesus taught in the Temple, and at night he went back to the Mount of Olives. When he had finished speaking of all these things, it was nearly time for the Passover.

He said to his disciples: "You know that in two days is the Passover feast. Then the Son of Man will be crucified."

The Plot

Matthew 26, Mark 14, Luke 22

Two days before the Passover feast, the elders, the priests and scribes gathered together before the high priest. They discussed how they might arrest Jesus, perhaps by trickery, and have him killed. They wanted to put Lazarus to death also, for Jesus had raised Lazarus from the dead and many people believed in Jesus because of this.

They decided that it could not be done on the feast day when thousands of pilgrims would be in Jerusalem because many of the people believed in him and would cause an uproar.

Then one of the twelve disciples, Judas Iscariot, went before the chief priests and asked: "What will you give me if I bring Jesus to you?"

They made an agreement to pay him thirty pieces of silver. From that moment Judas watched for a chance to betray Jesus.

The Anointing

Matthew 26, Mark 14, John 12

When Jesus had been at Bethany six days before the Passover, a woman had come to him with a jar of very fine ointment. She had broken the jar and poured the ointment over his head.

Some thought the ointment was wasted and said: "This ointment could have been sold, for it was very fine. And the money could have been given to the poor."

Jesus said: "Leave her alone. She has done a beautiful thing to me. The poor will always be with you, but you will not always have me. She has prepared my body for burying. What she has done will be told wherever the gospel is preached."

The Last Supper

Matthew 26, Mark 14, Luke 22, John 13

On the first day of Passover, Jesus sent two of his disciples into the city to prepare the feast of the unleavened bread.

The two asked: "Where will we prepare it?"

He answered: "In the city you will meet a man carrying a pitcher of water. Follow him to his house. He will show you a large room already furnished. You will prepare it there."

They went into the city and found everything as Jesus had said, and they prepared the Passover meal.

When evening came, Jesus sat down with the twelve apostles. As they were eating, he took

the bread and blessed it, broke it into pieces and gave it to them, saying: "Take this and eat; this is my body. Do this in remembrance of me."

Then he took the cup and blessed it and said to them: "Drink of the cup, all of you; for this is my blood which is poured out for many for the forgiveness of sins."

After supper Jesus got up from the table and poured water into a basin. Kneeling down, he began to wash the feet of the apostles, wiping them with a towel.

He came to Simon Peter who asked: "Lord, why do you wash my feet?"

Jesus answered: "Afterwards you will understand, though you do not now."

Peter said: "You shall not wash my feet."

Jesus answered: "If I do not, you will have no part in me."

Peter said to him: "Then, not only my feet, but my hands and head also."

Jesus said: "One who has bathed does not need to wash except for his feet; you are clean, but not all of you."

He added: "Not all of you," for he knew one was to betray him.

After washing their feet, Jesus sat at his place once more and spoke, saying: "Do you know what I have done? You call me Lord and Master and you are right. If I, your Lord and Master, have washed your feet, you should wash each other's. I have given you an example so that you may do as I have done.

"A servant is not greater than his master, and the one who is sent is not greater than the one who sends him."

Then Jesus spoke to them of scripture, saying: "It has been written that he who eats bread with me will rise up against me. So I say to you that one of you will betray me."

The twelve looked at each other and one of them leaned toward Jesus and asked: "Lord, who is it?"

Jesus answered: "It is the one to whom I shall give a piece of bread."

Then he dipped a piece of bread into a bowl and gave it to Judas Iscariot.

When Judas took the bread, Satan entered into him.

Jesus said: "Do what you must do; do it quickly."

Judas left immediately and went out into the night.

No one knew why. Judas had the purse, so they thought he was going to buy things for the festival or to give something to the poor.

A New Commandment
John 13-14

When Judas had left the Passover feast, Jesus said: "I will be with you for only a little while longer. You will seek me, but where I am going, you cannot come. But you will come later.

"I now give you a new commandment: love one another. As I have loved you, so you should love each other. From this, all will know that you are my disciples.

"Do not let your hearts be troubled. Believe in God and believe in me also. In my Father's house are many rooms and I go to prepare a place for you. Then I will come again and take you where I am going."

Thomas asked: "We do not know where you are going. How can we know the way?"

Jesus answered: "I am the way, the truth and the life. The way to the Father is through me. If you have known me, you have known my Father also."

Philip said: "Show us the Father."

Jesus answered: "He who has seen me has also seen the Father. Do you not believe that I am in the Father and the Father is in me? What I say to you I say not on my own authority but from the Father. Whoever believes in me will do as I do. Whatever you ask in my name, I will do."

The Holy Spirit
John 14-17

Jesus continued speaking to the disciples of many things, saying:

"If you love me, you will keep my commandments. Whoever loves me will be loved by my Father. And I will love him and show myself to him.

"Greater love has no man than this: that he give his life for his friends. You are my friends if you do what I command. I will call you servants no longer but friends, for all that my Father has said to me I have told you."

Jesus asked: "Will you lay down your life for me? When you went out without purses or shoes or weapons, you lacked nothing. But now let him who has no sword sell his robe to buy one. For the Scriptures must be fulfilled; everything concerning me has a purpose."

They said: "We have two swords."

And he answered: "That is enough."

Jesus spoke to them further, saying: "Although I leave you, I do not leave you alone. When the world sees me no more, another will be with you forever: the Spirit of truth. The Holy Spirit will teach you all things and remind you of all that I have taught. He will teach about sin and righteousness and judgement.

"In a little while you will see me no more. Then in another little while you will see me again."

They did not understand, so Jesus explained: "You will weep and mourn, and the world will rejoice; then your sorrow will turn to joy. I came from the Father and I am going to the Father. If you ask anything of Him, He will give it to you in my name. Ask and you will receive.

"The hour has come when I will be left alone. But I will not be alone, for the Father will be with me. I say this to you so you will have peace. There are many troubles in the world, but be of good cheer, for I have overcome the world."

Then he lifted his eyes to heaven, saying: "Father, the hour has come. Glorify Your son so that the son may glorify You. This shall be eternal life: that they know You as the only true God and Jesus Christ whom You have sent.

"I have given Your word to the world, and now I pray to You for all those who believe in me."

The Garden of Gethsemane
Matthew 26, Mark 14, Luke 22, John 18

When Jesus had spoken to the disciples of love and the Holy Spirit, they sang a hymn and went out of the city to the Mount of Olives.

There Jesus said to them: "Tonight you will leave me. But after I have risen I will go before you to Galilee."

Peter said: "Even if all the others leave you, I will never desert you."

Jesus answered: "You say that, but tonight before the cock crows in the morning, you will deny me three times."

Peter said: "Even if I must die with you, I will never deny you." And the others agreed.

Then they crossed a brook into a garden called Gethsemane, where Jesus said to the disciples: "Stay here while I go to pray."

He took Peter, James and John with him, saying: "I am sorrowful, and troubled. Stay here and watch with me."

Walking a little further, he fell to his knees and prayed: "My Father, if it is possible, let my cup pass from me. Nevertheless, let Your will be done."

It was evening, and when he went back to the disciples, they were asleep. To Peter he said: "Could you not watch with me even an hour?

Watch now, and pray that you will not fall into temptation. Indeed the spirit is willing, but the flesh is weak."

For a second time Jesus went away and prayed: "Father, if the cup of suffering cannot be passed on unless I drink it, let Your will be done."

Again he returned to the three disciples and found them asleep.

Then for the third time he left them and prayed the same words.

When he returned the third time he found them still asleep, and he said: "Are you still sleeping? The time has come, the hour is here, when the Son of Man is betrayed.

"Get up, he that betrays me is here."

The Betrayal
Matthew 26, Mark 14, Luke 22, John 18

While Jesus was still speaking, Judas came with a great crowd carrying swords and clubs.

Judas gave them a sign, saying: "The one I kiss is the man you must seize."

Then he went to Jesus, greeted him and kissed him. Those who were with Judas seized Jesus.

Simon Peter drew his sword and struck the servant of the high priest, cutting off his ear.

Jesus said: "Put away your sword. Those who use the sword will die by the sword. Do you not believe that I could pray to my Father to send help? But then the prophecies of scripture would not come true."

Saying this, he touched the man's ear and he was healed.

Then Jesus spoke to the crowd: "You have come out with swords and clubs, as you would to catch a thief or a robber. I sat with you in the Temple and you did not seize me there."

Those who had seized Jesus took him to the house of Caiaphas, the high priest, where the elders and scribes had gathered.

All the disciples fled, except Peter who followed at a distance. He sat inside the courtyard with the guards.

The chief priests and elders called witnesses to testify against Jesus. Although many came and testified falsely, the Council found nothing against Jesus that could cause his death.

Finally two false witnesses accused him, say-

ing: "This man said he would destroy the Temple of God and then rebuild it in three days."

The high priest asked Jesus: "Have you no answer for what these men say?"

Jesus remained silent.

Then the high priest said: "Now I ask you to tell us whether you are the Christ, the Son of God."

Jesus answered: "You have said so. In the days to come, the Son of Man will be at the right hand of power, coming on the clouds of heaven."

The high priest had his answer. He declared: "This man has spoken blasphemy. We need no more witnesses. You have heard him. What is your judgement?"

They answered: "He deserves to die."

Then they spat in his face and struck him and mocked him.

Peter's Denial

Matthew 26, Mark 14, Luke 22, John 18

As Peter was sitting in the courtyard, a maidservant came out and asked him: "Are you one of the followers of Jesus?"

He answered: "I am not."

It was night and getting cold. The officers made a fire to warm themselves and Peter stood with them. One of the men asked: "Are you not a disciple of Jesus?"

Peter denied it, saying: "I do not know the man."

Then a servant of the high priest came to Peter and asked: "Were you not in the garden with Jesus of Nazareth?"

Again Peter denied knowing Jesus and said: "I do not know what you are talking about."

Immediately the cock crowed. Then Peter remembered the words of Jesus: "Before the cock crows, you will deny me three times."

And he went out and wept bitterly.

The Death of Judas

Matthew 27

When Judas saw that Jesus had been con-demned, he regretted what he had done. He took the thirty pieces of silver back to the priests and elders, saying: "I have sinned. I have caused the innocent to be condemned."

They answered: "That is your affair. It has nothing to do with us."

Judas threw the money on the floor of the Temple. Then he went out and hanged himself.

The priests took the money, saying: "We cannot put this in the treasury; it is blood money."

After discussing it among themselves, they decided to use it to buy a potter's field to bury strangers in. To this day that place has been called the Field of Blood.

Jesus and Pontius Pilate

Matthew 26, Mark 15, Luke 23, John 18

In the morning the chief priests and elders and scribes bound Jesus and led him to the Roman governor, Pontius Pilate, saying: "This man is causing trouble in the land. He says he is Christ, the King."

Pilate asked Jesus: "Are you the King of the Jews?"

Jesus answered: "You have said so. Do you ask this for yourself or because others have said it?"

Pilate spoke, saying: "Your own people have brought you to me and accuse you."

Jesus answered: "You say I am a king, but my kingdom is not of this world. I came into the world to speak and show the truth. Everyone who believes in truth believes in me and listens to me."

The priests urged the governor again, saying: "Jesus has been stirring up the people and preaching throughout the land so that they follow him and listen to him."

Pilate asked: "Why did you not judge him according to your own law?"

The priests answered: "Because it is against the law for us to judge against a man or put a man to death."

Pilate said: "I find no fault with this man."

But the priests insisted, saying: "This Galilean stirs up the people, teaching and preaching throughout Judea."

When Pilate learned that Jesus was from Galilee, he sent him to Herod, ruler of Galilee. Herod was in Jerusalem and was glad to see Jesus, for he had heard much about him and hoped to see him perform some sign or miracle.

Herod questioned Jesus, but Jesus made no answer. The priests and scribes still accused him and Herod and his soldiers mocked him. Then they dressed him in fine clothes and sent him back to Pilate.

Again Pilate spoke to the priests and scribes, saying: "It is the custom at this time of the year for the governor to release one prisoner whom the crowd will name. Shall I release Jesus to you?"

They answered: "Not Jesus, but Barabbas." Barabbas was a murderer and a thief, and the governor did not understand.

So he asked again, and the crowd answered: "Release Barabbas."

"What shall be done with Jesus?" asked Pilate.

They answered: "Nail him to a cross! Let him be crucified!"

Then Pilate took a basin of water and washed his hands in it, saying: "I wash my hands of this man's blood. I am innocent of causing his death."

Before the crowd Pilate sentenced Jesus to be crucified and released Barabbas.

The Crucifixion

Matthew 27, Mark 15, Luke 23, John 19

The soldiers of the governor took Jesus away. They braided a crown of thorns and placed it on his head, pushing it down. They put a reed in his hand and then mocked him by kneeling before him and saying: "Hail, bow down to him, for he is King of the Jews!"

They spat on him and struck him. They took the reed from him and struck him with that also. Then they led him away to Golgotha, called the Place of the Skull, to be crucified.

On the way they seized a man coming in from the country, Simon of Cyrene. They gave him the heavy wooden cross to carry, and he walked behind Jesus.

Following them was a great multitude of people, among them women who wept and lamented. Jesus turned to them and said: "Daughters of Jerusalem, do not weep for me, but for yourselves and your children. The days will come when you will wish the mountains to fall on you and the hills to cover you. If they do this thing, what will they not do?"

Two others were led away also, criminals to be put to death.

When they reached Golgotha, they crucified Jesus there, and the criminals also: one to the right of Jesus and one to his left.

Jesus said: "Father, forgive them for they know not what they do."

After they had crucified him, the soldiers took his garments from him, tore them into pieces and divided the pieces among themselves. They took his robe also, and they said: "It has no seams. Let us draw lots for it and not tear it. Whoever wins shall have the robe to keep."

Then the soldiers sat down to keep watch over him. Above his head was a sign which said: "King of the Jews."

Near the cross of Jesus was Mary, his mother. Among others who had followed him there were Mary Magdalene, Mary the wife of Cleophas and Mary the mother of James and John the fishermen.

Jesus, seeing his mother there, called to her: "Woman, behold your son!" And to the disciple he said: "Behold your mother!" Then the disciple took her to his own home.

Many people stayed to mock Jesus on the cross, shouting at him and calling:

"If you are truly the Son of God, come down from there. You saved others, can you not save yourself? If you are the King of the Jews, come down and we will believe you. You trusted God; where is He now?"

One of the criminals crucified with him mocked him in the same way, saying: "If you are the Christ, save yourself and save us."

Then the other one said: "We are here justly, but you are innocent. Lord, remember me when you enter the kingdom of God."

Jesus answered: "You shall be with me in heaven."

From noon until three in the afternoon the land was covered with darkness.

Then Jesus called with a loud voice: "My God, my God, why have You forsaken me?"

The Death and Burial of Jesus

Matthew 27, Mark 15, Luke 23, John 19

There was darkness over the land, the earth shook, rocks split, graves opened, and the veil of the Temple was torn in half.

With a loud cry, Jesus said: "Father, I commit my spirit into Your hands." Then he breathed his last. He bowed his head and gave up the ghost.

When the Roman guard saw and heard this, he praised God, saying: "Surely this man was innocent."

All the people who had been watching there beat their breasts and went away. Those who knew him and had followed him stood at a distance and witnessed the death of Jesus.

The next day was the sabbath, so the people asked Pilate to remove the bodies for burial before the sabbath.

When the soldiers came to take down the body of Jesus, one of them pierced his side with a spear, causing blood and water to pour forth.

After this, a rich man and a disciple of Jesus, Joseph of Arimathea, secretly asked Pilate for the body of Jesus to bury it. Pilate gave his permission. Then Joseph wrapped it in clean linen and placed it in his own tomb. He rolled a great stone to the door of the tomb and returned home.

Mary, the mother of Jesus, and Mary Magdalene followed Joseph. They saw the tomb and how Jesus was laid in it. They stayed for a while and then, because it was the eve of the sabbath, they also went home. On the sabbath they rested.

The next day the chief priests and the Pharisees went to Pilate, saying: "We remember what Jesus said before he died, that after three days he would rise again. Therefore, place guards at the tomb, or his disciples will come to take the body away and tell the people that he has risen. That would be the greatest deception of all."

Pilate agreed and sent his soldiers to seal the tomb and watch over it.

The Resurrection
Matthew 28, Mark 16, Luke 24, John 20

After the sabbath Mary Magdalene and the other Mary came to sit by the tomb of Jesus.

Early in the morning on the first day of the week an angel of the Lord appeared and rolled the stone away from the front of the tomb.

When the guards saw the angel dressed in clothes as white as snow, they trembled with fear and fainted.

The angel spoke to the women, saying: "Do not be afraid. Jesus is no longer here; he has risen. Go quickly and tell his disciples that he has gone to Galilee. You will see him there."

They ran from the tomb, nearly overcome with fear and joy. On their way to tell the disciples, Jesus appeared to them. They bowed down and worshipped him, and he said: "Tell my brothers to go to Galilee, they shall see me there."

Jesus Appears
Luke 24, John 20

That same day two of the disciples went to the village of Emmaus, about seven miles from Jerusalem. While they were discussing all the events of the last few days, Jesus joined them. They did not know who he was.

Jesus asked: "What are you speaking of that makes you so sad?"

One of them, named Cleophas, was surprised, saying: "Have you just arrived? Have you not heard all that has happened these past few days?"

Jesus asked: "What things?"

They answered: "About Jesus of Nazareth, a mighty prophet of God who was condemned to death and crucified. We hoped he would rule Israel.

Today is the third day since the crucifixion and we have heard from women that they went to the tomb and found it empty. They had a

vision: an angel saying that Jesus is alive. Some of our men went to the tomb and found it just as the women said.

Then Jesus spoke to them, saying: "Men are foolish and slow to believe what the prophets have said. Was it not written that the Christ would suffer all these things?"

As they walked together, Jesus explained to them all the scriptures that had been written concerning him.

The three men came near the village of Emmaus and went in together to eat. When they sat down, Jesus took the bread and blessed it, broke it and gave it to the others. At once their eyes were opened and they knew him. Then he disappeared.

They returned to Jerusalem immediately to join the rest of the apostles.

"Truly the Lord has risen," they said. "He has appeared to Simon." Then they told all that had happened.

As they were speaking, Jesus himself appeared among them and said: "Peace be with you."

The disciples were terrified and thought they had seen a spirit. But Jesus showed them his hands and feet. And he said: "Touch me. A spirit does not have flesh and bones as I have."

They still did not believe, but they rejoiced and wondered.

He asked: "Have you any food?"

They gave him some fish and he ate it before them.

Then he spoke to them and said: "I told you when I was still with you that everything must be done as it is written in the Books of Moses, in the Prophets and in the Psalms. It is written that it was necessary for Christ to suffer and rise from the dead on the third day.

Repentance and forgiveness of sins should be preached in the name of Christ among all the nations. You are witnesses of all these things."

Doubting Thomas
John 20

Now Thomas, one of the apostles, had not been with them when Jesus first appeared. And he doubted that Jesus was truly alive, saying: "Unless I see his hands and feet and touch the places where the nails were, I cannot believe."

Eight days later the disciples were all together, Thomas with them. The door was shut but Jesus came among them, saying: "Peace be with you."

To Thomas he said: "Put your finger on my hands, touch my side. Have faith and believe."

Thomas answered, saying: "My Lord and my God."

Jesus said to him: "You have believed because you see me. Blessed are those who believe, though they had not seen."

At the Sea of Tiberius
John 21

Another time Jesus appeared to his disciples at the Sea of Tiberius. Simon Peter, Thomas, Nathaniel of Cana, the sons of Zebedee (James and John) and two others were together.

They got into a boat to go fishing. They fished all night and caught nothing.

At dawn, Jesus came to the shore, but they did not know it was Jesus. He called to them: "Children, have you any fish?"

They answered that they had none.

He said: "Cast your net on the right side of the boat."

They did and the net became so full and heavy with fish that they could not pull it in.

John said to Peter: "It is the Lord!"

Hearing this, Simon Peter, who had taken off his shirt, put it on and jumped into the water. The others came to shore in the boat dragging the net filled with fish.

When they landed, they saw a fire there, with fish on it and bread.

Jesus said: "Bring some of your fish." Simon Peter brought the net full of fish, one hundred fifty-three altogether.

Jesus said: "Come and eat." None asked who he was; they knew he was the Lord. He gave them bread and fish and they ate.

This was the third time that Jesus was revealed to them after he had risen.

After they had finished breakfast, Jesus said to Simon Peter: "Simon, do you love me?"

He answered: "Yes, Lord, you know that I do."

Then Jesus said: "Feed my lambs."

Again Jesus asked: "Simon, do you love me?"

Again he answered: "Yes, Lord, you know that I love you."

Jesus said: "Tend my sheep."

A third time Jesus asked: "Simon, do you love me?"

Peter was worried when he was asked the same question again. He answered: "Lord, you who know everything, know that I love you."

Jesus said: Feed my sheep. Surely, when you were young you girded yourself and walked about wherever you wanted. But when you are old, another will bind you and take you even where you do not want to go."

In saying this, Jesus foretold the way in which Peter would give his life.

Then he said: "Follow me."

The Ascension

Matthew 28, Mark 16, Luke 24, Acts 1

Jesus spoke to his disciples for forty days about the kingdom of God.

He told them many things. He said: "John baptized with water; before long, you will be baptized with the Holy Spirit. Then you will have power. All authority on heaven and earth will be given to you. You will be my witnesses in Jerusalem and in Judea and Samaria and throughout all the earth.

"Go to all the nations, making disciples of

them and baptizing them in the name of the Father and the Son and the Holy Spirit. Teach them all that I have commanded you, for I am with you forever until the end of days."

Then Jesus led his disciples to Bethany, lifted up his hands and blessed them. While giving his blessing, he was taken up and a cloud took him from their sight.

As they watched him disappear, two men in white robes appeared, asking: "Why are you gazing into heaven? Jesus, who was taken from you into heaven, will come again in the same way that you saw him go."

The disciples returned joyfully to Jerusalem and went into the Temple praising and blessing the name of God.

The Acts of the Apostles

The second book written by Luke. It tells of the spread of the Christian message from Jerusalem to Rome. The first part is about the apostle Peter, the second about Paul.

The Holy Spirit
Acts 1-2

After the apostles had seen the ascension of Jesus into heaven, they returned to Jerusalem. Staying together in one place, they prayed together for several days.

There were twelve apostles now, for Matthias had been chosen to take the place of the traitor Judas. Fifty days after the Passover, on the feast of the first harvest, also called Pentecost, the twelve were praying.

Suddenly there was the sound of a rushing wind in the house. Tongues of flame appeared, a single flame resting on each of the apostles. Then they were filled with the Holy Spirit and began to speak in different languages.

At that time Jews from every land were in Jerusalem. When they heard that the apostles were speaking all the languages on earth, they came together in a great crowd to listen. Each one heard his own language being spoken. They were astonished and wondered how these

men from Galilee could know so many different tongues.

Some marvelled and others mocked, saying: "They must have had too much new wine."

Then Peter spoke to the crowd and said: "These men are not drunk. It is too early in the day for that. They are carrying out the word of the prophet Joel who said: 'It shall come to pass that My Spirit will be upon all men. And whoever calls on the name of the Lord shall be heard and shall be saved.'

"Men of Israel, know that Jesus is the Christ, the Son of God. Therefore, repent and be baptized. Then you will receive the gift of the Holy Spirit."

All those that gladly received the words of Peter were baptized that day, altogether about three thousand people. They followed the teachings of the apostles, sharing fellowship, breaking bread and praying together.

Many wonders were done by the apostles. They stayed together and owned things together. They sold their belongings and divided the money among the people according to their need. Day after day they attended the Temple and ate together, praising God.

Every day more people were baptized and the number of believers continued to grow.

Healing the Lame Beggar
Acts 3

One day as Peter and John were going into the Temple to pray, they passed a man who had been lame from birth. He sat at the door begging from those who entered.

Peter saw the man and said to him: "Look at us."

204

The man looked, expecting them to give him something. But Peter said: "I have no silver or gold, but I will give you what I have. Therefore, in the name of Jesus Christ of Nazareth, rise up now and walk."

Having spoken, Peter reached out, took the man's right hand and helped him up. At once the man's feet and ankles became strong and he stood up. Walking and leaping joyfully, he entered the Temple praising God.

All who had seen the man healed were astonished and filled with wonder.

Peter, seeing their amazement, asked: "Why do you marvel? Why are you surprised that this man has been made to walk? As if it were through our power!

"The faith that comes through Jesus has made him able to walk. The God of our fathers, the God of Abraham, Isaac and Jacob, is glorifying His son Jesus whom you denied to Pontius Pilate and allowed to be crucified. God sent Jesus to bless you in turning away from your wickedness."

The Arrest of the Apostles
Acts 4-5

Peter and John continued speaking to the people, teaching the gospel and the resurrection of Jesus from the dead. Many who heard them believed. The number grew to about five thousand.

The priests and the Sadducees had Peter and John arrested because of their teaching, for the Sadducees had never believed in the coming of a Messiah or in resurrection.

The next day the scribes and elders, the high

priest and all those of the priestly family met together to decide what to do about Peter and John. They charged the two to stop their teaching and preaching in the name of Jesus.

Peter and John answered that they must continue to speak out about what they had seen and heard. They said: "Whether it is right to listen to you rather than to God, you will have to judge; but we must speak."

Then they let Peter and John go. They could not punish them because of all the people who believed.

Peter and John returned to the others and they all worked great wonders among the people, curing the sick and encouraging the rich to give so the poor could be helped.

Many people from towns outside Jerusalem brought their sick, those troubled with evil spirits and those in need. All these, too, were healed. Each day more people came to the apostles and became believers.

Once again the high priest and the Sadducees arrested the apostles and put them in the common prison.

Escape from Prison

Acts 5

At night while the apostles were in prison, an angel of the Lord opened the doors so that they could leave. The angel said: "Go into the Temple and speak to the people."

In the morning the high priest called the Council together and ordered the prisoners to be brought.

When the officers went to the prison and found the apostles gone, they hurried back to tell the high priest. Just then, someone ran in to the Council, saying that the apostles were in the Temple teaching the people.

The officers went to the Temple and brought the apostles back without violence, because they were afraid of the people. Then the high priest questioned the apostles.

Peter answered: "We must obey God rather than men. God raised Jesus to give repentance to Israel and to give forgiveness of sins. We are witnesses to these things and we must speak."

The members of the Council were angry, but one of the Pharisees, Gamaliel, warned them to leave the men alone, saying: "If their plan is of men, it will fail. If it is of God, we will never be able to overcome them. Let them go."

The Council took his advice; they charged the apostles not to speak in the name of Jesus and dismissed them.

Stephen, the First Martyr

Acts 6-8

The apostles continued to teach and preach in Jerusalem. They chose seven men to help them with their duties. Among these was Stephen, a man who had great faith and wisdom, a man full of the Holy Spirit who travelled among the people, performing miracles.

Some men of the synagogue for freed men disputed with Stephen, but with no success. Then they secretly got some others to say that he was speaking out against God and Moses.

When the elders and scribes heard this, they ordered him to appear before the Council. There, false witnesses said: "This man has been speaking out against the law and the synagogue. He says that Jesus of Nazareth will change the customs of Moses."

The high priest asked: "Are these things true?"

Stephen answered: "You are stubborn people, always resisting the Holy Spirit. Your fathers persecuted the prophets. And they killed those who announced the coming of Jesus, whom you betrayed and murdered. You received the laws, but you have not kept them."

The men of the Council were greatly angered when they heard Stephen speak.

All who looked at him saw that his face was like that of an angel. He was full of the Holy Spirit and gazed into heaven, saying: "I see the glory of God and I see Jesus at His right hand."

Members of the Council cried out against him and refused to listen. They rushed toward him, cast him out of the city and stoned him.

As Stephen was being stoned, he prayed: "Lord Jesus, receive my spirit." Then he kneeled and called in a loud voice: "Lord, do not hold this sin against them." There he died and the believers buried him and mourned.

A young man named Saul was among those who agreed to Stephen's death. In fact, he crusaded against the Christian cause, searching for believers and having them committed to prison.

The Conversion of Saul
Acts 9

Saul was a rabbi and teacher of the law. He had come to Jerusalem from Tarsus where he was born a Jew and a Roman citizen. He had

never believed in Jesus and was continually threatening and persecuting the disciples.

Saul asked the Council for authority to go to Damascus to seek out men and women who followed the way of Jesus, and to have them bound and brought to Jerusalem.

On the road to Damascus suddenly a light from heaven flashed around him. He fell to the ground and heard a voice saying: "Saul, why do you persecute me?"

Saul asked: "Who are you, Lord?"

The answer came: "I am Jesus, the one you continue to persecute. Now, go into the city and you will be told what you must do."

Saul got up, but he could not see. The men who were travelling with him led him into Damascus. For three days he neither ate nor drank and still could not see.

In Damascus there was a disciple named Ananias. The Lord came to him in a vision, saying: "Go to the street called Straight, to the house of Judas. Ask for Saul of Tarsus. He is praying there and he has seen you in a vision, coming to him and touching him to restore his sight."

Ananias answered the Lord, saying: "I have heard of this man and how much evil he has done, persecuting your followers. In fact, he has come here to arrest all who call on the name of Jesus."

But the Lord said: "I have chosen him to go to the Gentiles and kings and the children of Israel to spread the gospel. I will show him how he must suffer for the sake of my name."

Ananias went to the house. Placing his hands on Saul, he said: "Brother Saul, the Lord Jesus who appeared to you on the road has sent me here so you may regain your sight and be filled with the Holy Spirit."

Immediately Saul could see, as if scales had been removed from his eyes. Then he was baptized. And he ate and became strong.

For several days Saul stayed in Damascus, preaching in the synagogues, saying: "Jesus is the Son of God."

Those who heard him were amazed and wondered: "Is this the man who destroyed believers of Christ in Jerusalem?"

Saul increased in strength, preaching that Jesus was the Christ. And he continued to confuse and astonish the Jews of Damascus.

After a time, they plotted to kill him. He learned of their plan, so his disciples took him out of the city at night, letting him down over the wall in a basket.

When Saul arrived in Jerusalem, he joined the disciples there, preaching in the name of the Lord. When his life was again threatened, he went to Caesarea and then to Tarsus.

Soon after his conversion, Saul became known as Paul, his Roman name.

By now, the church was being built up in peace in Galilee, Judea and Samaria.

Peter and the Centurion
Acts 10

In Caesarea there was a man named Cornelius, a man of the Roman army, a centurion. He was a religious man, fearing God, praying constantly and giving generously to charity.

An angel came to him in a vision, saying: "Your prayers and good deeds have come before God as a memorial. Now, send to Joppa to bring back Simon who is called Peter. He is with Simon the tanner at the seashore."

The angel left. Then Cornelius sent two of his servants and a devout soldier to Joppa, after telling them what the angel had said.

As the men neared Joppa, Simon Peter went up the the housetop to pray.

It was mealtime and he was hungry. He went into a trance. He saw the heavens open and a great sheet came down; in it were all kinds of animals and birds and reptiles. A voice said: "Eat, Peter. Kill and eat."

Peter answered: "No, for I have never eaten anything unclean or forbidden."

The voice said: "What God has cleansed, you must not call unclean."

This happened three times; then the thing was taken into heaven.

While Peter was trying to understand the vision, the men sent by Cornelius arrived at the house.

The Spirit came to Peter and said: "Three men I have sent are looking for you. You must go with them."

So Peter went to meet the men and asked why they had come. They answered, saying: "Cornelius the centurion was told by an angel to send for you. He is a just man who fears God and he is well thought of by the whole Jewish nation. You must come to his house so he can hear what you have to say."

Peter invited the three to be his guests that night. The next day, they set out together and some of the brethren from Joppa went with them. They journeyed a whole day, stopping for the night.

The following day they arrived in Caesarea. Cornelius had gathered together his family and close friends.

When Peter entered, Cornelius bowed down at his feet and worshipped him. But Peter lifted him up, saying: "I too am a man. Stand up."

They went in where all the others were gathered and Peter spoke to them: "You know it is unlawful for a Jew to associate with those of other nations. But God has come to me and said that I should not call any man unclean. So I have come to you. Why have you sent for me?"

Then Cornelius told Peter about his vision and said: "We are here in the sight of God to hear all that the Lord has commanded you."

Peter began to speak, saying: "I can see that God accepts all people, that anyone who fears Him and does what is right is acceptable to Him."

Then he told them about Jesus and the Holy Spirit. While Peter was speaking, the Holy Spirit came to those who heard him. The believers were amazed that the gift of the Holy Spirit should be given even to the Gentiles.

Then Peter asked: "Can water be denied them? They must be baptized, they who have received the Holy Spirit." Then he commanded them to be baptized in the name of Jesus.

The Arrest of Peter

Acts 11-12

The apostles continued to travel and to preach about the Lord Jesus. They travelled to Phoenicea and Cyprus and Antioch, speaking to the Jews and to the Greeks. Many became believers.

In Antioch, the disciples were called Christians for the first time.

King Herod heard and saw the growth of the church and the number of believers. He had John, the brother of James, killed; and he had Peter arrested during the season of unleavened bread.

Peter was sent to prison to be guarded by four groups of soldiers until after the Passover,

when Herod expected to release him. The church continually prayed to God for him.

The very night that he was to be set free, Peter, in chains, was sleeping between two soldiers. And there were sentries guarding the doors of the prison.

Suddenly a light shone in the prison and an angel of the Lord appeared, touching Peter and waking him. The angel spoke to him, saying: "Get up quickly." The chains fell from Peter's hands.

Then the angel said: "Get dressed, put on your sandals; wrap your mantle around you and follow me."

Peter did all this, but he did not know whether it was real or a vision.

They passed the first and second prison guards and came to the gate of the city. It opened before them and they passed through. On the first street the angel left him.

Peter knew then that the Lord had sent the angel to rescue him from Herod.

He went to the house of Mary, the mother of Mark who had been called John. There many people were gathered together praying. When they saw him, they were amazed and questioned him. But he silenced them and told them how the Lord had brought him out of prison.

"Go and tell all this to the brethren," he said. Then he left them, going to another place.

When morning came, there was much confusion at the prison over what had happened to Peter. Herod questioned the guards and had them put to death.

Paul's First Missionary Journey

Acts 13

At Antioch in Syria prophets and teachers of the church had gathered together, worshipping the Lord and spreading the word of Jesus. There the Holy Spirit came to them, saying: "I have called Barnabas and Paul, who was called Saul, to be set apart from the rest to do the work that I have for them."

After praying and fasting, Barnabas and Paul, taking John Mark with them, went to Salamis and Paphos on Cyprus. There they preached and spread the gospel. Then they came back to the mainland to Perga and Antioch in Pisidia, and John Mark returned to Jerusalem.

At Antioch Paul and Barnabas went into the synagogue on the sabbath. After the reading of the law and the prophets, they were asked if they had anything to preach.

Then Paul stood up and spoke about the history of Israel, saying that the prophecies of the Old Testament had come true through Jesus.

"Men of Israel," said Paul, "the God of Israel chose our fathers and made them great when they lived as strangers in Egypt. He delivered them from slavery and looked after them for forty years in the wilderness. He overcame seven nations in Canaan to give them the land He had promised.

"He sent them judges for about four hundred fifty years, until Samuel the prophet. And He sent other prophets to teach them.

"The people wanted a king, so He gave them Saul and David and Solomon. And from the house of David, He said one would come to do His will and be a saviour.

"Now, according to His promises, God raised up Jesus of Nazareth. Through him the word of salvation has come. Even though he was crucified, God raised him from the dead. We are now his witnesses to the people. We bring you the good news that what God promised has been done.

"You must know that through Jesus forgiveness of sins is proclaimed and everyone who believes is freed. Therefore, you must believe and continue in the grace of God."

The following sabbath, a great crowd gathered to hear Paul preach the word of God.

When the Jews saw the crowd, they were upset and spoke out against him. Paul and Barnabas replied, saying: "The Lord has commanded us to be a light unto the nations, to bring salvation throughout the whole earth."

The Gentiles were glad and became believers, glorifying the name of God. But the leaders of the city rose up against Paul and Barnabas and drove them out of the district.

They went to Iconium. There too they went into the synagogue and preached. And a great number of Jews and Greeks became believers.

Again, the unbelieving Jews stirred up trouble and spoke out against the teachings of Paul and Barnabas. An attempt was made to stone them, so they fled to Lystra, and travelled through other cities of Galatia where they continued to preach the gospel.

Paul and Barnabas in Lystra

Acts 14

In Lystra was a man who had been crippled from birth and had never walked. He heard Paul speak, and Paul saw that he had faith enough to be made well. In a loud voice Paul said: "Stand on your feet."

The man stood up and walked.

When the people saw what Paul had done, they cried out: "The gods have come to us in the shape of men. Let us make sacrifices to them."

When Paul and Barnabas heard this, they said: "Do not sacrifice to us. We are only human, men like you. You should worship the living God, the God that made heaven and earth, the sea and everything that is in the world. For many generations He let nations go in their own ways, but He continued to do good, sending the rain and the sun, giving us food and filling our hearts with gladness. Turn to the true God."

With these words, the people were kept from making sacrifices to them.

Then, men of Antioch and Iconium came and turned the people away from Paul and Barnabas, stoning them and dragging them out of the city until they thought that Paul was dead. But disciples gathered around him, and he went with Barnabas to Derbe. After preaching there, they went back to Lystra and Iconium and Antioch. They appointed elders in every church, urging them to continue their faith in the Lord and to convert believers.

They travelled and spread the word throughout Pisidia, Pamphylia and Perga; then into Attalia. From there they sailed again to Antioch in Cilicia where they stayed a long time with the disciples there.

The Council of Jerusalem

Acts 15

From Antioch, Paul and Barnabas returned to Jerusalem where there was a debate going on among church leaders. The question had been raised whether Gentiles should become Jews before they could become Christians.

Some asked: "Must believers keep the laws of Moses before they accept the word of Jesus?"

Paul and Barnabas spoke to the Council saying: "We believe that God makes no distinction between them and us, but that He cleanses all hearts by faith. We believe that we shall all be saved through the grace of the Lord Jesus."

Saying this, Paul persuaded the church leaders that Gentiles could be accepted directly as Christians, as long as they put aside idol worship and observed a few other laws of cleanliness. Then Paul and Barnabas, along with Judas and Silas, returned to Antioch.

Paul's Second Journey

Acts 15-16

Paul spoke to Barnabas, saying: "Let us go back to every city where we have preached the gospel and see how the people are doing."

Barnabas wanted to take John Mark, but Paul disagreed. Then they decided to separate: Barnabas and Mark sailed to Cyprus, Paul chose Silas and travelled with him through Syria and Cilicia and part of Phrygia and Galatia.

Paul and Silas in Macedonia

Acts 16

Throughout their travels, Paul and Silas strengthened the churches and increased the number of believers.

The Spirit forbade Paul to go into Asia so they went to Troas. There, a vision appeared to Paul: a man of Macedonia called to him, saying: "Come to Macedonia and help us."

Immediately Paul and Silas set out for

Macedonia. They travelled through Samothrace and Neapolis to Philippi, the chief city of Macedonia and a Roman colony in Europe.

On the sabbath they went to the synagogue to pray. A slave girl who had special powers, which helped to bring her owners great riches, began to follow them. She called out, saying: "These men are the servants of God. They show us the way of salvation."

Paul turned then and said to the spirit within her: "Come out, in the name of Jesus Christ." And it came out.

When her masters saw that her power to make them rich was gone, they became angry. They seized Paul and Silas, brought them before the rulers of the city and charged them with breaking the law, with teaching Romans the customs and ideas of the Jews.

Paul and Silas in Prison
Acts 16

The rulers of Philippi ordered Paul and Silas to be beaten, thrown into prison and kept securely. So the jailers locked them in an inner cell and clamped their feet into the stocks.

Paul and Silas prayed continually and sang praises to God. All the other prisoners heard them.

Suddenly at midnight there was a great earthquake. The foundations of the prison shook, the doors opened and every prisoner's bonds became unfastened.

The keeper of the prison, seeing the open doors, thought all the prisoners had escaped. He feared the anger of the rulers and was just about to kill himself when Paul called to him: "We are all here. Do not be afraid."

Then the jailer ran and bowed down before Paul and Silas and asked: "What must I do to be saved?"

They answered: "Believe in the Lord Jesus and you will be saved, you and all your household."

Then he cleaned their wounds and took them to his house, where they baptized his family.

In the morning, the magistrates sent a

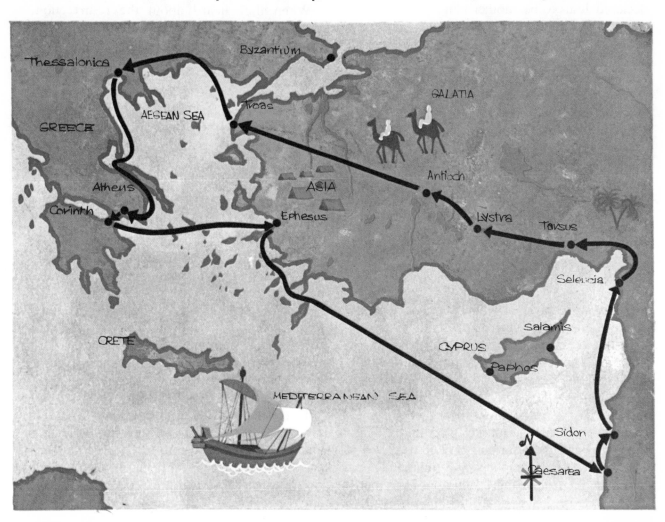

message that Paul and Silas should be released. But Paul said: "They beat us openly and should not forgive secretly. We are Roman citizens. Let them come themselves to set us free."

So they came and apologized. They released Paul and Silas from prison and asked them to leave the city.

Preaching in the Synagogues
Acts 17

Paul and Silas travelled through Amphipolis and Apollonia and went to Thessalonica where there was a synagogue. On three sabbaths Paul went there, discussing and arguing and explaining the meaning of the scriptures. He said: "Jesus is the Christ." And he preached the gospel.

Many in the synagogues believed and so did many Greeks. But those Jews that did not believe caused trouble by gathering a crowd until the whole city was in an uproar. They spoke out against Paul and Silas, saying: "These men are breaking the laws of Caesar. They have declared Jesus to be another king."

Then the rulers became alarmed, and the believers thought it best to send Paul and Silas away at once.

They went to Berea by night. There, too, they went into the synagogue. Many of the Jews received the word eagerly and believed. And Greek women as well as men also believed.

When the Jews of Thessalonika heard of Paul's success in Berea, they came and stirred up the crowds against him. The brethren took Paul away, but Silas and Timothy remained to preach.

In the Market Place in Athens
Acts 17

Those who travelled with Paul took him to Athens. Then they returned to send Silas and Timothy to join him as soon as possible.

Athens was the artistic and intellectual capital of the Greek world. There, Paul was greatly disturbed, for he saw that the city was full of idols. Every day he argued in the synagogue and in the market place, preaching the gospel and the resurrection of Jesus.

The Greek philosophers and thinkers met him and listened, asking: "What does this man babble? He preaches about foreign gods."

They took him to the market place and asked him to tell them about his new teaching, for they loved to explore new ideas. Paul spoke to them at great length, saying:

"Men of Athens, I know that you are very religious. I have seen your idols and an altar inscription which says 'To an unknown god.' What you worship as unknown, I shall make known to you.

"God who made heaven and earth, the world and everything in it, does not live in temples built by men. He does not need men to serve Him. He has made all the nations on earth and has said that they should seek Him and they will find Him. He is not far from us, for in Him we live and move and have our being.

"God is not like gold or silver or stone, to be made in images. Times have passed when these things were allowed. Now God has commanded all men to repent.

"He has set a time when He will judge the world in righteousness by a man whom He has sent and raised up from the dead."

When they heard about the resurrection, some joined Paul and believed; others mocked him. After this, Paul left Athens and went to Corinth, also in Greece.

Paul's Return to Corinth
Acts 18

In Corinth he argued in the synagogue every sabbath and he convinced both Jews and Greeks that Jesus was the Christ. He stayed a year and a half, teaching the word of God.

Then the Jews attacked Paul and brought him before the Greek tribunal, saying: "This man is telling men to worship God in ways that are not according to the law."

But the tribunal said: "This is not a matter for the court to decide. It is about your own beliefs; judge him yourselves."

The crowd seized the leader of the synagogue and beat him and the rulers did nothing about it.

Paul left Corinth and sailed to Syria. He went to Ephesus where he stayed only a short time and promised to return. Then he travelled back to Caesarea and Antioch, through Galatia and Phrygia, greeting and strengthening the disciples. After this, he returned to Ephesus.

Paul's Third Journey

Acts 19

Paul spent more than two years in and around Ephesus, speaking and arguing about the kingdom of God. Some people would not believe and spoke evil of the Way. But Paul continued to speak so that everyone in Asia, Jews and Greeks, heard the word of the Lord.

Paul performed miracles through the help of God, healing and casting out evil spirits. Many magicians burned their books and became believers. Altogether, the word of the Lord grew.

Paul decided that he should return to Jerusalem and go to Rome. But about that time, an argument arose about the Way.

The Riot at Ephesus

Acts 19

A silversmith named Demetrius called together all of his fellow workers, saying: "This man Paul has come here and preached that people shall not have silver gods or idols. Because of him we have little work these days, and even the great temple of our gods is in danger."

The metal workers agreed with Demetrius. They rushed into the streets and seized two of Paul's companions, dragging them into the assembly and causing great confusion. There was shouting and accusation, some saying one thing and some another.

Finally the town clerk quieted the people, saying: "Everyone knows that the city of Ephesus worships the goddess Diana. You should do nothing foolish. These men have not insulted our goddess. They have not destroyed the temple.

"Now, if anyone has a complaint, let him come before the court and bring charges. Do not be guilty of causing a riot for which there seems to be no cause."

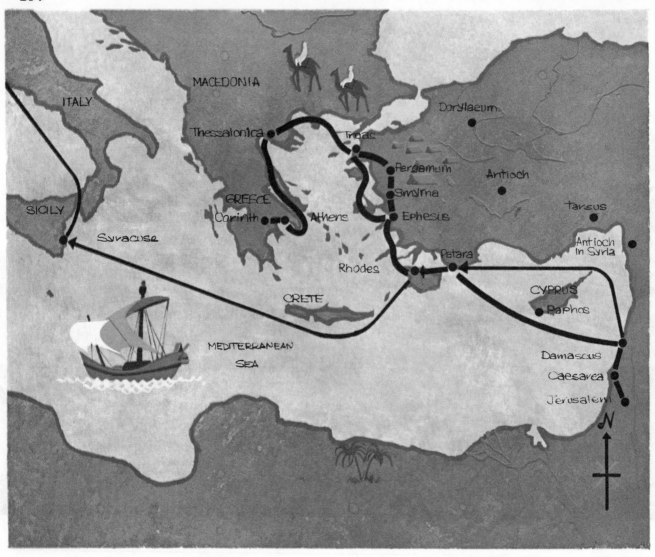

Having said this, he dismissed the assembly.

Then Paul sent for his disciples, urged them to continue their work and he left for Macedonia. There, too, he gave the disciples encouragement. Then he went to Greece.

Preaching in Troas
Acts 20

After three months in Greece, Paul's enemies rose up against him. He left Philippi and returned to Troas, travelling through Macedonia.

Paul stayed in Troas seven days. The day before he was to leave, all the disciples were gathered together, and he spoke to them until midnight.

A certain young man named Eutychus had sat on the window sill listening intently all evening. When it was nearly midnight he fell sound asleep, tumbled from the third floor window and was picked up dead.

Paul ran down and, putting his arm around the fellow, said: "Never fear, he is still alive." The young man was taken home alive and well.

Then Paul returned to the upper room and ate and talked until dawn, when he left Troas. He was hurrying to try to get to Jerusalem on the day of Pentecost.

He sailed from Assos stopping along the coast at Mitylene, Chios, Samos, Trogyllium and Miletus.

Paul's Farewell to Ephesus
Acts 20-21

At Miletus Paul sent for the church elders of Ephesus. When they arrived, he spoke to them for some time, saying: "You know how I lived with you when I first went to Asia, serving the Lord and being disturbed by persecutions. I testified and taught both Jews and Greeks about repentance to God and faith in Jesus.

"Now I am on my way to Jerusalem, not knowing what will happen there, for the Holy Spirit has warned me that trouble and imprisonment lie ahead. You may never see me again, but I must go to accomplish the ministry I have set out to do.

"You must take care of yourselves and the flock which the Holy Spirit has given you to look after. Trouble will arise, but you must be alert. Continue to help the weak and remember the words and deeds of the Lord Jesus. I commend you to the grace of God."

So saying, he knelt down with them and prayed. They wept, embraced Paul and led him to his ship.

He and the few who travelled with him went to Cos, Rhodes and Patara. Passing Cyprus, they sailed to Syria and landed at Tyre where they stayed for seven days.

From Tyre they went to Ptolemais, and then to Caesarea where they stayed at the house of Philip the evangelist. While they were there, a prophet named Agabus came from Judea.

Agabus took Paul's belt and tied his own hands and feet with it, saying: "The Holy Spirit says that the Jews at Jerusalem will bind the owner of this belt as I am bound. Then they will hand him over to the Gentiles."

All who heard this begged Paul not to go to Jerusalem. Paul answered: "Why are you weeping? I am ready to be imprisoned or even to die for the name of the Lord Jesus."

They said: "Let the Lord's will be done."

Then they bid him good-bye.

Paul in Jerusalem
Acts 21

Paul went to Jerusalem, some disciples from Caesarea travelling with him. When he arrived, the brethren welcomed him.

Some of those who were strict followers of the laws of Moses rose up against him, shouting and accusing him of false teaching and of bringing Greeks into the Temple. They dragged him out of the Temple and began beating him.

When the captain of the Roman soldiers heard about the riot, he ordered his soldiers to that place. The crowd, seeing the soldiers, stopped beating Paul.

The captain ordered Paul arrested and put in chains. Then he asked who Paul was and what he had done.

Some of the crowd shouted one thing and some another, so that there was great confusion. The captain ordered Paul taken to prison. On the steps, Paul asked if he could speak to the people.

He was given permission to speak and raised his hand to silence the crowd. He spoke to them in Hebrew and they listened.

"I am a Jew from Tarsus, brought up to live by the laws of our fathers. I persecuted the followers of Jesus, committing many men and women to prison. I even went to Damascus to seek out the disciples of Christ.

"On my way to Damascus a great light from heaven came to me and Jesus spoke."

Then Paul told of his conversion and baptism and repentance. The crowd listened intently.

Paul continued: "When I returned to Jerusalem, the word of the Lord came to me and said that I must be a witness to all men. 'Go from here to preach among the Gentiles,' said the Lord."

Hearing this, the crowd became enraged, shouting: "Take him away; he should be put to death!"

The captain then ordered Paul to be thrown into prison and questioned by torture.

Paul in Prison
Acts 22-23

As Paul was being tied up, he asked one of the soldiers: "Is it lawful to torture a Roman citizen who has not been tried and sentenced?"

The soldier immediately went to the captain, saying: "Be careful; the man is a Roman citizen."

When the captain heard this, he ordered Paul's bonds to be loosened. He was afraid, for he had ordered a Roman citizen to be bound without a trial.

The next day Paul was questioned by the Council of priests in the Temple. Again there was such an uproar that no judgement could be made and Paul was taken back to prison.

A group of his enemies then plotted to kill him, saying: "We will not eat until he dies. Let us see that he is brought before the Council again and we will kill him."

Paul's nephew heard about the plan and in-

formed the soldiers. The captain, fearing for the safety of his prisoner, ordered him taken to Caesarea by two hundred soldiers to appear before the governor.

The Hearing before Felix

Acts 24

The governor ordered Paul's accusers to come to Caesarea to testify. The high priest and a few elders arrived. Their spokesman was Tertullus, a gifted speaker, who said:

"Your excellency, we have found this man to be a trouble-maker, stirring up Jews throughout the world. He is a leader of the Nazarenes. He has even defiled the Temple and has not lived according to the laws. For these reasons we accuse him.

"Question him yourself and you will see that what we have said is true."

The governor gave Paul permission to speak,

and he began: "Since you have been judge over this nation for many years, I would speak on my own behalf.

"When I went in to the Temple to worship, I did not argue or dispute with anyone there. Nor did I cause any trouble among the people.

"I admit that I worship the God of our fathers according to the Way, hoping that there will be a resurrection of both the just and the unjust. I believe everything in the law and the prophets. Those who accuse me cannot prove what they have said against me."

Felix, himself knowing something about the Way, put off making a decision until the chief judge should arrive in Caesarea. He gave orders for Paul to be watched over and kept in custody. But he allowed Paul some freedom, letting him have visitors and friends to care for him.

Paul's Appeal to Caesar
Acts 25-27

Paul remained a prisoner on Caesarea for two years. Then Felix was replaced by a new governor, Porcius Festus.

Soon after the new governor arrived, he ordered Paul to be brought before him.

When Paul was allowed to speak, he said: "I have done no wrong to the Jews or against Caesar. If I have done anything to deserve death, I am not afraid to die. But let me be tried where I should be judged; I appeal to Caesar."

The governor and his council agreed, saying: "You have appealed to Caesar; you shall go."

A few days later Agrippa the king and his sister Bernice came to Caesarea. Festus told them about Paul.

The king said: "I would like to hear the man myself."

Festus ordered Paul brought before the king and Paul spoke at great length about his conversion. He talked of repentance, of the gospel and of the Way.

Agrippa and Bernice and the governor all agreed that Paul had done nothing to deserve imprisonment or death. They would have set him free if he had not asked to appear before the emperor.

Then they arranged to send him to Rome by ship.

The Journey to Rome
Acts 27-28

Paul and some other prisoners were taken to a ship and put in charge of a centurion named Julius. It was a long, slow journey for there was little wind. Much time was lost and it was nearly winter, when the sea would be too stormy to travel.

Paul warned the captain of coming danger, but the captain decided to take a chance and sail on to the island of Crete, to spend the winter anchored there. Then they would continue to Rome after the bad weather.

They set sail and, almost immediately, a great wind began to blow. The ship was tossed around by high waves. The storm raged for many days.

One night an angel of the Lord came to Paul, saying: "Do not be afraid. You will appear before Caesar, and all with you will be saved."

On the fourteenth night, the captain thought they were nearing land. Paul took some bread and gave thanks to God; then they all ate. Altogether there were two hundred and twenty-six people on the ship.

In the morning they saw land and attempted to take the ship into port, but the ship ran aground and was wrecked. Everyone had to scramble for the shore, some swimming and others holding onto broken pieces of board.

The island where they found themselves was called Malita, or Malta. The people who lived there were kind and welcomed them, building a fire for them because of the rain and the cold.

A leader of the people was a man named Publius, whose father was sick with fever. Paul visited him and prayed. He placed his hands on the sick man and he was healed. After this all the people who were sick came to Paul and were cured. They gave Paul and his followers gifts and supplies when the time came for them to set sail once more.

Paul had spent three months in Malta when they finally boarded a ship and set sail for Italy. They stopped several times: at Syracuse, Rhegium and Puteoli before they got to Rome.

Paul's Last Years
Acts 28

When the brethren in Rome heard of Paul's arrival, they went to meet him. He greeted

them, gave thanks to God and was greatly encouraged.

The centurion delivered all his other prisoners to the captain in charge, but Paul was allowed to live alone with one soldier to guard him.

After he had been in Rome three days, he called together all the leaders of the Jews. He told them of his having been delivered to the Romans as a prisoner and of his appeal to Caesar for justice.

The people said: "Tell us of your teaching, for we know that everywhere people are speaking out against your group, the Nazarenes."

Paul answered them, speaking for a whole day, from morning until night. He spoke about the laws of Moses and about the prophets, telling them of the kingdom of God. He tried to convince them about Jesus. Some believed and others did not.

Then he said: "The Holy Spirit was right when he told Isaiah the prophet: 'You can go to the people, but hearing, they may not understand and seeing, they may not perceive. Their hearts have become heavy, their ears and their eyes are closed.'

"The Gentiles have also been told about the salvation of God and they will hear."

For two years Paul lived in a rented house in Rome with a soldier to guard him. Many people came to him and he received them all, preaching the kingdom of God, teaching about the life and resurrection of Jesus, spreading the gospel. All this he did quite openly and no one kept him from speaking.

The date and place of Paul's death is not sure. Some believe he was released from prison after his two years in Rome and later arrested during the persecution of Christians by the Emperor Nero.

Others believe he was still in Rome when the persecutions began. It is presumed that he was beheaded after being sentenced to die.

Paul's Letters

Paul wrote many letters during his journeys and imprisonments. They reveal his thoughts, beliefs and teachings about Jesus and the church, giving advice and encouragement to the early Christians about life and worship.

Most of the writings are informal letters written to a specific group of person for a particular purpose.

To the Romans

The letter to the Romans is the most formal of Paul's letters. Some believe it to be the most important. It was written from Corinth, Greece, toward the end of Paul's third journey, before he went to Jerusalem where he was arrested.

Paul begins by telling who he is: "a servant of Jesus Christ, called to be an apostle, set apart for the gospel."

The letter is addressed: "To all in Rome who have been called to be saints: grace to you and peace from God our Father and the Lord Jesus Christ.

"I thank God through Jesus for your faith. Somehow I hope to come and preach the gospel to you. The gospel is the power of God for salvation for all who have faith. In it the righteousness of God is revealed through faith."

Then he wrote that the way a man lives his life is important to God, even though all men fall short. "It is not the bearers of the law, but the doers of the law who are righteous."

Continuing to write of sin, Paul spoke of the eternal and internal struggle within man between sin and the law of God, between the flesh and the spirit.

"God has shown His love for us: while we were sinners, Christ died for us. Through baptism we share in the death and resurrection of Jesus. We have been set free from sin and have become as slaves of God. The wages of sin is death; the gift of God is eternal life in Christ.

"Nothing can separate us from the love of God, neither death nor life, neither angels nor powers, neither things present nor things to come, neither height nor depth, nor any creature."

About the Jews, Paul said. "The Jewish people were given the law, but now both Jews and Gentiles can look to Jesus as their Saviour."

How to live as a Christian? Paul answered the Romans: "I appeal to you not to conform to this world, but be transformed that you may do and be what is good and acceptable and perfect. Hate evil, hold onto what is good. Love one another, be aglow with the Spirit, serve the Lord.

"Rejoice in hope, be patient in trial, be constant in prayer.

"Now I am on my way to Jerusalem with help for the saints there. I appeal to you to pray for me that I may be delivered from the unbelievers in Judea so I may come to you.

"The God of peace be with you. Amen."

To the Corinthians

After leaving Athens, Paul had travelled to Corinth, another important city of Greece. He preached the Christian message there and established a strong church. Later, he heard that conflicts had arisen within the church and that many questions were being asked. For these reasons he wrote stern letters to the Corinthians.

"I appeal to you," wrote Paul, "in the name of our Lord Jesus Christ, that you all agree and that there be no divisions among you. Instead be united of the same mind and the same judgement.

"Christ sent me to preach the gospel, not to baptize, though I did baptize a few believers.

"The word is foolishness to those who perish, but to those of us who are saved, it is the power of God.

"In the wisdom of God, the world did not come to know God through wisdom. The foolishness of God is wiser than men; the weakness of God is stronger than men.

"To all those who are called, Jews and Greeks, Christ is the power and the wisdom of God.

"You, each of you, is God's temple and God's spirit lives within you. If anyone destroys God's temple, God will destroy him. God's temple is holy and you are that temple.

"Therefore," said Paul, "the body is sacred.

"Do not associate with immoral men who call themselves brothers; drive out the wicked from among you. It is those inside the church that you are to judge; God judges those outside.

"Let everyone lead the life assigned to him and in which God has called him. He who was called as a slave is a freed-man of the Lord; he who was free when called is a slave of Christ. Do not become slaves of men. Do whatever you do to the glory of God."

Then Paul wrote answers to questions that had been asked, such as: "Women should pray with their heads covered and men with bare heads; the bread and the cup which are taken in remembrance of Christ must be taken in a worthy manner, proclaiming the Lord's death.

"You are the body of Christ and members of it. If one member suffers, all suffer together; if one is honoured, all rejoice together.

"In the church God has named first apostles, second prophets, then teachers, workers of miracles, healers, helpers, administrators and speakers. Each should desire the higher gifts, and I will tell you a more excellent way.

"Though I speak with the tongues of men and of angels and have not love, I am as a noise of clanging cymbals. Though I have the gift of prophecy and understand all mysteries and all knowledge, and though I have all faith and can move mountains, but have not love, I am nothing.

"Though I give all my belongings to feed the poor and my body to be burned, and have not love, it gains me nothing.

"Love suffers long and is kind; love envies not, love boasts not and is not puffed up.

"Love is not easily provoked, thinks no evil. Love rejoices not in wickedness, but rejoices in truth.

"Love hears all things, believes all things, hopes all things, endures all things.

"When I was a child I spoke as a child, understood as a child, thought as a child. When I became a man, I put away childish things.

"Now abides these three: faith, hope, love, but the greatest of these is love.

"Brethren, be not children in understanding; in understanding be men."

In this letter, too, Paul wrote about the resurrection of Jesus who "died for our sins according to the scriptures," saying that Christians need never fear death because "God gives us victory through our Lord Jesus Christ. For the trumpet will sound and the dead will be raised.

He continued: "Therefore be steadfast, watchful, courageous and strong in your faith. Let all that you do be done in love."

Paul's second letter to the Corinthians was written to defend his work as an ambassador of Christ. In it he also defended his beliefs, stating again and again that the grace of Jesus leads a person toward the love of God, and the love of God given by the Spirit produces fellowship.

Here, too, he told of all that he had suffered up to this time because of his preaching: imprisonment, beatings, shipwreck, hunger, insults and dangers of all kinds.

"For the sake of Jesus," wrote Paul, "I am content with hardships, weakness and persecutions; for when I am weak, then I am strong."

Then he made a plea for the Corinthians to contribute to a fund for poor Christians and "the saints" in Jerusalem.

Paul ended with a warning and a blessing: "Mend your ways, agree with one another, live in peace.

"The grace of the Lord Jesus Christ and the love of God and the communion of the Holy Spirit be with you all. Amen."

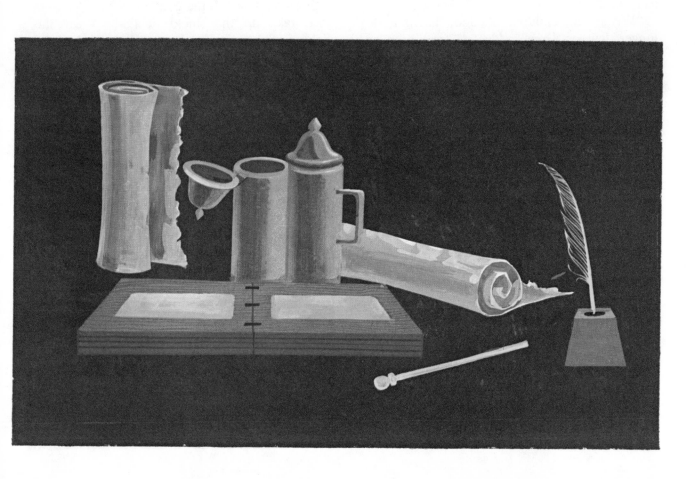

222

To the Galatians

After leaving Galatia in Asia Minor, Paul heard of disagreements among the people there. He wrote to them showing his displeasure and concern. The letter speaks of a controversy that had arisen: some believed that Gentiles had to become Jews first and then Christians. The letter declares Christian independence and tells of the rewards that will come to those who live according to the Spirit.

Paul's letter to the Galatians begins: "Grace to you and peace from God the Father our Lord Jesus Christ who gave his life for our sins.

"I am surprised that you turn away from the gospel so quickly. I want you to know that the gospel I preach is not man's gospel, but it came through a revelation of Jesus. You know of my early life and how I persecuted believers. Then I was called by God to preach the faith I once tried to destroy.

"Some think that only those who accept and live by the laws of Moses can be Christians. Consider: did you receive the Spirit through the law or through faith?

"Before faith came, we lived under the law. Now faith has come and Christ has redeemed us from the law.

"We are all children of God. There is no longer Jew or Greek, slave or free, man or woman. We are all one in Jesus Christ.

"I have confidence in the Lord that you will become as I am and believe as I do, living by the Spirit and doing good to all.

"If a man has any fault, restore him in the spirit of gentleness. Look to yourself too, lest you be tempted. Each man will have to answer for his own deeds. God is not deceived: whatever a man sows, so shall he reap."

To the Ephesians

It was in the great city of Ephesus that Paul worked the longest and lived through many dangers. Most of the Christians there had been Gentiles and not Jews. The letter, written from prison in Rome, begins by reminding them that Jesus came to save all people.

"I continually give thanks and remember you in my prayers that the God of our Lord Jesus Christ may give you wisdom and revelation, opening your hearts.

"By grace you have been saved through faith. You were Gentiles, strangers to the covenant and with no hope, for you were without God.

"You are no longer strangers, but you are fellow members of the household of God, along with the prophets and apostles and with Christ himself who is the cornerstone. We have all come alive through God's mercy.

"I am a prisoner because of my beliefs concerning you, the Gentiles. Do not be discouraged but continue to lead lives worthy of that to which you have been called.

"Act with patience, love and meekness. Maintain unity of the Spirit in the bond of peace. There is one body and one Spirit, one Lord, one faith, one baptism and one God and Father above us all. Grace is given to each of us according to the gift of Christ.

"Being a Christian makes a difference in thinking, believing and doing. Children should obey their parents, parents should discipline their children, slaves and masters should respect one another and show no partiality.

"Be strong in the Lord, in the power of the Lord against the devil. Protect yourselves with the ways of God; fight against wickedness. Cover yourself with truth and the breastplate of righteousness. With the gospel of peace on your feet, take up the shield of faith. Wear the helmet of salvation and carry the sword of the Spirit which is the word of God."

To the Philippians

Philippi was the first city in Europe in which Paul preached the gospel. He had looked for a synagogue there to preach to his own Jewish people about the coming of the Messiah. But, there were so few Jews that they met together at the river's edge.

By the time Paul left Philippi, many people had become Christians and the church was established.

This letter expresses joy and gratitude for "your truthfulness and partnership in the gospel."

"Let your lives be worthy of Christ; stand firm. Believe in him; even suffer for his sake. Rejoice in the Lord; watch out for evil-doers.

"Whatever is true, honest and just; whatever is pure, lovely and good; if there is anything excellent and worthy of praise, think about these things and seek after them.

"I rejoice in the Lord and do not complain. I have learned to be content and can do all things in him who strengthens me. You can have that same trust.

"It was kind of you to share my trouble . . . you have sent me help . . . the gifts you sent, the offering and sacrifice are pleasing and acceptable and pleasing to God. And God will fill your every need."

To the Colossians

Although Paul had never been to Colossae, other Christians had preached there. This letter was written from prison in Rome to the "saints and faithful brethren in Colossae" explaining the uniqueness of creation and of Jesus and to combat the teaching about "elements of the world" that influenced men's lives.

He wrote to them of his prayers for them, hoping that they would be "filled with spiritual wisdom and understanding, to lead lives worthy of the Lord and pleasing to Him."

"I rejoice in my suffering for your sake and for the sake of the church. Though I am not with you in body, I am with you in spirit, rejoicing in your faith in Christ. Let no one deceive you or judge you or disqualify you.

"Put earthly things aside: evil desire, impurity, passion, jealousy, anger, greed, foul talk and lies. Instead seek kindness, patience, forgiveness, meekness, thankfulness and above all, love.

"Whatever you do, in word or deed, do it in the name of the Lord Jesus, giving thanks to God the Father. Remember my bonds. Grace be with you."

To the Thessalonians

Paul wrote two letters to the church in Thessalonika, the capital of Macedonia. Paul reminded the Thessalonians of what a wonderful life they had begun when they were converted. They were few in number and most of them were poor and had been persecuted because of their new faith. He wrote to give them encouragement and hope.

"As followers of Jesus, you must love one another and all the brethren as well. Live quietly, work hard and depend on no one.

"Do not mourn the dead like others who have no hope. Since Jesus died and rose again, so through Jesus God will bring to Him all those who have died.

"The Lord will descend from heaven with the sound of trumpets and the dead in Christ will rise first. Then we who are alive and those who are in the clouds will be caught up together to meet the Lord in the air. And we will be with the Lord forever."

Many people thought that Christ would soon return to earth and that they could just wait for his coming. Paul wrote that there would be troubled times before the coming and that the way to be ready was to live each day doing what was right.

"It may be a long time," wrote Paul, "but you must be patient and steady, having faith.

"Encourage one another, be at peace together and help the weak. Rejoice always, pray constantly and give thanks. Hold fast to what is good, keep away from all evil so you will be blameless at the coming of the Lord.

"The grace of our Lord Jesus be with you all. Amen."

To Timothy and Titus

The two letters to Timothy and the one to Titus are more formal and official than

Paul's other letters. They speak of the work and duties of a minister in dealing with his people. Some scholars think they were not written by Paul but by someone else who put Paul's ideas into letter form.

Timothy lived in Lystra and was the son of a Greek father and a Jewish mother. He and his mother and grandmother had already become Christians when Paul visited Lystra. Timothy became Paul's friend and travelling companion. Paul took him on missionary voyages and sent him on difficult missions alone. He is mentioned in several of Paul's letters.

Titus, too, was a companion of Paul's. He had gone to the meeting of the apostles in Jerusalem with Paul and Barnabas. Later he went to Crete to establish the church there. This letter, too, outlines the duties of the elders and bishops and includes advice about dealing with "members of the flock."

"Timothy, my son," wrote Paul, "wage the good warfare with faith and a good conscience. Pray for all men, for God desires all men to be saved and come to the truth.

"There is one God and one mediator between God and men: the man Christ Jesus, who gave himself as ransom for all."

Paul then went on to describe how one should get into "the household of God, the church of the living God":

"A bishop, deacon or elder must be above reproach. He must be sensible, dignified, gentle, the husband of one wife, a good teacher, not quarrelsome or a lover of money. He should manage well his household and his children and be well thought of by others. Be a good example in every way.

"As for the rich: they must do good and be rich in good deeds and generous."

The second letter, in a very personal message, states Paul's love for Timothy, and is a reminder to:

"Remember Jesus Christ risen from the dead as preached in the gospel for which I am now suffering and imprisoned like a criminal. I urge you to preach the word, be convincing and unfailing. Endure suffering, teach patiently. Take your share of suffering as a good soldier of Christ.

"The time of my departure is near. I have fought the good fight and kept the faith.

"Try to come to me soon, and bring the cloak I left at Troas, the books and especially the parchments . . ."

To Titus, faced with opposition in Crete, Paul wrote: "Be a good example for the sake of the gospel and be a model of good deeds. Preach and declare the glory of God and of Jesus Christ who gave himself for us.

"Avoid controversy and quarrels. Insist on the teachings of the church."

To Philemon

Paul wrote the letter to Philemon during his imprisonment in Rome. Philemon, who had become a Christian due to Paul's preaching, was the master of a slave who had run away. The slave was then converted to Christianity by Paul.

The letter was to be taken by the slave, Onesimus, to his master, urging Philemon to take him back "not as a slave, but more than a slave, as a beloved brother...Receive him as you would receive me."

To the Hebrews

Most scholars think this letter was not written by Paul; some think it was written as a sermon and not a letter, expressing many of Paul's views.

Some of the Jews who had been converted to Judaism were about to return to their earlier beliefs. They were asking what more they needed to know besides their belief in God and the laws of the Old Testament.

The writer was a believing Christian who preached the gospel as a better way of life.

"In the old times," he wrote, "God spoke through Moses and the prophets. Now, through Christ, God has spoken in a new and perfect way. Through Jesus all people can come near to God and know that their sins will be forgiven."

"Jesus is above the angels and Moses and the high priests; the new covenant is superior to the old for if the first had been perfect, there would have been no need for a second.

"Christ has entered heaven to appear in our behalf in the presence of God, and will appear a second time to save those who wait for him.

"If we sin after receiving the new truth, there is a fearful prospect of judgement and fire.

"Faith is the assurance of things hoped for, the conviction of things not seen. By faith much has been done: we understood creation through faith, Abraham acted through faith, and Isaac and Jacob and the judges and prophets and David, all acted through faith.

"Yet none of these received what was promised. Now Jesus is the pioneer and the perfecter of our faith. Through him let us continually offer praise to God, a sacrifice of tongues to speak and acknowledge his name.

"Do good and share what you have; do what is pleasing to God.

"Pray for us, for we have a clear conscience.

"The Lord is my helper, I will not be afraid; what can man do to me?"

"Remember and obey your leaders; imitate their faith.

"Grace be with all of you. Amen."

Letters of James, Peter and John

These letters were all written as "epistles," or public letters, intended for many churches in general and directed to no group in particular.

James, "a servant of God and of the Lord Jesus Christ," was leader of the church in Jerusalem. His letter is directed to all the Jews who had become Christians. It is a collection of teachings, plain and practical:

"Do not be hearers of the word only, be doers. Faith without good deeds is dead."

James then wrote of wars, economic evils and of the power of prayer: prayers of the sick and of the sinner.

Peter was one of the first disciples and worked to spread the gospel after Jesus was crucified. He was put to death during the persecutions of Christians by Nero, the Roman Emperor.

Peter's first letter was written to followers of Jesus who were being persecuted in Asia. It reminded them of how Jesus had suffered and been raised from the dead "by the love and power of God" in which they should trust.

"Now you are God's people," wrote Peter, "and you must live as free men, believing in the Lord."

His second letter deals with false teachers in the church and explains the second coming of Christ, saying: "The day of the Lord will come, the heavens will open with a loud noise, the earth and everything on it will be burned up.

"Until that time you should live lives of holiness and godliness."

The writer of the next three letters is probably John the fisherman, the son of Zebedee, one of the very first followers of Jesus and the same John who wrote the Gospel.

The letters are written to make certain truths perfectly clear: that with God there is light, that one should not sin and that love is above all else: "God is love and the Son of God has come to give us understanding.

"He who does good is of God; he who does evil has not seen God."

The Revelation to John — John's Vision

The Book of Revelation is also called the Apocalypse, from the Greek word which means "revealing" or "vision." It is a collection of visions about God's justice and mercy and assured the followers of Jesus that he will appear again.

"The revelation of Jesus Christ was given by God to show what would take place," according to the writer, John, who was the leader of the churches in Asia.

"Grace to you and peace from him who is and was and is to come, and from the seven spirits who are before his throne, and from Jesus Christ the witness, the firstborn of the dead and the ruler of kings on earth.

"I, John, am on the island of Patmos because of the word of God and the testimony of Jesus." That is: in exile because persecutions of Christians had begun. Christians had refused to set up and bow down to statues of the Roman Emperors and were accused of being disloyal and dangerous.

The vision was to reassure and encourage the churches in Asia Minor that were being per-secuted and treated with hostility. The great message was that "the Lord Jesus is alive forever" and would outlast even the greatness of Rome. Called "Babylon" in John's visions, Rome would fall and God will judge the earth.

The power of Satan too would be des-troyed and the saints would be saved to stand with God and Christ, the Lamb who had been sacrificed.

The vision is described, from the beginning: "It was the Lord's day. I was in the Spirit and heard a loud voice like a trumpet behind me telling me to write what I see in a book and send it to the seven churches of Ephesus, Smyrna, Pergamum, Thyatira, Sardis, Philadelphia and Laodicea.

"I turned and saw seven golden lampstands and in the midst of them one like a son of man, dressed in a long robe. His head and hair were white as snow, his eyes like a flame. In his right hand were seven stars and from his mouth was a two-edged sword. His face was like the sun shining with full strength.

"I fell at his feet as though dead. He touched me with his right hand, saying: 'Do not fear, I am the first and the last, the living one. I died, yet am alive forevermore. I have the keys of death and Hades. The seven lampstands are the seven churches and the seven stars are their angels. Now write to the seven churches all the words which I will tell you. Write that I know the works of each church, and urge the followers to hold fast to their belief. I am coming soon!'

"After this, I looked into heaven and saw a door. I heard a voice like a trumpet calling me to come and see what would happen in the future.

"I saw a throne and one seated on the throne. Around it were twenty-four thrones with men seated on them wearing golden crowns and white clothes. From the throne came lightning and thunder. Before the throne were seven flaming torches which are the seven spirits of God and there was a sea of glass, like crystal.

"Around the throne were four living creatures full of eyes looking in every direction: the first like a lion, the second like an ox, the third with the face of a man, the fourth like a flying eagle.

"In the right hand of the one on the throne was a scroll written on and sealed with seven seals. An angel called in a loud voice: 'Who is worthy to break the seals and open the scroll?'

"Then I saw a lamb with seven horns and seven eyes like the seven spirits of God. He took the scroll. At once the four creatures and the twenty-four elders fell down before him, each with a harp and golden bowl of incense.

And I heard the voices of many angels proclaiming: 'He is worthy to receive power and might and wealth and wisdom and glory and blessing!'"

In the vision, as each of the first four seals was opened, a horse and rider appeared.

These have been called the "Four Horsemen of the Apocalypse." The four stand for the judgements of man because of his sins. They are the white horse, the terror of war; the red horse and rider, chaos and murder; the black one, famine and disease; the last one, a pale sickly green, is death and hell.

The fifth seal revealed the martyrs, those who died for their beliefs. The sixth seal revealed the punishments of all those who have done evil and are afraid to face judgement.

"When the seventh seal was opened, there was silence in heaven and seven angels with seven trumpets appeared. Each of the first six caused different calamities to take place in the universe, then the seventh blew his trumpet and there were loud voices, saying: 'The kingdom of the world has become the kingdom of our Lord and of His Christ!'

"Then God's temple in heaven was opened and the ark of His covenant was seen. And there were flashes of lightning, peals of thunder, an earthquake and hail."

228

Next came the casting out from heaven of Satan and his devils, a symbol of the struggle between good and evil:

"Those who were worthy and have been redeemed follow the Lamb and are blessed. Those who have followed the beast shall receive God's wrath and be tormented with fire and brimstone forever.

"After all these things I saw another angel calling with a loud voice: 'The great city, Babylon, has been thrown down with violence and will be no more.' "

Then, the last judgement: "I saw the dead standing before the throne; the books were opened, and the book of life also. The dead were judged by what was written in the books and what they had done. If anyone's name was not in the book of life, he was thrown into the fire.

"After this I heard the voice of a great multitude in heaven, crying:

'Hallelujah! Salvation and glory and honour to our God.
We rejoice and glorify Him,
For the marriage of the Lamb of God has come.
His Bride is ready, clothed with bright pure linen.
Her garment is the goodness of the saints of God.
Happy are those who are invited to the marriage of the Lamb.'

"Then I saw a new heaven and a new earth and the holy city Jerusalem coming down from heaven.

"And a voice came from heaven saying: 'Behold, God now lives among men and He will dwell with them and they will be His people. There shall be no more death or tears or pain or suffering for these have all passed away.'

"Jerusalem had a great high wall around it with twelve gates and twelve angels. The gates were the names of the twelve tribes of Israel. The foundations also numbered twelve. On these were written the names of the twelve apostles of the Lamb.

"The city was square, of pure gold and jewelled.

"There was no temple in the city for its temple is the Lord God Almighty and the Lamb. There is no need for moon or sun for the glory of God is its light.

"The gates shall always be open. Nothing unclean shall enter the city, only those written in the Lamb's book of life.

"Then I saw the river of the water of life, clear as crystal, flowing from the throne and the tree of life on either side of the river, its leaves for the healing of nations.

"I, John, heard and saw these things.

"The Lord is coming soon to repay everyone for what he has done. Blessed are those that may enter the city.

"The grace of the Lord Jesus be with you all. Amen."

BIBLICAL
MAPS

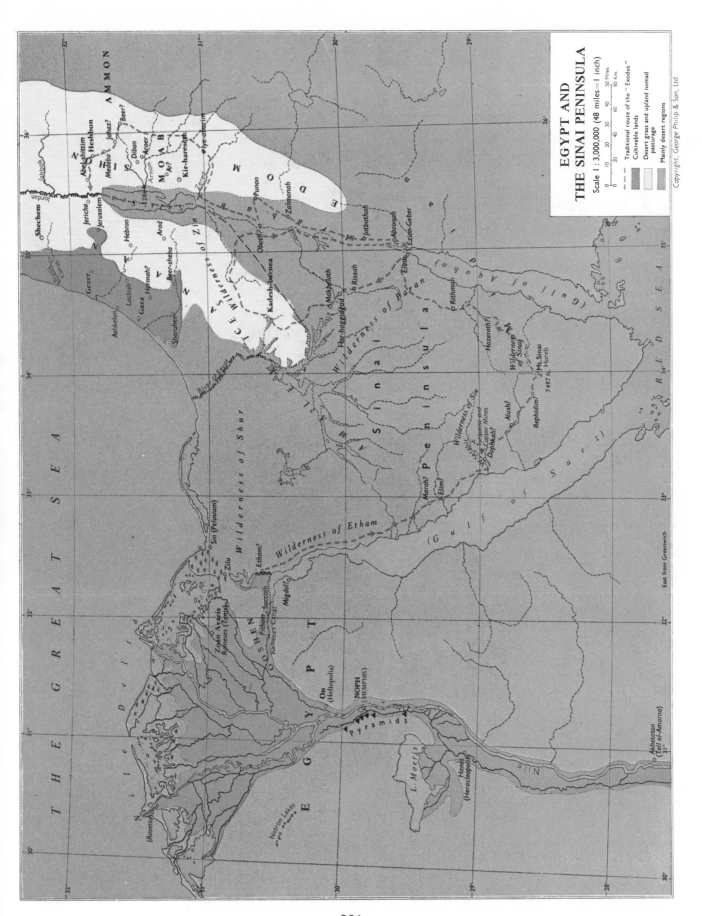

EGYPT AND
THE SINAI PENINSULA

Scale 1 : 3,000,000 (48 miles = 1 inch)

Traditional route of the "Exodus"
Cultivable lands
Desert grass and upland nomad pasturage
Mainly desert regions

Copyright, George Philip & Son, Ltd.

East from Greenwich

231

HEBREW SETTLEMENT
OF THE
PROMISED LAND

Scale 1 : 1,500,000 (24 miles = 1 inch)

0   5   10   15   20   25   30 Miles
0   10   20   30   40   50 Km.

Hebrew settlements c. 1200 B.C.
Land subsequently occupied
Boundaries of Israelite tribal allotments
Cities of Refuge
Philistine settlements
Territory under direct domination
of Philistines c. 1050 B.C.

SIDON

DAMASCUS

Zarephath

Abana

Hermon 9232 ft

Pharpar

TYRE

Laish, Dan DAN
Baal-gad?

Misrephoth-maim
Achzib
Kedesh
Hazor
Waters of Merom

Acco
Ramah

Argob
(KINGDOM OF

Aphek
Madon
Sea of Chinnereth -695 ft.
Golan? Ashtaroth
Karnaim
OG, BASHAN)
Kenath Nobah

Haroshëth
Shimron
Mt. Tabor 1929 ft.
Havvoth-jairs

Dor
Jokneam
Megiddo
Hill of Moreh
ISSACHAR
Jezreel
Well of Harod
Mt. Gilboa 1640 ft.
Edrei
Tob?
Salecah
Ramoth-gilead

Taanach
Ibleam
Beth-shean
Pella

THE
Dothan
MANASSEH
Jabesh-gilead
Mahanaim?

GREAT
Thebez
Mizpeh?

SEA
Shechem
Mt. Ebal 3084 ft.
Jacob's Well
Penuel

Pirathon?
2890 ft.
Mt. Gerizim
Arumah?

Kanah
Aphek
Tappuah
Shiloh
Adam

Joppa
EPHRAIM
Mt. Ephraim

DAN
Mt. Gaash
Ophrah
Jogbehah

Luz
Beth-el
Rock Rimmon
Ai, Beth-aven

Bezek?
BENJAMIN
Jericho -820 ft.
Rabbath-ammon
(KINGDOM

Gezer
Beth-horon
Gibeah
Gilgal
Abel-shittim
Heshbon

Gibbethon
Aijalon
Gibeon
Kiriath-jearim
Beth-jeshimoth
Bezer
OF

Ekron
Sorek
Eshtaol
Jebus
Jerusalem
Mt. Pisgah 2644 ft.

Ashdod
Beth-shemesh
Medeba
AMMON)

Makkedah?
Jarmuth
Beth-lehem
Mts. Abarim
Jahaz?

Ashkelon
Libnah
Azekah
Adullam
Kiriathaim

Gath?
Mateshah
JUDAH
Kiriath-arba
Hebron
En-gedi -1286 ft.
REUBEN

Lachish
Dibon

Gaza
Eglon
Aroer

Kiriath-sepher
Debir
Juttah

Zephath?
Gerar?
Hormah?
Anab
Arad

Ziklag?

Sharuhen
Beer-sheba
Aroer
KINGDOM OF
MOAB
Kir-hareseth

Besor

SIMEON

Mt. Halak
Ascent of Akrabbim
KINGDOM OF

Wilderness of Zin

Wilderness of Kedemoth

Zered

Arnon

Bozrah

Wilderness of Zin
EDOM

Kadesh-barnea
Punon
East from Greenwich

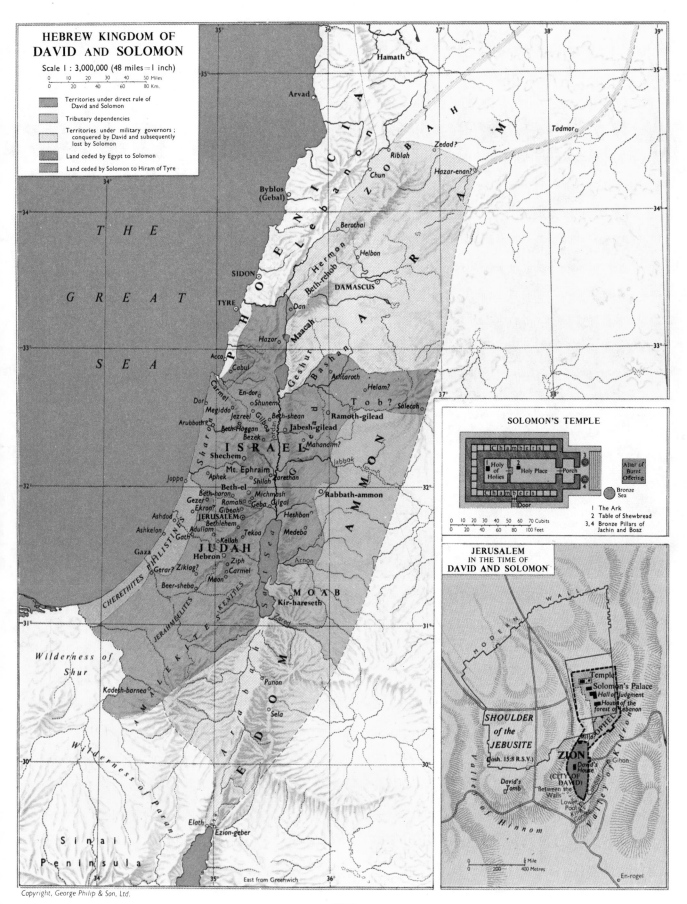

HEBREW KINGDOM OF DAVID AND SOLOMON

Scale 1 : 3,000,000 (48 miles = 1 inch)

0 10 20 30 40 50 Miles
0 20 40 60 80 Km.

Territories under direct rule of David and Solomon

Tributary dependencies

Territories under military governors; conquered by David and subsequently lost by Solomon

Land ceded by Egypt to Solomon

Land ceded by Solomon to Hiram of Tyre

Hamath

Arvad

Byblos (Gebal)

Riblah

Zedad?

Tadmor

Chun

Hazar-enan?

Berothai

Helbon

SIDON

Beth-rehob

Hermon

DAMASCUS

TYRE

Dan

Maacah

Hazor

Acco

Cabul

Geshur

Bashan

Ashtaroth

Helam?

Salecah

Dor

Carmel

En-dor

Shunem

Megiddo

Jezreel

Gilboa

Beth-shean

Tob?

Arubboth?

Beth-Hoggan

Bezek

Jabesh-gilead

Ramoth-gilead

ISRAEL

Shechem

Mahanaim?

Mt. Ephraim

Jabbok

Joppa

Aphek

Shiloh

Zarethan

Beth-el

Michmash

Beth-horon

Gezer

Ramah

Geba

Gilgal

Heshbon

Ekron?

Gibeah

JERUSALEM

Bethlehem

Rabbath-ammon

Ashdod

Adullam

Tekoa

Medeba

Ashkelon

Gath

Keilah

AMMON

Gaza

JUDAH

Hebron

Ziph

Carmel

Gerar?

Ziklag?

Maon

Arnon

MOAB

Beer-sheba

Kir-haresheth

Zered

THE GREAT SEA

PHOENICIA

L e b a n o n

Z O B A H

A R A M

THE GREAT SEA

SHARON

PHILISTINES

CHERETHITES

JERAHMEELITES

AMALEKITES

KENITES

EDOM

Wilderness of Shur

Kadesh-barnea

Punon

Sela

Wilderness of Paran

Elath

Ezion-geber

Sinai Peninsula

East from Greenwich

SOLOMON'S TEMPLE

Chambers

Holy of Holies

Holy Place

Porch

Chambers

Door

Altar of Burnt Offering

Bronze Sea

0 10 20 30 40 50 60 70 Cubits
0 20 40 60 80 100 Feet

1 The Ark
2 Table of Shewbread
3, 4 Bronze Pillars of Jachin and Boaz

JERUSALEM IN THE TIME OF DAVID AND SOLOMON

MODERN WALL

Temple

Solomon's Palace

Hall of Judgment

House of the forest of Lebanon

SHOULDER of the JEBUSITE (Josh. 15:8 R.S.V.)

Valley of Hinnom

ZION (CITY OF DAVID)

David's House

"Between the Walls"

Gihon

David's Tomb

Lower Pool

Valley of Kidron

En-rogel

0 ½ Mile
0 200 400 Metres

233

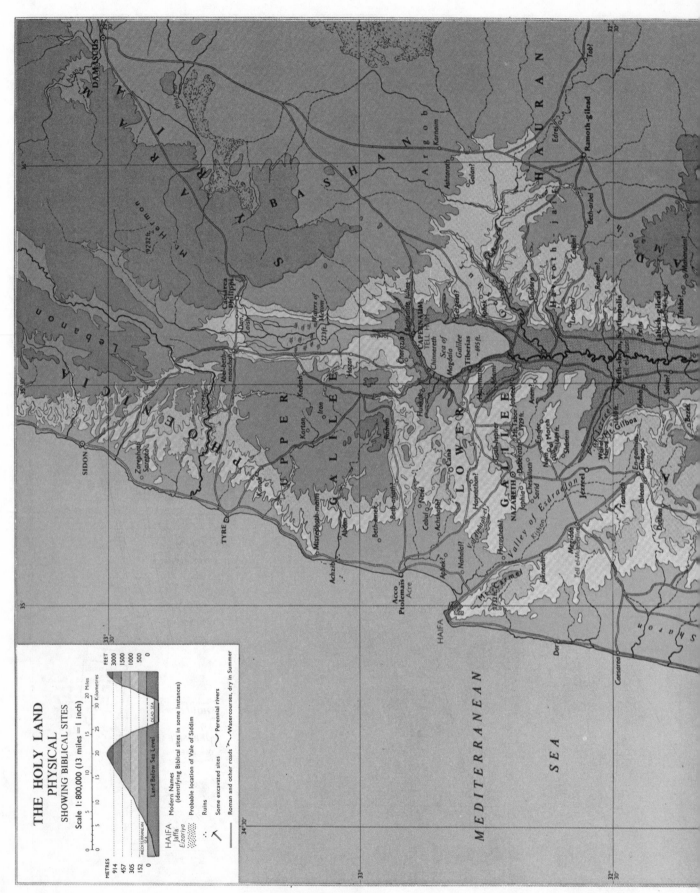

THE HOLY LAND
PHYSICAL
SHOWING BIBLICAL SITES

Scale 1: 800,000 (13 miles = 1 inch)

HAIFA   Modern Names
Jaffa   (identifying Biblical sites in some instances)
El-zariya

⠂⠒⠂ Probable location of Vale of Siddim

∴   Ruins

⅄   Some excavated sites   ~ Perennial rivers
──   Roman and other roads ~ Watercourses, dry in Summer

METRES	FEET
914	3000
457	1500
305	1000
152	500
0	0

Land Below Sea Level

MODERN JERUSALEM

THE OLD CITY

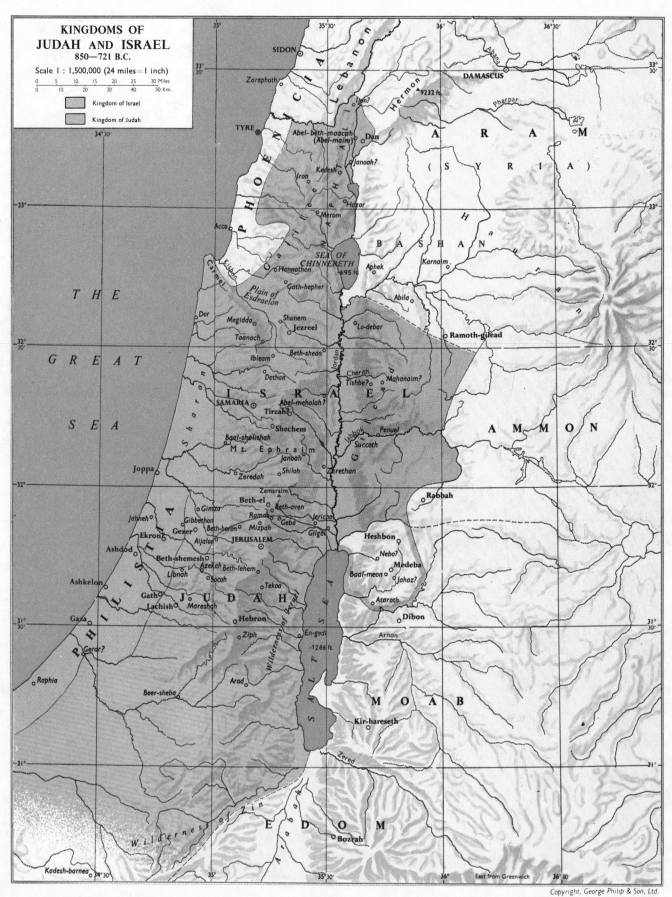

KINGDOMS OF
JUDAH AND ISRAEL
850—721 B.C.

Scale 1 : 1,500,000 (24 miles=1 inch)

0   5   10   15   20   25   30 Miles
0   10   20   30   40   50 Km.

Kingdom of Israel
Kingdom of Judah

SIDON
Zarephath
DAMASCUS
PHOENICIA
TYRE
Abel-beth-maacah
(Abel-maim)
Dan
Janoah?
Iron
Kedesh
Hazor
Merom
Acco
Carmel
SEA OF
CHINNERETH
-695 ft.
Aphek
Karnaim
Abila
Hannathon
Gath-hepher
Plain of
Esdraelon
Dor
Megiddo
Shunem
Jezreel
Lo-debar
Ramoth-gilead
Taanach
Beth-shean
Ibleam
Dothan
Cherith
Tishbe?
Mahanaim?
SAMARIA
ISRAEL
Abel-meholah?
Tirzah?
Shechem
Penuel
Baal-shalishah
Mt. Ephraim
Succoth
Janoah
Joppa
Zeredah
Shiloh
Zarethan
AMMON
Zemaraim
Beth-el
Gimzo
Beth-aven
Ramah
Rabbah
Jabneh
Gibbethon
Geba
Gezer
Beth-horon
Mizpah
Jericho
Ekron
Aijalon
JERUSALEM
Gilgal
Heshbon
Ashdod
Beth-shemesh
Nebo?
Medeba
Azekah
Beth-lehem
Baal-meon
Jahaz?
Ashkelon
Libnah
Socoh
Tekoa
Gath
JUDAH
Mareshah
Ataroth
Lachish
Dibon
Gaza
Hebron
En-gedi
-1286 ft.
Arnon
Gerar?
Ziph
SALT SEA
Raphia
Arad
MOAB
Beer-sheba
Kir-hareseth
THE
GREAT
SEA
PHILISTIA
Wilderness of Judah
Wilderness of Zin
Arabah
Zered
EDOM
Bozrah
Kadesh-barnea
ARAM
(SYRIA)
Hermon 9232 ft.
Abana
Pharpar
BASHAN
Jordan

East from Greenwich

Copyright, George Philip & Son, Ltd.

236